INFORMATION TECHNOLOGY
in the
SERVICE SOCIETY

A Twenty-First Century Lever

Committee to Study the Impact of Information Technology on
the Performance of Service Activities

Computer Science and Telecommunications Board

Commission on Physical Sciences, Mathematics, and Applications

National Research Council

NATIONAL ACADEMY PRESS
Washington, D.C. 1994

NOTICE: The project that is the subject of this report was approved by the Governing Board of the National Research Council, whose members are drawn from the councils of the National Academy of Sciences, the National Academy of Engineering, and the Institute of Medicine. The members of the committee responsible for the report were chosen for their special competences and with regard for appropriate balance.

This report has been reviewed by a group other than the authors according to procedures approved by a Report Review Committee consisting of members of the National Academy of Sciences, the National Academy of Engineering, and the Institute of Medicine.

The National Academy of Sciences is a private, nonprofit, self-perpetuating society of distinguished scholars engaged in scientific and engineering research, dedicated to the furtherance of science and technology and to their use for the general welfare. Upon the authority of the charter granted to it by Congress in 1863, the Academy has a mandate that requires it to advise the federal government on scientific and technical matters. Dr. Bruce Alberts is president of the National Academy of Sciences.

The National Academy of Engineering was established in 1964, under the charter of the National Academy of Sciences, as a parallel organization of outstanding engineers. It is autonomous in its administration and in the selection of its members, sharing with the National Academy of Sciences the responsibility for advising the federal government. The National Academy of Engineering also sponsors engineering programs aimed at meeting national needs, encourages education and research, and recognizes the superior achievements of engineers. Dr. Robert M. White is president of the National Academy of Engineering.

The Institute of Medicine was established in 1970 by the National Academy of Sciences to secure the services of eminent members of appropriate professions in the examination of policy matters pertaining to the health of the public. The Institute acts under the responsibility given to the National Academy of Sciences by its congressional charter to be an adviser to the federal government and, upon its own initiative, to identify issues of medical care, research, and education. Dr. Kenneth I. Shine is president of the Institute of Medicine.

The National Research Council was organized by the National Academy of Sciences in 1916 to associate the broad community of science and technology with the Academy's purposes of furthering knowledge and advising the federal government. Functioning in accordance with general policies determined by the Academy, the Council has become the principal operating agency of both the National Academy of Sciences and the National Academy of Engineering in providing services to the government, the public, and the scientific and engineering communities. The Council is administered jointly by both Academies and the Institute of Medicine. Dr. Bruce Alberts and Dr. Robert M. White are chairman and vice chairman, respectively, of the National Research Council.

Support for this project was provided by the following organizations: the Alfred P. Sloan Foundation (under Grant No. 90-10-4) and Apple Computer Inc., International Business Machines Corporation, the AT&T Foundation, Digital Equipment Corporation, and Xerox Corporation, under unnumbered contracts.

Library of Congress Catalog Card Number 92-85596
International Standard Book Number 0-309-04876-1
Copyright 1994 by the National Academy of Sciences. All rights reserved.

Available from:

National Academy Press
2101 Constitution Avenue, N.W.
Washington, D.C. 20418

B-132

Printed in the United States of America

COMMITTEE TO STUDY THE IMPACT OF INFORMATION TECHNOLOGY ON THE PERFORMANCE OF SERVICE ACTIVITIES

J. BRIAN QUINN, Dartmouth College, *Chair*
MARTIN BAILY, McKinsey & Co., *Vice Chair*
JORDAN BARUCH, Jordan Baruch Consulting
TORA BIKSON, RAND Corporation
DAVID CARLSON, Kmart Corporation
DENNIS CHAMOT, AFL-CIO
KENNETH COATES, Ford Motor Credit Company
WILLIAM CURTIS, Carnegie Mellon University
ROBERT ELMORE, Arthur Andersen & Co.
CHARLES GOLD, Ernst & Young
MAX HOPPER, American Airlines
ELLEN KNAPP, Coopers & Lybrand
HENRY LICHSTEIN, Citibank
JEROME MARK, Bureau of Labor Statistics (Retired)
STEPHEN ROACH, Morgan Stanley & Co.
IRWIN SITKIN, Aetna Life and Casualty (Retired)
MICHAEL ZUBKOFF, Dartmouth Medical School

Special Advisors

JOHN OPEL, IBM Corporation (Retired)
MORRIS TANENBAUM, AT&T (Retired)
WALTER WRISTON, Citibank (Retired)

Staff

MARJORY S. BLUMENTHAL, Director
HERBERT S. LIN, Senior Staff Officer
LESLIE M. WADE, Project Assistant

COMPUTER SCIENCE AND TELECOMMUNICATIONS BOARD

WILLIAM WULF, University of Virginia, *Chair*
RUZENA BAJCSY, University of Pennsylvania
JEFF DOZIER, University of California at Santa Barbara
DAVID J. FARBER, University of Pennsylvania
HENRY FUCHS, University of North Carolina
CHARLES GESCHKE, Adobe Systems Inc.
JAMES GRAY, Digital Equipment Corporation
JOHN L. HENNESSY, Stanford University
DEBORAH A. JOSEPH, University of Wisconsin
RICHARD M. KARP, University of California at Berkeley
KEN KENNEDY, Rice University
BUTLER W. LAMPSON, Digital Equipment Corporation
BARBARA H. LISKOV, Massachusetts Institute of Technology
ROBERT L. MARTIN, Bell Communications Research
DAVID G. MESSERSCHMITT, University of California at Berkeley
ABRAHAM PELED, IBM T.J. Watson Research Center (until August 1993)
WILLIAM PRESS, Harvard University
CHARLES L. SEITZ, California Institute of Technology
EDWARD SHORTLIFFE, Stanford University School of Medicine
CASMIR S. SKRZYPCZAK, NYNEX Corporation
LAWRENCE T. TESLER, Apple Computer Inc.
LESLIE L. VADASZ, Intel Corporation

MARJORY S. BLUMENTHAL, Director
HERBERT S. LIN, Senior Staff Officer
JAMES MALLORY, Staff Officer
GREG MEDALIE, Staff Officer
RENEE A. HAWKINS, Staff Associate
GLORIA BEMAH, Administrative Assistant
JANET QUARLES, Project Assistant
LESLIE M. WADE, Project Assistant

COMMISSION ON PHYSICAL SCIENCES, MATHEMATICS, AND APPLICATIONS

RICHARD N. ZARE, Stanford University, *Chair*
RICHARD S. NICHOLSON, American Association for the Advancement of Science, *Vice Chair*
STEPHEN L. ADLER, Institute for Advanced Study
JOHN A. ARMSTRONG, IBM Corporation (retired)
SYLVIA T. CEYER, Massachusetts Institute of Technology
AVNER FRIEDMAN, University of Minnesota
SUSAN L. GRAHAM, University of California at Berkeley
ROBERT J. HERMANN, United Technologies Corporation
HANS MARK, University of Texas at Austin
CLAIRE E. MAX, Lawrence Livermore National Laboratory
CHRISTOPHER F. McKEE, University of California at Berkeley
JAMES W. MITCHELL, AT&T Bell Laboratories
JEROME SACKS, National Institute of Statistical Sciences
A. RICHARD SEEBASS III, University of Colorado
CHARLES P. SLICHTER, University of Illinois at Urbana-Champaign
ALVIN W. TRIVELPIECE, Oak Ridge National Laboratory

NORMAN METZGER, Executive Director

Preface

In the spring of 1991, The Computer Science and Telecommunications Board (CSTB) of the National Research Council (NRC) convened the Committee to Study the Impact of Information Technology on the Performance of Service Activities. Asked initially to assess the impact of information technology (IT) on productivity in the service sector, the committee met five times over a 16-month period, deliberating over concepts and the analyses of subgroups convened to assess specific issues.

In addition to using the standard macroeconomic data collected and developed by government agencies, the committee drew on observations from managers and executives in industry (a group including some of the committee's own members, as well as numerous others). These observations were obtained through interviews that were used to develop and check insights, not to generate quantitative data. Appendixes A through D provide methodological and supporting details about the committee's sources of information and its approach to using this information. Appendix E lists the interviewed executives, whose observations helped the committee to understand the processes by which IT projects are planned, implemented, and evaluated.

At the macroeconomic level, the committee was concerned about the constraining effects of looking at services from the traditional perspectives of goods-producing industries (Chapter 1). At present, most of the terminology, methodology, and data for analyzing productivity (and performance) derive from earlier studies in the goods-producing industries, but to the committee, most of these seemed inadequate for understanding trends in the service sector. For example, whereas productivity in goods-producing activities is measured in terms that refer to relatively concrete units of output, dollar sales, or profits, performance in services may relate best to more subjective qualities such as timing, quality, comfort, or convenience. Measurement difficulties are a theme that runs through the entire report.

In refining its approach to reflect its initial findings, the committee chose to investigate the full range of impacts of the use of IT on performance in the service sector. Thus, the committee examined the nature and measurement of performance in services at progressively less aggregated levels of analysis: the macroeconomic level (Chapter 1), the industry level (Chapter 2), the enterprise level (Chapter 3), and the activity level (Chapter 4). Chapters 1 through 4 culminate in Chapter 5, which discusses implications for managers in organizations wishing to improve their management of information technology, and Chapter 6, which presents issues and recommendations for public policy.

To put this report in perspective, some observations on the committee's operation and scope of concern are appropriate. First, this report was shaped by interactions within a multidisciplinary committee that included business executives, economists, behavioral scientists, management theorists, and technologists. Second, the committee considered the context of international competitiveness in conducting its analysis, but detailed investigation of international conditions was beyond its scope. Third, although smaller companies were represented in the data that supports industry- and macroeconomic-level analyses, the committee's resources did not permit a systematic examination of the distinguishing characteristics of smaller enterprises.

Many parties outside the committee contributed to this report. First and foremost were the executives of major service companies who participated in the committee's extensive series of interviews. The time, thoughtfulness, and candor of these executives were invaluable to the committee in understanding a variety of complex and otherwise hidden experiences. The anonymous reviewers convened by the NRC also played a key role; their probing comments on the initial draft resulted in a much stronger final report. The contributions of Patricia Higgins (Dartmouth College) in providing research, moral, and logistic support throughout the project were essential to its successful completion. Penny Paquette and Scott Anfinson of Dartmouth College, Debbie Perrault of Kmart, and Ashley Maddox (intern at Arthur Andersen) also contributed to this report.

The committee chair, James Brian Quinn, integrated the contributions from those inside and outside the committee. He also demonstrated a significant personal involvement in shaping the ideas, the concepts, and even the detailed wording of this report. As importantly, his involvement demonstrated a central finding of the study—that good work and high performance demand strong and enlightened management and leadership.

CSTB is grateful for the support of the Alfred P. Sloan Foundation, Apple Computer Inc., International Business Machines Corporation, the AT&T Foundation, Digital Equipment Corporation, and Xerox Corporation, which made this project possible. In accordance with NRC policy, the majority of the funding for this study did not come from private industry.

> William Wulf
> Chair
> Computer Science and Telecommunications Board

Contents

SUMMARY AND OVERVIEW 1

1 INTRODUCTION AND IMPACT OF INFORMATION
   TECHNOLOGY AT THE MACROECONOMIC LEVEL.......... 24

   This Study—Approach, Scope, and Terms, 29
   Current Data and Measures of Productivity, 30
       National Income and Product Accounts Prepared by the
           Bureau of Economic Analysis, 31
       Industry-specific Measures of Productivity Developed by the
           Bureau of Labor Statistics, 40
   Alternate Measures of Productivity and Performance, 44
   Observations and Conclusions, 45
       Many Factors Influence Productivity: IT Affects Many
           Aspects of Performance, 45
   Organization and Scope of This Report, 47
   Notes and References, 49
   Bibliography for Chapter 1, 51

2 IMPACTS OF INFORMATION TECHNOLOGY AT
   THE INDUSTRY LEVEL 52

   Air Transport, 57
   Telecommunications, 62
   Retail and Wholesale Trade, 69
   Health Care, 75

Banking, 80
Insurance, 86
Observations and Conclusions, 91
Notes and References, 93

3   IMPACTS OF INFORMATION TECHNOLOGY AT
    THE ENTERPRISE LEVEL 97

Why Firms Invest in IT, 98
How Companies Use and Invest in IT, 100
    Types of Applications, 100
    Decision Making About Investing in IT and the Rigor of
        Program Evaluation, 118
Cross-cutting Observations Regarding All Uses of Information
    Technology, 122
    Controlling the Costs of IT, 122
    Enhancing Technological Sophistication and Developing
        Standards 124
    Problems in Assessing Enterprise Performance, 125
Summary and Conclusions, 132
Notes and References, 133

4   IMPACTS OF INFORMATION TECHNOLOGY AT
    THE ACTIVITY LEVEL 136

Introduction, 136
What Is an Activity?, 139
Some Observations About Service Activities, 141
    Service Activities Are Everywhere, 141
    Service Activities Are Increasingly Important, 141
    Service Activities Are Generic and Elemental, 142
Roles for Information Technology in the Evolution of Activities, 143
    New Tools and Tasks, 144
    New Linkages and Transformations in Firms, 148
    Outsourcing and Industry Transformation, 153
Consequences for Employees, 155
Conclusions, 160
Notes and References, 163

5   IMPROVING DECISION MAKING ABOUT INFORMATION
    TECHNOLOGY 165

Common Problem Areas in the Management of Information
    Technology, 168
    Lack of Competition, 168
    Inadequate Planning and Follow-up, 169

Resistance and Inefficiencies in Work Practices, 170
Excessive Project Scope, 171
Technology-driven Investments in IT, 172
Difficulties in Software Development, 172
Critical Issues in the Management of Information Technology, 173
Information and IT Strategy Seeking Competitive Advantage, 174
Cross-Functional Reengineering and Reorganization, 175
Continuous User and Customer Involvement, 181
Customer-driven Measures of Quality, 182
Compressing Project Scope and Payback Time, 185
Postproject Audits, 186
Benchmarking Against Specialized Outside Providers, 187
Customer and Knowledge-driven Performance Evaluation and Reward Systems, 190
Summary and Conclusions, 191
Notes and References, 192

6 INFORMATION TECHNOLOGY IN SERVICES: IMPLICATIONS FOR PUBLIC POLICY.................... 193

Implications for Macroeconomic and Fiscal Policy, 194
Background on Employment Issues Raised by Information Technology in Services, 195
The Need for Policy Intervention to Ease Employment Transitions, 199
The Need for Additional Research to Guide Policy Making, 201
Improving Federal Macroeconomic Data Gathering and Analysis, 203
Improving Data and Accounting Principles Related to Investments in Information Technology, 205
Increasing Awareness of and Investments in Research Related to Information Technology in Services and Service Quality Measurements, 206
Other Policy Issues Identified by This Study, 207
Notes and References, 209

APPENDIXES

A Selected Research on Economic and Strategic Impacts of Information Technology, 217
B Methods for Deriving Bureau of Economic Analysis Measures of Output, 228
C Procedures for Deriving Bureau of Labor Statistics Measures of Productivity for Service Industries, 234
D How the Committee Conducted Its Study, 247
E List of Executives Interviewed, 266

INFORMATION TECHNOLOGY
in the
SERVICE SOCIETY

Summary and Overview

The use of information technology (IT) has revolutionized the structure of management and the nature of competition in a variety of industries.[1] IT is especially important in the service sector, which now accounts for about 74 percent of the value added in the U.S. gross domestic product (GDP) and about 76 percent of national employment (Table S.1) and enjoys a healthy $52 billion trade surplus. Estimates indicate that about 85 percent of all measured investments in IT hardware are in services. Contrary to the widespread misconception of services as predominantly simple, labor-intensive activities, the service industries include many large, technology-intensive and technically sophisticated firms in transportation, financial services, banking, insurance, retail and wholesale trade, telecommunications, health care, and professional and personal services. As IT becomes less expensive, more portable, better integrated and interconnected, and embedded in a wider variety of devices, new applications in these fields and whole new industries—such as interactive multimedia systems for business, home entertainment, and communications purposes—are likely to evolve and to have profound effects on industry structures, employment, and economic growth.

Moreover, the U.S. economy revolves increasingly around various important white-collar service activities (e.g., research, design, financing, education, accounting, marketing, logistics planning, communications, and information management) rather than blue-collar shop floor production. These activities are central to the individual service indus-

TABLE S.1 The Scale of Services and Investments in IT in 1991

Industry	Value Added (billions of 1991 dollars)	Employment (millions of FTE jobs)	Investment in IT (billions of 1991 dollars)
Nation	4,587.5	103.3	
Agriculture, Forestry, Fisheries	90.9	1.6	
Mining	36.7	0.7	0.9
Construction	210.1	4.5	0.5
Manufacturing	841.0	18.0	25.3
Total goods sector	1,178.7	24.8	
Transportation	140.8	3.3	3.8
Communications[a]	95.3	1.2	21.1
Utilities[b]	99.0	0.9	8.0
Wholesale Trade	266.0	5.9	17.0
Retail Trade	403.3	16.2	17.9
FIRE[c]	685.0	6.5	38.7
Other services[d]	1,002.4	26.1	20.3
Government	699.4	18.6	
Total service sector	3,391.2	78.7	

NOTE: All figures presented are for calendar year 1991.

[a]Includes telephone, telegraph, and broadcasting.
[b]Includes electric, gas, and sanitary services.
[c]Includes financial services, insurance, and real estate.
[d]Includes health care and delivery, business services, legal services, hotels, and recreation.

SOURCES: U.S. Department of Commerce, Bureau of Economic Analysis. 1992. *Survey of Current Business,* July. Data on value added are from Table 6.1C (National Income Without Capital Consumption Adjustment), p. 82. The relationship between national income without capital consumption adjustment and gross domestic product (or gross product originating by industry) is specified in Table 1.9, p. 52, and is essentially gross domestic product without capital consumption or property and sales tax. Data on employment are from Table 6.5C, p. 84.

Data on investment in IT include hardware costs only and are from Stephen Roach, Morgan Stanley & Co.

tries and are critical in producing value within manufacturing and other goods-producing companies. The effectiveness with which IT is deployed in services thus strongly influences U.S. standards of living and competitiveness in world trade.

THE INFORMATION TECHNOLOGY PARADOX

The magnitude of the investment in IT in the past decade (as measured roughly by investment in hardware; Figure S.1) has prompted questions about payoff for both the nation and individual enterprises. Because IT is

SUMMARY AND OVERVIEW

often used to automate processes (that is, to perform tasks that might otherwise require substantial human intervention), and because automation is popularly associated with efficiency and cost reduction, questions about payoff have usually centered on productivity. Productivity is a concept that relates the level of outputs to the level of inputs used in their production. In particular, some economic studies have suggested that the large investment in IT by the service sector has not been associated with substantial gains in productivity as measured by national macroeconomic statistics—the so-called IT paradox. While some studies indicate that U.S. productivity levels themselves compare quite favorably with those of international competitors in several important service industries, others suggest little correlation between investments in IT and productivity, profitability, or return on investment at the industry or enterprise level.

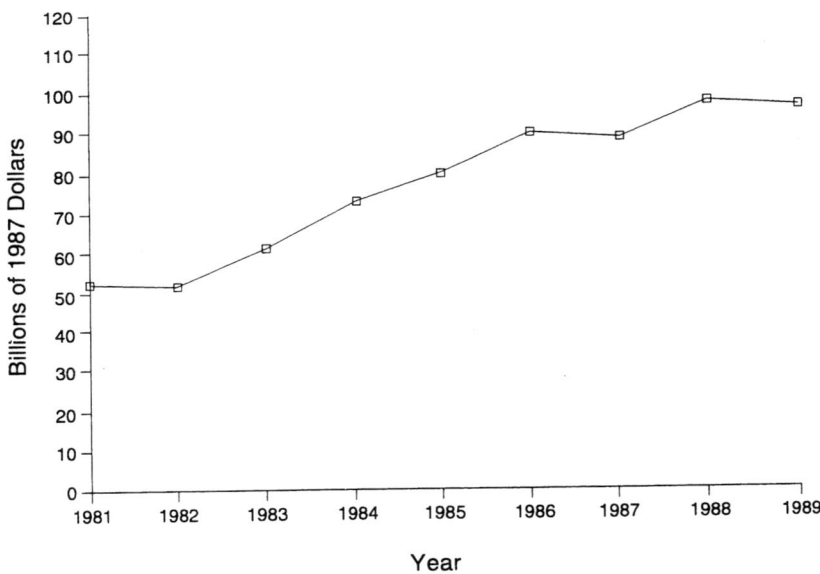

FIGURE S.1 Growing investment in information technology (IT) by the service sector. The only systematic data available on IT expenditures account for hardware components but exclude software and services. Thus this figure shows expenditures only for office, computing, and accounting equipment, communications equipment, instruments, and photocopy and related equipment; it does not include expenditures for software, electronic information services, data processing and network services, computer professional services, custom programming, systems integration, consulting, or training services. SOURCE: Stephen Roach, Morgan Stanley & Co.

The committee concluded, however, that these studies by themselves provide an overly narrow picture of what is happening in services. Macroeconomic data and traditional measures of productivity do not capture many of the crucial performance elements that are important to customers and are critical to service industry executives when they invest in IT. For most service companies, the use of IT now appears more essential than optional, because IT is often an integral part of the infrastructures on which such organizations depend. Obvious elements of such information infrastructures are the telephone and transaction-processing systems without which most businesses could not function, the electronic navigation and control systems without which airlines could not operate, and the interconnected networks of computers that are increasingly necessary to compete at all in financial services, wholesale and retail distribution, transportation, entertainment, and health care. In addition, highly sophisticated systems can provide some innovators with important strategic leadership positions.

The committee believes that understanding the impact of IT on the overall performance of service activities, not simply determining how the use of IT affects productivity in services, is the real challenge. And in contrast to what one would conclude based on the results of studies mentioned earlier, many observers of the service industries (including several members of the committee) and many service industry executives (including the majority of those interviewed in the course of this study) believe that IT has had and will continue to have a real and significantly positive impact on overall service-sector performance.

ANALYZING THE IMPACTS OF INFORMATION TECHNOLOGY

To understand more fully how IT has changed the service sector and what the societal impacts of that transformation have been, the committee examined these issues at four different levels of analysis and considered both quantitative and qualitative observations (primarily collected during an extensive series of interviews with industry executives).

Macroeconomic Analysis

From the standpoint of readily available government statistics on the U.S. economy, during the 1980s the service sector showed limited gains in productivity despite an extraordinary burst of spending on IT. The service sector spent over $750 billion on IT hardware alone in that decade (Figure S.1)—enough to result in the virtual doubling of the IT endowment of the average white-collar worker. At the same time, government economic statistics point to only a 0.7 percent average growth in productivity in the service sector during this period—a distinct slowdown compared to that of previous years and far short of the average gains in the manufacturing sector during the same period.

However, as mentioned earlier, there are various reasons why the readily available government statistics may not accurately reflect the full impact of IT on performance in the service sector. It is well known, for example, that the existing data on productivity do not capture important elements of service quality, e.g., how well a hospital, airline, restaurant, hotel, or bank has satisfied its customers. In addition, statistics on industry productivity are available for only a limited set of service industries that accounts for only 42 percent of all service workers. For some major service industries—notably banking and other financial services, education, health care, and government—output is imputed solely on the basis of input; thus, by definition, output divided by input is a constant for these industries. This imputation affects measurement of output in about 25 to 30 percent of the service sector. Data collected at the industry level also tend to understate or ignore the influence of whole new service markets, even though a primary use of IT is to enable new services.

Another factor that may distort the macroeconomic picture of IT's impact on performance in service industries (particularly telecommunications, transportation, and finance) is the fact that such impacts may be reflected more in measurements of the productivity of customers of these service industries (often manufacturing) than in those of the service industries themselves. Competitive pressures often constrain service pricing, with the result that benefits enjoyed by customers may not appear in the revenue measures of the service-providing industry, while the costs of providing such benefits (e.g., the costs of IT) always will appear. For example, margins and prices in the wholesale trade, finance, and transportation industries have dropped in real terms, although companies now provide a much more complex array of services to customers.

Two other factors should be recognized when interpreting macroeconomic data on productivity and the use of IT. First, the effects on productivity of investing in and using IT cannot be isolated from other things that significantly influence productivity, such as the quality of the work force and management, training efforts, and most importantly, investment in other (non-IT) technologies necessary to achieve a desired result. Second, although the same is true for any other type of investment, macroeconomic data cannot account for the alternative costs and potential risks that companies and industries might have encountered if they had not invested in IT.

However, the central limitation of macroeconomic analysis is the fact that the usual measure of *productivity*—industry or sector output (usually as assessed by some dollar measure such as deflated revenue or price) divided by input (often as assessed by hours of work or number of employees)—ignores important dimensions of *performance* in service industries (and goods-producing ones as well) that are critical to customers and to the managers of individual businesses making decisions about investments in IT. High among these dimensions of performance is the availability of new service functions that would be impossible without IT—such as the rapid deployment of hospital emergency services or 24-hour-per-day securities trading. Of perhaps greater importance are the handling of increased complexity and the provision of the greater quality, convenience, reliability, timeliness, safety, flexibility, and variety that use of IT makes possible in services. As firms begin to compete along these dimensions, the very nature of a service often changes in ways that make comparisons of service output—and hence productivity measures—increasingly problematic.

Because of the above limitations, generalizing from macroeconomic data about the impact of IT on *overall* service-sector performance is likely to be misleading. Significant improvements have been made in macroeconomic data and analysis techniques relative to measuring IT's impacts on performance in the service sector. However, major challenges remain. Chapter 1 is devoted to exploring these issues.

Industry-level Analysis

Nearly all service industries make substantial use of IT. However, patterns of IT's use and impact vary widely across industries, in part because of differences in and limitations posed by industry structures, degrees of regulation, the timing of IT's introduction, and the adaptability of processes and products to change. In some service industries like transportation, communications, utilities, and wholesale trade, growth in productivity (in GDP per labor-hour) from 1948 to 1973 led that of the construction, durable goods, and nonelectrical machinery manufacturing industries; in other service industries, it did not (Table S.2). Nevertheless, since 1973, measured growth in productivity in most services appeared to drop despite large investments in IT, although there were still great variations among industries.

Within the major service industries, increases in productivity (as measured by GDP per labor-hour) ranged from a very respectable 4.6 percent per year in communications to an anemic 0.17 percent in the finance, insurance, and real estate segment from 1973 to 1989 (Table S.2). The committee examined the impact of IT on service performance in six more disaggregated service industries: air transport, telecommunications, retail and wholesale trade, health care, banking, and insurance. Within these industries, some showed strong growth in GDP per labor-hour. Others,

TABLE S.2 Average Annual Growth in Gross Domestic Product Per Labor-Hour for Major Sectors of the U.S. Economy, 1948 to 1989

Industry	1948-73	1973-89
Business		
Goods producing		
Farming	4.64	2.04
Mining	4.02	-0.82
Construction	0.58	-1.20
Manufacturing	2.87	2.75
Durable goods excluding nonelectrical machinery	2.56	2.05
Nonelectrical machinery[a]	2.03	6.01
Nondurable goods	3.40	2.37
Service producing		
Transportation	2.31	0.65
Communication	5.22	4.63
Utilities	5.87	2.46
Trade	2.74	1.18
Wholesale	3.14	1.18
Retail	2.40	1.13
FIRE[b]	1.44	0.17
Other services	2.17	0.32
Government enterprise	-0.15	0.26
General government	0.21	0.34

[a]Nonelectrical machinery hours from Bureau of Labor Statistics.
[b]Finance, insurance, and real estate.

SOURCE: U.S. Department of Commerce, Bureau of Economic Analysis. 1991. *Survey of Current Business,* April, Tables 6.2 and 6.11.

notably insurance and health care, showed negative growth in GDP per labor-hour from 1981 to 1989 (Table S.3). Many service industries are currently undergoing significant restructuring at least partially enabled by their IT systems.

However, available data on industry-level productivity do not convey important aspects of the ways IT has affected these industries and their overall performance:

• In airlines, innovations using IT have been associated with competitive leadership and with survival as complexity has increased. Airlines depend on IT within aircraft and airports, in air traffic control systems, and for sales, marketing, maintenance, and safety systems, as well as for capacity, load management, and logistics planning. Computerized

TABLE S.3 A Comparison of Various U.S. Service Industries in 1991

Industry	Revenues (billions of current dollars)	Employment (millions of FTE employees)	IT Capital Stock (billions of current dollars)	Average Annual Rate of Change in GPO per Labor-Hour, 1981 to 1989 (% per year)[a]	Compound Annual Rate of Growth in Investment in IT, 1981 to 1989 (% per year)
Air transport	87.5	0.7	11.1	3.1	14.1
Telecommunications	129.7[b]	0.9	114.0	5.7	-5.1
Wholesale trade	469.5	5.9	60.2	2.8	11.0
Retail trade	884.5[c]	16.2	58.8	2.3	9.6
Health care	475.0[b]	7.4	19.6	-1.3	9.3
Banking[d]	209.5[b]	2.1	28.5	0.1	27.9
Insurance (carriers plus agents)	226.7[b]	2.2	17.1	-1.4	30.8

[a]Labor productivity is often measured in terms of gross product originating (GPO) per hour of labor input. The GPO of an industry is a value-added measure of that industry's contribution to the gross domestic product.
[b]1990 figure.
[c]Includes restaurant trade.
[d]Includes depository institutions only; excludes federal credit agencies, security commodity brokers, and mortgage bankers.

SOURCES: Unpublished data on revenues are from the Bureau of Labor Statistics. Employment data are from U.S. Department of Commerce, Bureau of Economic Analysis, 1992, *Survey of Current Business,* July, Table 6.5C (Full-Time-Equivalent Employees by Industry), p. 84. IT capital stock data are from Stephen Roach, Morgan Stanley & Co.

reservation systems have changed the entire pattern of competition and profit making in the airlines industry, although in the 1980s, airline profits were highly erratic in the shakeout that resulted from the deregulation of the industry. Competition has forced airlines to pass on to customers the savings gained through increased efficiency, but new route structures enabled by the use of IT have also allowed airlines to pass certain costs (notably inconveniences caused by the "hub-and-spoke" system) on to customers.

• Telecommunications companies depend on IT for operations management, billing and customer service, product differentiation, and new-product development. These companies further provide the infrastructures of telephone, cable television, satellite, microwave, and fiber-optic-cable connections that enable other industries to operate effectively. They provide the pathways over which a variety of new concepts and products have been (and can be) introduced by the financial services, entertainment, data services, software, direct distribution, education, travel, and health care industries, among others. Deregulation in the 1980s increased the variety of services available and decreased their costs for most customers. Improved communications have allowed companies to manage materials and services purchased anywhere in the world, control inventories on a just-in-time basis, gather information, and manage diversified producing locations in ways that have changed basic premises about industry boundaries, the organization of enterprises, and many traditional management techniques. At the same time, the use of IT has enabled telecommunications companies to shift to the consumer much of the labor of placing calls, although consumers themselves often find self-service dialing a convenience.

- Retailers and wholesalers have used IT to collect and analyze sales data more quickly and effectively, to plan purchasing and marketing activities better, to communicate more rapidly with their suppliers, and to offer more differentiated services to customers. To improve the cost, quality, and timeliness of their offerings, many maintain worldwide sourcing and logistics systems that use IT. The variety of items carried and the hours retail stores remained open increased substantially during the 1980s. However, the industry found it difficult to convert its investments in IT into financially measurable gains in productivity because of heavy and rapidly changing competition. The basic structure of retail competition, sourcing of products, inventory management, and retailers' power relative to that of manufacturers shifted during the 1980s. In some cases, wholesaling and retailing merged. In addition to powerful general-merchandise and supermarket chains, highly specialized "category-killer" chains (e.g., Toys "R" Us or Foot Locker), warehouse clubs, superstores, and chain boutiques emerged as new forms of competition. All were highly dependent on IT and broad geographical sourcing.

- In health care, the use of IT has become increasingly important in diagnosis and therapy (e.g., medical imaging, radiation therapy, and patient monitoring). For business operations, IT has generally been less well used in health care than in other industries, and there may be great untapped potentials for its use in such operations as well as in new clinical applications, outpatient care, and monitoring of outcomes. Measures of economic output in health care are extremely tenuous because of the presence of many nonmarket forces and problems in defining quality. Although numerous new and improved cures, therapies, and diagnostics have been introduced since 1970, there is wide consensus that measured productivity in health care has been dropping. Yet few would like to do without the potentially better diagnosis and treatment that electronic devices permit in health care today. And the costs of dealing with today's complex reporting requirements would soar further without electronic systems.

- The banking industry has used IT to enable increases in the volume of transactions as well as the development of new products; applications have ranged from back-office (check and accounts) processing, mortgage and loan application processing, and electronic funds transfer to more strategic innovations such as automated teller machines and new kinds of securities. IT has been used to interlink financial services, banking, and investment systems worldwide—thus decreasing a nation's capacity to control its currency value or its economy by conventional policy interventions. IT has also been used to manage trillions of dollars in daily transactions by the securities markets of the world, functions that physically could not be handled without IT. Yet despite the fact that customers have benefited from the greater variety, convenience, and accuracy of services as the result of expanded use of IT in the 1980s, measured productivity in banking has grown only slightly, although this is at least partly because the output of banking is difficult to measure. Banks now compete with many other (nonbank) enterprises to provide credit card, investment, and other services. Systems for personal savings, credit extension, and management of financial transactions have been substantially improved.
- Insurance companies have relied on IT for back-office claims processing and account updating and now use IT to enhance links to agents, to customize policies, to manage risks globally, and to develop new services (e.g., managed health care systems) nationally. Although industry-level data indicate that the insurance industry did not capture measurable productivity benefits during the 1980s from its use of IT (Table S.3), the industry did introduce a variety of complex new services much more specifically tailored to individual customers' needs. The use of IT also radically improved in the cycles of new-product introduction in the insurance industry, and increased the scale and accuracy of the services provided.

IT has been associated with growing complexity and customization in each of these different industries. At the same time, growth in the volume of transactions, in the number, variety, and linkages among enterprises, and in the kinds of equipment available has led to demands for greater technical standardization. Across all industries studied, lags in the development of standards, software, and management systems—rather than hardware limitations—have been the main constraints to progress. Cycle times for the introduction of products in all major service industries have dropped, and greater control over the mix and size of inventories (whether of airline seats, financial holdings, or distributed products) has become essential to success.

The economies of scale offered by back-office automation have led to waves of mergers and acquisitions and increased concentration in financial services, health care, and air transport. IT has been used effectively to centralize these new larger enterprises and also to facilitate later geographical decentralization into networks of local affiliates and branch offices. Chapter 2 discusses the impact of IT at the industry level in greater detail.

Enterprise-level Analysis

The enterprise level is where most of the decisions are made about the use of IT. Executives who actually make such decisions find that measures related to revenue, profitability, alternative costs, growth potentials, market share, and return on investment (ROI) are more relevant than the more abstract measures of "productivity" used at the industry and macroeconomic levels. When meaningful financial measures are not available, executives use engineering or quality metrics such as response time, reliability, and customer satisfaction to estimate IT's impact. For most investments in IT, executives interviewed by the committee tended to use decision-making processes (such as capital budgeting) similar to those used for investments in any other type of advanced technology. But, as for investments in R&D and other new technologies, their decision making relied on intuitive and nonfinancial measures as well as formal ROI analyses and financial justifications. The committee found that the companies it interviewed were not consistent in their use of postproject audits to determine benefits received from IT investments and projects.

For some uses of IT, results are readily measurable. For others they are not. Companies interviewed by the committee often reported great difficulties in predicting strategic effects precisely, measuring certain types of output (such as increased flexibility), assessing benefits that might be diffuse or delayed (such as those made possible by desktop communications, spreadsheets, and word processing), and separating the contributions of IT from those of other factors.

IT has often been used (especially in early applications) to reduce personnel costs in large paper-intensive departments such as accounting or purchasing, and in some cases even to eliminate or consolidate certain back-office operations. Better information-handling capabilities have also helped decrease other costs such as excessive capital float or inventories, billing or payment errors, logistics costs, and customer complaints. In addition, IT has been used to create new or improved services that a firm can offer to the public, such as the call-waiting service made available to residential telephone customers or the new "synthetic securities" offered by the investment banking community. Providing more customized insurance policies to customers with special needs or reducing the time needed for a retail-store cashier to tally a customer's total purchase are examples of improved services.

Although such benefits are often captured by available data, the committee found that managers invest in IT to achieve a variety of impacts that are not reflected in industry-level or macroeconomic measures of productivity. These include:

- *Preserving or expanding market share.* While aggregate industry output is a key issue for national policymakers, individual companies care more about their individual firm's performance than about that of the industry as a whole. Market share is a key measure of competitive success and a basis for gaining relative marketing or purchasing power as well as improved economies of scale or scope. To maintain their market share, all companies in an industry may be forced to install an IT system even though it does not increase their own or the industry's output. Thus investments increase, but company or industry volume and profits may not.

- *Avoiding risks or alternative costs.* Executives often invest to avoid risks, for example, malpractice suits in health care or accidents in the airline industry. The benefits of avoiding losses by using better processes or controls are very real to a company, but only the costs of achieving them show up in company or national accounts. It is difficult to imagine how most companies in industries such as financial services, large-scale retailing and wholesaling, airlines, lodging and restaurant chain operations, health care, or communications could operate without the benefit of IT. Yet the losses they would incur if they did not use IT appear nowhere in company or national accounts.

- *Creating flexibility for changing business environments.* Changes in the business environment (e.g., increased regulation, marketing, or operational complexity) may require unforeseeable changes in the way a company operates. As many financial services and banking firms have learned, a flexible IT system may be essential to the very survival of the company as it attempts to cope with rapidly changing environments. In other cases, companies invest in IT to provide a flexible future platform for creating new products that may not yet have been planned or even conceived.

- *Improving the internal environment.* Firms often invest in IT to obtain and analyze information that will provide a greater degree of predictability or stability for their operations. Such investments help companies to avoid undue fluctuations in sales or profitability as well as catastrophic failures caused by inadequate information. Other firms invest in IT to improve employee relations. Properly installed, IT can be used to eliminate burdensome tasks, make jobs more attractive, shorten the training cycles needed before an employee becomes productive, and improve worker morale.

- *Improving the quality of products and interactions with customers.* Companies increasingly compete on the quality of their customer service and have used IT to serve customers more rapidly, accurately, efficiently, and with more customized service products. Such improvements help to generate long-term loyalty among customers. IT has been especially important in helping to improve reliability, ensuring more consistent levels of performance, minimizing errors, and improving customers' and employees' perceptions about companies and their products. IT is also a powerful tool for companies with life-critical operations in which real-time systems help to improve the safety of employees, customers, and the public.

An important common finding was that, in the companies surveyed, decision-making processes for IT projects were comparable to those used for other complex advanced-technology projects. In many instances, decisions about investments in IT are like decisions about R&D. Payoffs from both R&D and IT are likely to be uncertain in both scale and timing. Companies readily admitted that they had made investment errors. Expected value is often not quantifiable or even estimable, let alone predictable. It is not surprising that the experience of firms investing in IT varies considerably within an industry and by type of investment.

When IT is used to reduce costs or to provide a specific new service, managers are often able to calculate rates of return and payback times with relative accuracy. However, for many other investments in IT—like the strategic and infrastructure expenditures noted above—it is nearly impossible to estimate such figures. Strategic uses of IT can change a firm's entire competitive or risk posture within an industry, affecting many different elements of customer, cost, and competitive relationships simultaneously—not just revenues or costs. Programs or systems such as MCI's Friends and Family program, American Airlines' SABRE computerized reservations system, Morgan Stanley's TAPS system for integrated trading, and McKesson's ECONOMOST system for ordering and inventory control affect those firms' quality of customer service, flexibility, reliability, breakeven points, response times, and market positioning in ways that cannot be measured in precise financial terms.

When IT is used in this fashion, a firm's most valuable assets may become the professional know-how, flexible response and capabilities for innovation, information and management systems, and knowledge about customers and markets embodied in its IT and supporting systems. These assets also are not reflected in the firm's accounting statements or in the nation's accounting system. When successful, such companies can redefine the standard to which other firms in the industry (and all cross-competing industries) are held by consumers of their services. A firm's use of IT may affect the entire structure of the firm's industry, its competitiveness with other industries, and even the nation's international competitiveness. Competitors may be forced to choose between making similar investments or being forced out of the business. Entirely new subindustries can result from particularly fortuitous strategic changes, as cellular telephone, overnight package delivery, "swaps" and synthetic securities, and facsimile services demonstrate. But, as the failed experiments of Zap-mail, videotext, and AMRIS's CONFIRM system also show, favorable outcomes are far from assured. Chapter 3 deals in depth with these issues.

Finally, IT has become a significant element in the cost structure of many companies. Even the service sector's $750 billion expenditure on IT in the last decade understates by a substantial amount the total cost of IT, since it includes only hardware and excludes essential elements such as software, training and support, and maintenance and upgrading; the costs of these excluded elements may well be substantially greater than the costs of the hardware. The costs of a significant IT infrastructure become more fixed than variable in nature and are especially burdensome when revenues and margins are squeezed by recessions or competitive pressures and overcapacity results. In some cases, this problem leads to sizable financial losses even though the services being provided using the IT infrastructure may be of higher absolute value to the customer. The problem of overcapacity applies to entire industries and not just individual enterprises, since IT systems, especially large, complex ones, must be purchased in predetermined sizes that are not in direct proportion to demand and therefore usually provide more capacity than warranted by average levels of demand.

Activity-level Analysis

Although it is perhaps easiest to evaluate IT's impact on performance in services at the enterprise level by considering a firm's profitability, growth in market share, or survival, many of the impacts of IT can be understood only by an examination of IT's application in specific activities within enterprises, such as customer service, product design, image creation, quality and cost control, and R&D. These activities may be performed within one functional organization or cut across several functional areas within one enterprise. Moreover, these activities may not all be performed within a single enterprise, but may be spread between the enterprise, its suppliers, and its customers. Because measures of performance at the enterprise level aggregate the effects of all activities within an enterprise, they may frequently miss critical shifts in structure or performance occurring at the activity level. Those shifts, however, may affect the structure and performance of many enterprises and industries.

Examining the use of IT at the activity level allows more penetrating insight into why and how IT has been associated with major changes in job content, forms of internal organization, industry structures, and cross-industry competition. For example, most overhead functions are merely services an enterprise has chosen to produce internally. If desired, many could easily be purchased externally. In fact, this is the way many service industries started. Important tasks in services and manufacturing often resemble each other so much that the lines separating the two sectors are becoming arbitrary—if not misleading—for policy purposes.

Within companies, an obvious impact of using IT in service activities is in providing specialized tools that enable more effective performance of particular activities (e.g., substituting on-line databases for paper records). Firms may also invest in IT-based systems that lower internal costs and prices but require more effort by the customer, a concept fundamental to many of the do-it-yourself "services" provided by businesses (e.g., credit-card gas pumps, long-distance dialing, machine-operated parking facilities, automated teller machines). Since these firms gain at the expense of the customer, the net performance gains (taking the customer into account) are clearly less than the gains to the firms themselves. In other instances, firms have used IT to rework how they perform service activities such as logistics activities that cut across individual functional organizations such as purchasing, inventory control, manufacturing, and distribution.

IT is also used to facilitate the separation, reorganization, and recombination of activities without regard to their location in space or time. This had led to the widespread development of "network" organizations. Flexibilities enabled by IT may also result in the flattening of organizations or the decentralizing of decision-making authority, thereby allowing more autonomy at lower levels and broadening the mix of tasks for which individuals are responsible. At the same time, managers have used IT to enhance dimensions of performance that depend on greater centralization (e.g., the consistency of fast foods or the accuracy of bank reports).

IT-based linkages now allow managers to separate out many traditional activities (like payroll or accounting) from their core operations, procure them from outside suppliers, and still integrate them with important activities that continue to be performed internally. Decisions to use "outsourcing" often rest on the fact that outside providers of highly specialized service activities—who may have invested in or developed specialized IT technology and applications—can often perform them more effectively or at less cost than firms that do not specialize in that activity. IT-based linkages often provide an opportunity to expand such choices by facilitating the monitoring and integration of service activities provided off-site with those kept in-house. Not only are large enterprises reorganizing or shedding entire departments and divisions, but they are also in some instances selling some of their skills in internal activities to outsiders, becoming the external service providers for other firms (as Federal Express has done with its telephone answering service). Electronic data interchanges now bind many firms in a web of worldwide purchasing, shipping, billing, and receiving connections.

IT-based linkages have also been used to establish broader and more complex patterns of interconnections or alliances among different firms (which themselves may or may not be in the same industry). Entire industries such as telecommunications and investment banking compete largely as networks of independent enterprises temporarily linked to accomplish a specific task, for example, building a new telecommunications system for a country. Such interconnections are frequently established to improve the performance of tasks by taking advantage of each enterprise's expertise in performing particular activity-level tasks.

As the use of IT alters the nature and location of activities, it also alters the nature and location of work. Use of IT is one important force facilitating realignment of work flows, job redesign, organizational restructuring, and work relocation. As a result, the nature of jobs, skill requirements, and requirements for training are changing rapidly.

Radically revised organizational structures—entailing different lines of managerial authority and different flows of information—have emerged. Restructurings affect the tasks of personnel at all organizational levels, but middle-level technical and administrative managers may face the greatest challenges in retraining and adjusting to faster, less bureaucratic decision-making structures. These trends have been the focus of much commentary in business publications. The committee's analysis underscores how using IT has amplified these trends. Chapter 4 expands on these vital issues.

KEY FINDINGS

In the course of its deliberations, the committee examined the impact of IT on performance in the service sector not only from the standpoint of understanding the IT paradox, but also in terms of broader implications for decision making by business executives and government policymakers. Detailed below are the committee's overall findings. The broader implications of these key findings as well as more specific findings as they relate to management and policy decision making are described in the remainder of this summary.

• **Traditional macroeconomic data collected to date do not capture many important benefits or costs that accrue to firms from deploying IT.** Accordingly, it is not appropriate to use these data as a basis for judging the impact of service-sector investments in IT on the sector's performance. Even if growth in service-sector productivity were uniformly poor, which it is not, traditional measures rarely take into account improvements in quality, convenience, and reliability for customers, or losses that using IT has helped avoid—all important issues to individual firms. Moreover, as with other important technological advances (such as electrification and telephones), it may take decades before aggregated measures fully reflect the results achieved by the use of IT.

- **The use of IT has had a direct and positive operational impact on the performance of services by many individual firms, but the financial impact of the use of IT has not always been as positive.** Although it is often difficult to isolate the effects of IT use from other factors that may influence operational performance in service activities (e.g., quality of the work force), individual firms have used IT to improve efficiency by reducing costs (e.g., through better logistics scheduling in airlines or more efficient routing in deliveries from suppliers to retail stores). In nearly all of the service industries, including those examined by the committee, firms have used IT to handle tremendous volumes of transactions. IT has been used to provide timely information that can substantially influence profits (e.g., investment bankers capture and analyze stock and bond price movements instantaneously; retail executives track sales from hour to hour; airlines perform real-time yield management). There are a variety of reasons why the use of IT has not always had a positive financial impact on service firms. One reason is that many applications have used new technologies and other applications of IT have been experimental, and a basic characteristic of innovation is that experiments and new technologies sometimes fail. A second reason is that the range of problems to which IT can be applied continues to expand so quickly that some companies are forced to invest in new technologies to obtain new capabilities even before they have captured the full anticipated benefits of their installed IT infrastructures.

- **The use of IT has had important customer-supplier effects.** For the customers of service providers, IT has been used to help improve the quality and variety of services in many industries, especially through its ability to amass, analyze, and control large quantities of specialized data. Such improvements include error reduction or increased precision (e.g., more reliable medical diagnostics and procedures, more accurate billing on checkout activities); faster or more convenient service (e.g., computer-aided repair services, credit-card purchases, automated teller machines); improved security, safety, and reliability (e.g., automated maintenance protocols, monitoring systems, or on-line audits). On the other hand, some important costs have been passed on to customers (e.g., while the hub-and-spoke routing systems and complex yield management strategies now used by airlines lower airline operating costs and sometimes the cost of tickets, they also may vastly increase the inconveniences associated with air travel; while certain users find automated communications systems and direct dialing procedures more convenient and private and they lower the price per call for everyone, many users are greatly frustrated by them) and on to suppliers (e.g., IT systems such as electronic data interchange have led to closer relationships and working partnerships between companies and their suppliers but also to greater costs for suppliers in terms of inventory carrying and coordination). The net effect of these changes is not always calculable.

- **IT has been an important element in promoting many broad restructuring and strategic changes in service industries.** IT has been used to create new industries (e.g., the cellular telephone business) and has contributed to changes in traditional relationships between industries (e.g., retailers dictating designs, packaging, and specifications to manufacturers). Entirely new lines of business have appeared, such as interest swaps, securitized mortgages, and indexed mutual funds. The economies of scale offered by back-office automation have supported some mergers and acquisitions, leading to reductions in the work force and increased concentration in some industries such as financial services or airlines. In other cases, the falling cost of IT has often facilitated the entry of relatively small businesses into new markets and the development of efficient local branches, franchises, or affiliates through which larger companies can service broader geographical areas or remote locations more effectively. IT has been used to increase cross-competition among various industries and among individual activities within companies in different industries. IT has been an enabling force in creating entirely new forms for economic activity (e.g., worldwide research networks, global sourcing arrangements, large-scale development and sharing of new databases, new training and educational capabilities, faster-response innovation systems, and competition through disaggregated alliances or networks of companies).

- **The widespread use of IT in services has a profound effect on employment patterns.** The committee's analysis of IT's roles at the activity and enterprise levels revealed changes in production processes, products, and lines of business that will produce substantial changes in employment patterns. When an industry's productivity increases and its output remains constant, jobs in that industry are of course lost. If that industry is committed to enhancing productivity through downsizing alone, those jobs will be lost permanently. However, if past patterns continue, total output is likely to grow, though jobs may well shift to different firms and industries or between geographical regions. Forecasts indicate that the new jobs created and old jobs restructured will demand a new mix of skills. Emerging new forms of organization often require a wider range of skills than traditional forms. Future jobs are predicted to be more knowledge-based than in the past. Forecasting

SUMMARY AND OVERVIEW   19

specific skill needs is complicated by the fact that the job displacements and skill changes that typically accompany any major technological change will unfold at the same time that international competitive pressures, deregulation, and other factors are causing major changes in the overall economy. Compounding analyses of these changes is the fact that many service activities can easily be physically separated from their producing clients. As it has in software, the creation of domestic demand for other services might well result in substantial export of certain jobs overseas.

MANAGEMENT IMPLICATIONS

The use of IT can have a significant impact on the performance of service firms, both strategically and operationally. However, successfully applying IT and reaping maximum payoffs from IT investments require good management. The question is not, Is IT useful? but rather, How can IT be successfully applied to enhance service performance? The committee's interviews with senior executives revealed several specific areas that affect the likelihood of successfully managing applications of IT. While not completely new, each provides an important focal point for concern and attention by managers investing in and using IT. The committee concludes that for maximum effectiveness:

• There needs to be a comprehensive IT-based strategy designed not only to support the basic business but to create competitive advantage. Top management must understand this strategy, be deeply involved in its generation, and be committed to its implementation if the strategy is to have company-wide significance and transcend divisional boundaries.

• Business processes should be examined and when appropriate redesigned before IT is installed, paying special attention to functions that cross existing organizational boundaries. New management techniques and performance-reward structures are generally needed to support cross-functional systems. And internal activities and formal organizations should be explicitly restructured to make the best use of these systems.

• Customer and user needs (especially those of external customers) should normally drive the design, installation, and evaluation of IT systems. Users and customers should be involved whenever possible in system designs, and customer-driven metrics of quality should be used whenever possible to assess the impacts of using IT. Customer-driven performance measurement systems (as opposed to hierarchically driven systems) should be important elements in evaluating cross-functional team performance.

• Most IT projects should focus on relatively short-term payoffs and should have well-defined goals within a long-term strategic framework. While "bet-the-company" IT projects have at times resulted in revolutionary changes that have benefited their initiators, mega-projects are likely to be overly complex, over budget, delayed, and mismatched to customer needs by the time they are implemented.

• The goals and desired outcomes of IT projects should be established using benchmarks for service performance established by extensive examination of possible "best-practice" processes as implemented in other firms, including specialized external service providers. Restricting searches for best-practice processes to peer firms may limit management perspectives severely.

As reported by executives interviewed by the committee, most of the problems in achieving payoffs from investment in IT came not from the investment decisions themselves but from inadequate planning and implementation of IT applications by management. Inadequate retraining and failure to continuously upgrade worker skills were a major problem. Another was a failure to follow up installations of IT with appropriate organizational structures, performance measurement systems, and reward and incentive plans. Details of the management implications of the committee's findings are found in Chapter 5.

POLICY CONCERNS

While the committee believed that it was beyond its scope and expertise to develop major policy or action recommendations, four primary areas of concern to policymakers were identified: enhancing the diffusion of IT throughout the service sector, dealing with the impacts of IT on employment patterns, obtaining better data as well as a better understanding of organizational and structural changes occurring in the economy as a result of IT, and reassessing the impact of these changes on the effectiveness of traditional policy measures. Detailed recommendations on how to address these areas of concern are explored in Chapter 6.

Diffusing the Benefits of IT in Services

In general, market mechanisms have worked well in developing IT for services. Many individual companies have reaped substantial economic benefits from using IT, notwithstanding the fact that these benefits are frequently not reflected in traditional economic data and that certain attempts to use IT have been undeniable failures. There are two key areas where policy stimuli might affect future economic benefits from investments in IT.

The first is IT's potential inclusion in—or exclusion from—investment incentives. To the extent that public policies are used to stimulate further investment (whether in new capital spending or in R&D), such policies should treat investment in IT in services as they would any other capital or R&D investment. Preference should not be accorded to other types of capital investment or process experimentation—such as those for manufacturing or fixed equipment—over IT applications. Since service activities are integral to both service and manufacturing industries, IT applications that lower service costs or improve service performance are likely to have a significant positive impact on competitiveness in both sectors—despite the low measured productivity increases seen to date. Moreover, given their importance, the nonhardware aspects of IT such as software and training should be included along with hardware in any definition of IT for investment and/or tax purposes.

The second relates to continued support for the development of information infrastructures, whether through public investment in certain critical areas (such as advanced R&D) or through changes in laws and regulations. The experiences of many large service enterprises illustrate the value of broad access to interactive computing systems connected by telecommunications and data communications systems or integrated voice and data communications between different facilities, localities, and countries. Large U.S. firms have often been world leaders in the development and use of information infrastructures, especially for their own multinational networks. Increasingly, however, the emergence of relatively inexpensive desktop IT can bring sophisticated information-processing capabilities into the reach of the private home, as well as small and medium-size enterprises. Such enterprises (and home users) will require affordable access to public information infrastructures if they are to develop to their fullest extent. In some geographical areas, selectively stimulating the growth of information infrastructures, particularly for small businesses and for homes, could enhance interactions among all enterprises, promote expansion in both the number and types of jobs in the service sector, and lead to the creation of entirely new service industries. Enabling homes to have broad access to IT may also stimulate markets for many affordable products (e.g., multimedia devices or services).

Coping with the Impact of IT on Employment Patterns

Large-scale changes in employment patterns have already occurred, and further changes seem inevitable. The real issue is how best to facilitate the continuing shift in job mix. Extensive retraining, education, and job creation are essential tools for such facilitation. In a humane society, steps should also be taken to minimize the disruption and hardship of displaced individuals. As in the past, the volume of training and education needed is likely to exceed the capabilities of private industry. In addition, the rapid evolution of IT and other new technologies suggests that the need for retraining during a person's lifetime will be periodic. All this supports the broad-based call for strengthening the literacy and numeracy provided by public K-12 education. Past studies indicate that education in general skills is likely to prove more beneficial in times of uncertainty and rapid change than education in specifically targeted and narrowly focused skills.

Obtaining Improved Data and Conducting Research on Structural Changes

The rapid growth of services and changes in the nature of service activities in the last two decades underscore the need for a better understanding of changing conditions. The analyses on which such understanding has traditionally rested have relied on statistical data collected by the Bureau of Labor Statistics and the Bureau of Economic Analysis. However, these data suffer from significant deficiencies. Efforts such as the Boskin Initiative to increase the disaggregation of federal data and statistics and to improve the scope of coverage (in terms of both price and quality measurements and the industries measured) were begun, and these efforts should continue.

Better statistical data is not the only need. Specific research and continuous monitoring are also needed to better understand (1) the nature of structural changes occurring within enterprises and industries, (2) those issues that are peculiar to small businesses, and (3) the large-scale impacts of IT on employment patterns at the activity and enterprise levels. Ironically, the United States funds research that addresses organizational and institutional changes overseas (e.g., change as the result of political or economic shifts in other nations), but funding for this kind of research tends to be difficult to find domestically.

Reassessing the Effectiveness of Traditional Policy Measures

Further research is also needed on the way information technologies affect the impact of traditional policy instruments. Some unintended results are possible, and their likelihood should be assessed. For example, because of integrated financial markets, interest rates lowered for policy reasons in the United States may merely (1) enable domestic or foreign companies to invest at lower costs overseas or (2) change the exchange rates for U.S. currency. Because of outsourcing abroad, increases in government purchases or government stimulation of consumer demand may simply increase imports and create jobs overseas. Enhanced data and communications networks generally have international connections that increase access by foreign competitors to U.S. markets as well as U.S. access to foreign resources, potentially increasing the pressure on and lowering returns for U.S. innovators and suppliers. The internationalization of financial markets spurred by worldwide IT networks makes it increasingly difficult to control a domestic economy using the standard macroeconomic levers and brings into question the entire concept of national sovereignty. Such subjects are worthy candidates for investigation.

Additional conclusions and suggestions of the committee may be found in the body of the report.

NOTE

[1] Throughout this report, unless otherwise specified, the term *information technology* includes computer and communications hardware, as well as the software and associated services required to effectively use that hardware.

1
Introduction and Impact of Information Technology at the Macroeconomic Level

Information technology has changed the way that most companies do business. It is hard to imagine returning to an era in which payroll accounting, check processing, airline reservations, or stock exchange trades were handled without computer technology. In a typical business day now, over 200 million shares are traded on the New York Stock Exchange alone; in 1989, U.S. commercial banks processed almost 58 billion payment transactions.[1] Transaction volumes of this magnitude would have been impossible to handle with the technology of 50 years ago. Innovations in electronics made over the past 40 years have been incorporated into new computers, office automation equipment, communications equipment, and their associated software systems. Information technology has revolutionized services both in service-sector industries and in the service activities that are an increasingly integral part of goods-producing industries.

For purposes of this report, the service industries consist primarily of transportation, communications, wholesale and retail trade, financial services, insurance, real estate, utilities, and personal and professional services; unless otherwise specified, information technology (IT) includes computer and communications hardware, as well as the software and associated services required to exploit that hardware.

Despite the obvious and dramatic changes in the economy brought about by use of IT, a strange paradox emerges from analysis of aggregate U.S. economic data. According to standard methods of calculation, productivity in the business sector has grown slowly since the widespread introduction of IT. However, the slow growth of measured U.S. productivity has not been occurring uniformly throughout the economy. Measured productivity in the manufacturing sector, after slowing in the 1970s, has been growing at a rate of about 3 percent a year, as gauged by the average annual rate of increase in measured output per labor-hour over the past 10 years. The farming sector has also achieved solid growth in productivity. Much of the rest of the economy, however, has lagged behind—especially construction and elements of the service sector. The result is that business as a whole has achieved only about a 1-percent-a-year improvement in output per hour in recent years. Particularly puzzling is the weak measured performance of the service sector, which has accounted for the bulk of the nation's expenditures in IT.

The dilemma is this: although data show that over $750 billion has been invested in IT hardware alone in the 1980s (Figure 1.1), and although

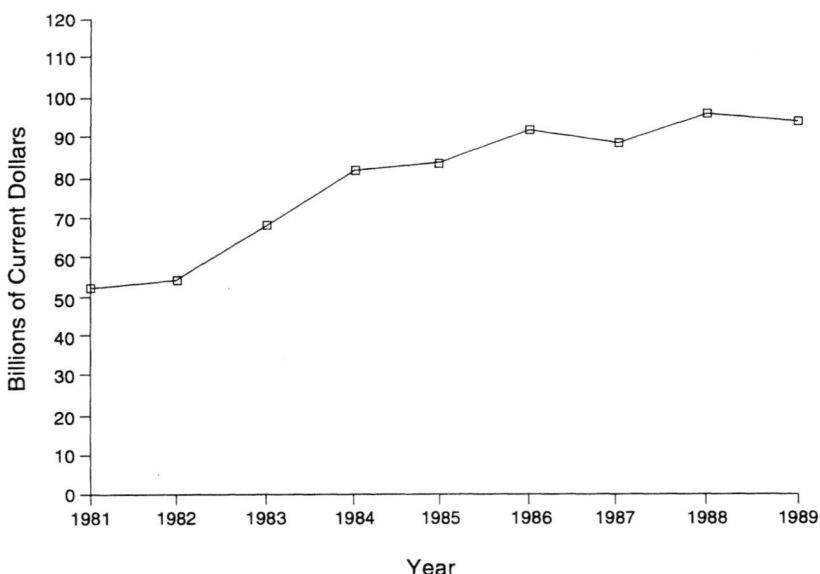

FIGURE 1.1 Growing investment in information technology (IT) by the service sector. The only systematic data available on IT expenditures account for hardware components but exclude software and services. Thus this figure shows expenditures only for office, computing, and accounting equipment, communications equipment, instruments, and photocopy and related equipment; it does not include expenditures for software, electronic information services, data processing and network services, computer professional services, custom programming, systems integration, consulting, or training services. SOURCE: Stephen Roach, Morgan Stanley & Co.

BOX 1.1 One Assessment of the Information Technology Paradox

Stephen Roach's assessment of the information technology (IT) paradox hinges on what he believes are the unique characteristics of the service sector's competitive environment. While U.S. manufacturing firms faced intense competition in the 1980s, service companies were protected by regulation, he says, and by the lack of foreign competition—in effect shielding them from the harsh realities of market pressures. In response, he maintains, service companies became complacent and allowed their costs to become increasingly bloated, leading to a most disappointing record of productivity growth that is consistent with the macroeconomic evidence presented in Chapter 1.

Roach points out that the service sector's lagging efficiencies are particularly disturbing because it is the segment of the economy that has invested most heavily in IT. Indeed, over the past 10 years, the service sector spent $862 billion on IT hardware alone—accounting for about 85 percent of the nation's total IT expenditures. This surge of spending has been enough to equip the average white-collar worker in the service sector with about $10,000 worth of IT hardware in 1991—essentially double the endowment that existed in 1980. Such extraordinary commitments to IT have not yielded measurable benefits for productivity, Roach maintains, because service companies have had little incentive to strive for efficiencies, given the unique protection they enjoyed from competitive realities.

As a result of this rapid spending on IT, Roach argues, the service sector has experienced an ominous transformation of its cost structure. Service companies used to be largely variable-cost producers, with the salaries of white-collar workers constituting the bulk of overall expenses. When business conditions toughened, white-collar job attrition was an effective means of cost control. Now, however, courtesy of the massive infrastructure of installed IT, service companies have a new layer of fixed costs—in effect transforming them from variable- to increasingly fixed-cost producers. The commitment to IT has, therefore, crimped the ability of service managers to adapt to changing business conditions.

Roach also stresses that this lack of flexibility has come at a most inopportune moment for services—a point in time when competitive pressures have intensified dramatically. Regulation has been replaced by deregulation. Moreover, the pressures of foreign competition have been increasingly evident in the form of a dramatic increase in foreign direct investment in the U.S. service sector—inflows of capital that have deepened the pockets of many players battling for market share in the world's richest and deepest service market.

In response to this intensified competition, a new wave of restructuring has been unleashed in the vast service sector—highlighted in the last 2 years by nearly a dozen mega-bank mergers, the failures of a number of major airlines, and dramatic downsizing in retailing, telecommunications, accounting, advertising, and the legal profession. In each of these industries, white-collar jobs are now being permanently eliminated. Roach maintains that this development would not be occurring if IT were delivering what it was intended to deliver—increased output through meaningful improvements in white-collar productivity. Thus, he views the reality of service-sector restructuring as an independent confirmation of the IT paradox—a growing recognition by managers that there is, in fact, considerable validity to the disturbing results conveyed through the macroeconomic data on measured productivity. At the same time, he also views restructuring as a powerful catalyst that is now forcing managers to rethink applications of IT—setting in motion a process that could well culminate in the long-awaited macroeconomic payback from the use of IT.

SOURCE: Stephen Roach, Morgan Stanley & Co.

experienced executives and observers of business note that IT has contributed to important positive changes in the way that business is conducted, standard measures of productivity at the macroeconomic level still reveal few benefits of such changes over the past two decades.[2] What are some possible explanations?[3]

- One possibility is that there has been wasteful or inefficient use of information technology in the service sector. Although it provides a powerful tool, IT can be used well or badly. The view that mismanagement has kept the new technology from providing much impetus toward improving productivity has been expressed in the past by Stephen Roach, a member of the committee (Box 1.1).[4]

- An alternative view is that the use of IT has in fact raised productivity significantly and that other problems have caused the slowdown in productivity growth. IT is only one of several factors that affect productivity. Thus the slow growth of measured productivity in services may be the result of such problems as poor performance in U.S. schools, weaknesses in technology development in areas other than IT, changed energy prices, generally inadequate investment in capital equipment or structures, including infrastructure, and/or a shift in employment to sectors that present limited opportunities for increasing productivity. Or perhaps a slowing of growth in measured productivity was inevitable as the economies of industrialized countries matured and the relatively easily obtained gains in productivity were realized. In fact, most other industrialized countries have also slowed in measured growth at about the same time as the U.S. economy.[5]

- A third perspective on this issue is that IT may have been used to transform business activities but that these changes are being missed by current methods of measuring productivity.[6] In this view, the use of IT is bringing about real increases in productivity that are not captured in the data. Thus the slowdown in productivity growth may be partly or wholly the result of errors in measurement.

- A fourth view argues that IT-based systems have the potential to raise the productivity of the economy significantly, but that this result will take time. Economic historians have pointed out that major changes in technology, such as the introduction of steam power or electrification, have affected productivity only after many years.[7] Thus, the payoff from investments in IT hardware may have been delayed because software development and systems reengineering have lagged behind and because it takes many years to train people to use new technology productively. This optimistic view of the potential for future growth in productivity suggests that payoffs can be expected in the years ahead as U.S. service industries learn to use IT more effectively.

- A fifth view underscores the importance of examining the impact of IT at much lower levels of aggregation than is possible using macroeconomic data. A 1993 study by Erik Brynjolfsson and Lorin Hitt[8] found that information technology "has made a substantial and significant contribution to the output of firms," with a return on investment for IT that is significantly greater than that of other capital investments.

These various alternative approaches to explaining the IT paradox are not mutually exclusive. It could well be that some mistakes were made in early adoptions of IT, leading to wasteful investment, but that as software development, worker retraining, and management understanding progress, investments will pay off in measurable forms. For example, IT may be applied initially to increase information about markets, whereas productivity may increase only later as the information is used to improve operations.

In considering these alternatives it may be useful to keep in mind the difference between the average and the marginal contribution of using IT. The average contribution of using IT can be determined, in principle if not in practice, by asking how much lower productivity in the economy might be if there had been no electronics revolution to bring down computing costs: what would the level of productivity be if companies did not have access to IT at all? Determining the marginal contribution of using IT requires asking a different question: Given the existing stock of IT capital, what increment to productivity is gained by adding another dollar of investment in additional IT? It is possible in principle that using IT has contributed greatly to productivity on average, but that overinvestment at the margin has led to a low return on the last dollar. Often without explicitly stating so, some discussions of the productivity paradox focus on the average contribution of using IT, whereas others actually address the question of overinvestment at the margin.

THIS STUDY—APPROACH, SCOPE, AND TERMS

Motivated by questions concerning how the use of information technology contributes to productivity in U.S. service industries and whether the potential benefits of information technology are being full realized, the committee initially sought to assess the impact of IT on productivity in the service sector. However, the committee soon determined that this was the wrong issue.

Although it attempted to investigate key factors in each of the five approaches to explaining the productivity paradox, the committee found no way to determine with precision the relative significance of the various alternatives as they pertain to use of IT. There was general agreement that existing methods for measuring productivity at the aggregate level do not entirely capture the changes taking place in the U.S. economy as a result of using IT and that focusing on the apparent productivity paradox gives an overly narrow picture of what is happening in services. Indeed some committee members argued that the whole concept of productivity, as it is currently measured, may be outmoded and that other measures of performance provide a better indication of the contribution of IT. There was a consensus that the use of IT has changed the way that businesses operate, and that the locus of innovation and of the production of value has shifted away from traditional manufacturing activities and toward service industries and service activities.

Based on its assessment of current knowledge, the committee concluded that productivity is an important but not a sufficient measure of benefit. As measured, productivity does not capture other important elements of performance such as the quality, flexibility, convenience, variety, responsiveness, reliability, and new opportunities that the use of IT in services can permit. In addition, data on assessments of service-sector productivity often do not reflect the substantial benefits customers or suppliers have received from service-sector investments in IT. If captured at all, these benefits have shown up in measures of the customer- or supplier-industries' productivity.

Finally, the use of IT in services has often transformed the structures of both manufacturing and service industries, created cross-competition among different industry segments, allowed development of global supplier and customer networks, created whole new industries, and changed the very way in which commerce and management are performed.

In addition, IT is a relatively new technology, and hence long delays can be expected before its effective deployment. Many of the service industries into which it has been deployed have not traditionally managed major technological changes. Even in industries inured to such changes, introduction of a new technology typically takes significant time and is accompanied by mistakes in implementation and evaluation and by lags in profitability increases.

In the course of its deliberations, the committee recognized that understanding and improving the impact of IT on the overall *performance* of services activities, not simply determining the *productivity* of IT in services, is the real challenge. Moreover, the committee came to believe that the primary impediments to the full exploitation of IT to improve service-sector business practices and performance were not as much issues of inadequate technology as they were issues of management. For this reason, the report focuses primarily on the roles of management in the exploitation of IT, although the remarkable dynamism that characterizes the evolution of information technology itself has not gone unnoticed.

To better understand these complex issues, the committee chose to investigate the full range of impacts of IT use on performance in the service industries, including measured productivity as only one element in overall performance. To do so, the committee analyzed the impacts of IT use at four levels: the macroeconomic level, the industry level, the enterprise level, and the activity level within the enterprise. The purpose of these inquiries was not so much to critique past studies or results as to offer practical insights to executives and policymakers concerning the utility of available data and the application of practices that might improve IT's impact on the performance of service activities in the future.

CURRENT DATA AND MEASURES OF PRODUCTIVITY

Based on existing data, it is impossible to determine exactly what payoff the U.S. economy has achieved from use of IT. To understand this point one must look at the ways in which productivity is currently measured, particularly in the service industries. There are both strengths and weaknesses in the current statistical base. The recently updated productivity series developed by the Bureau of Labor Statistics for selected industries shows strong growth in many service industries. The aggregate data from the Bureau of Economic Analysis also offer useful insights about the productivity of the service sector. But both series may ignore or understate some key factors that contribute to productivity in several service industries. Alternative measures of performance may be useful to supplement measures of productivity—or to substitute altogether for them—as indicators of economic performance.

National Income and Product Accounts Prepared by the Bureau of Economic Analysis

The Bureau of Economic Analysis (BEA) of the U.S. Department of Commerce has responsibility for preparing the National Income and Product Accounts (NIPA). The data in these accounts are comprehensive, covering economic activity throughout the U.S. economy. When the framework of the accounts was developed after World War II, the concern of public policy was to avoid a return to the disastrous period of the Great Depression. The data that are prepared are used when monetary and fiscal policy are adjusted in order to influence the level of demand in the overall economy. The need to be comprehensive and the focus on policies affecting demand influence in many ways the nature of the data collected. Thus, at times, the data are limited in their usefulness for studying aggregate supply—productivity and long-term growth.

Traditionally, the gross national product (GNP) has been the principal aggregate measure of all of the goods and services produced in the economy. How this figure is constructed is a factor in its limitations and general validity for assessing productivity. The basic data that go into GNP describe the sales of goods and services for consumption, the sales of goods (including construction) for investment, and government purchases of goods and services (including the services government itself produces). Included in GNP are final sales, that is, sales to consumers or to government or the sales of durable goods to businesses. Sales of components or raw materials that are then processed further are considered sales of "intermediate" goods and are not included directly in GNP. Additions to inventory are counted as part of investment and are added to final sales in computing GNP (or subtracted in the case of any depletion of inventories).

The GNP includes the income that is earned by U.S.-owned assets located overseas minus the earnings of foreign-owned assets located in the United States. When this net income is subtracted out, the resulting aggregate is called the gross domestic product (GDP). In its recent revisions of the NIPA, BEA has highlighted GDP rather than GNP. GDP gives the best aggregate indicator of economic activity within U.S. borders.

The BEA collects information on final sales and inventories to estimate GDP in current dollars, that is, with everything priced at its actual sales price. It then uses price information collected by the Bureau of Labor Statistics and, for some components, by BEA itself to construct an aggregate price deflator for GDP. This deflator is used to transform GDP in current dollars into GDP in constant dollars, also known as real GDP. Real GDP reflects the total of goods and services produced in the economy priced in base-year prices, currently 1987 prices. Putting everything in common prices is designed to remove the effect of inflation on GDP and leave only an index of the increase in the physical quantities of goods and services produced in the economy, often called the gross domestic product originating in the U.S. economy (GPO).

Once total GDP has been calculated, the activities of the government sector,[9] owner-occupied housing, and the nonprofit sector are often subtracted out, and the resulting measure of output is then described as the GDP originating in the private business sector of the economy (i.e., the GPO of the business sector).

Business GDP can be subdivided further into the GDP produced in each sector or industry in the economy (GPO by industry), based largely on the wage and capital income generated by the industry. Obtained in this way, the output of an industry reflects the *value added* produced within the industry, that is, the real value of the sales of the industry (adjusted for any change in inventory) minus the value of materials and services purchased from other industries.[10] Estimating the contribution to total GDP made by each constituent industry often involves some educated guesswork, because many companies have plants in several different industries, and so their income has to be divided up to account for their various activities.

Another difficulty encountered in determining the real (constant-dollar) output of each industry comes in developing suitable industry price deflators. The dollar value of income generated in each industry is divided by an industry price deflator in order to compute real output of the industry in 1987 dollars. This approach is analogous to the procedure used to compute aggregate real GDP in 1987 dollars, but some of the industry price deflators are more difficult to construct than the aggregate price deflator. The prices associated with both the outputs and the inputs of some industries are intrinsically hard to measure, or data are simply not collected that allow accurate measurement.[11]

Although it develops data on business GDP and GDP by industry, the BEA does not publish data on productivity. Instead, the responsibility for measuring productivity in the U.S. economy rests with the Bureau of Labor Statistics.

Productivity from the NIPA Data: What do the Numbers Show?

The Bureau of Labor Statistics (BLS) makes some adjustments to the NIPA data on output associated with business GDP and GDP by industry and combines those data with data on labor input by industry to give average labor productivity (Box 1.2), computed as real GDP per employee-hour. (Box 1.2 discusses different concepts of productivity, such as labor, capital, and multifactor productivity.) BLS publishes data on productivity only for the business sector as a whole, for nonfarm business, and for manufacturing. However, BLS will release on request the productivity data for individual industries, and the resulting productivity information is often widely quoted.

Table 1.1 shows the rates of growth of average labor productivity for the business sector as a whole and for the major industry sectors as prepared by BLS using the BEA data.[12] The figures for the productivity of the business sector show the pattern that has become familiar. Productivity grew at a rate of a little less than 3 percent a year in the business sector as a whole from 1948 to 1973 and then fell to 0.63 percent a year from 1973 to 1979 before making a partial recovery from 1979 to 1989.

The business sector is divided into goods- and service-producing industries, and shows solid growth in both parts of the economy over the period

TABLE 1.1 Average Annual Growth in Gross Domestic Product per Labor-Hour for Major Sectors of the U.S. Economy, 1948 to 1989

Sector	Average Annual Rate of Growth (% per year)				Difference in Rate of Growth, 1948-73 and 1973-89
	1948-73	1973-79	1979-89	1973-89	
Business	2.88	0.63	1.35	1.08	-1.80
Goods producing	3.21	0.71	2.31	1.71	-1.50
Farming	4.64	0.11	3.22	2.04	-2.60
Mining	4.02	-5.56	2.13	-0.82	-4.84
Construction	0.58	-2.02	-0.71	-1.20	-1.78
Manufacturing	2.87	1.80	3.33	2.75	-0.12
Durable goods excluding nonelectrical machinery	2.56	1.55	2.35	2.05	-0.51
Nonelectrical machinery[a]	2.03	1.06	9.10	6.01	3.98
Nondurable goods	3.40	2.37	2.37	2.37	-1.03
Service producing	2.49	0.58	0.84	0.74	-1.75
Transportation	2.31	0.15	0.95	0.65	-1.66
Communication	5.22	4.27	4.84	4.63	-0.59
Utilities	5.87	2.66	2.35	2.46	-3.41
Trade	2.74	-0.35	2.10	1.18	-1.56
Wholesale	3.14	-1.21	2.65	1.18	-1.96
Retail	2.40	0.14	1.72	1.13	-1.27
FIRE[b]	1.44	0.36	0.05	0.17	-1.27
Services	2.17	0.84	0.01	0.32	-1.85
Government enterprise	-0.15	0.62	0.04	0.26	0.41
General government	0.21	0.03	0.53	0.34	0.13

[a]Nonelectrical machinery hours from Bureau of Labor Statistics.
[b]Finance, insurance, and real estate.

SOURCE: U.S. Department of Commerce, Bureau of Economic Analysis. 1991. *Survey of Current Business,* April, Tables 6.2 and 6.11.

BOX 1.2 Measuring Capital and Multifactor Productivity

Measures of productivity relate physical output to physical input. As such, they encompass a family of measures ranging from measures of single-factor-input productivity, such as output per unit of labor input or output per unit of capital input, to measures of multifactor productivity, such as output per unit of labor and capital combined. In the form of indexes these measures present the change in output associated with the corresponding change in input. In other words, the indexes show the change in resources (labor, capital, materials, or all combined) used to produce the output of the activity being measured. They do not measure how much of the change in output came from any of the individual input factors, but rather how the many factors affecting the production process resulted in changes in resource use.

The most extensively developed and widely used measure of productivity is the one relating output to labor input—labor productivity. It is a tool relevant for analyzing labor costs, real income, and employment and, as a practical matter, is most easily measured. However, an increase or decrease in output per employee-hour does not imply that labor is solely or necessarily even primarily responsible for improved or worsened productivity. Movements in output per hour reflect technological innovations, changes in capital input, scale of production, education, management, and many other factors as well as the skills and efforts of the work force.

Average labor productivity is the ratio of output to labor input. Labor input is chosen as the most important factor of production—the compensation of labor is about two-thirds of total value added. But labor productivity can change for reasons that have nothing to do with the work force. Various factors can cause labor productivity to change over time. For example, there have been substantial increases in the amount of capital used per worker. Technology itself and the organization of work may change. These considerations do not invalidate the concept of labor productivity; they simply mean that it is important to interpret it correctly. Also, it may be necessary to choose among a family of measures relating output to labor, capital, and other inputs, some of which adjust for quality, and some of which do not.

Many economists prefer a concept called multifactor productivity or total-factor productivity. When the value-added measure of output is used, growth in multifactor productivity is computed as the growth rate of output minus a weighted average of the growth rates of labor and capital inputs. The weights are then shares of labor and capital costs in total cost. Increases in multifactor productivity reflect increases in the efficiency with which labor and capital are used to produce output.

When considering multifactor productivity, it is important to find a good measure of the capital input to production, but such measures are hard to find. So, in practice the main capital input measures reflect only physical capital—structures and equipment. The stock of physical capital in use is estimated from the history of investment over time and from estimates of the extent of scrapping and depreciation. Land use is also included in many capital measures.

These basic measures of productivity have been extended in several ways. A weighted or adjusted labor input can be used to reflect the changing level of human capital in the work force as a result of changes in age, experience, and years of schooling. For individual industries and sectors of the economy, there are measures of multifactor productivity that use the gross output of the industry rather than its value added. Materials, energy, and purchased services are then considered inputs into production, like capital and labor.

Human capital is one form of nonphysical or intangible capital, and there is some concern that other forms of nonphysical capital have become increasingly important but are not counted. Manufacturing industries spend heavily on R&D, and many industries in the manufacturing sector and in services spend heavily in developing software and computer systems. Members of the committee familiar with computer systems development estimate that these costs are two to three times or more the cost of computer hardware. These additional costs include software, hardware, and software to connect to other computers or to network PCs, support staff, and R&D support for new systems. It has been argued, for example, that to some airlines the value of their reservations systems is greater than the value of their airplanes.

Taking account of the full range of different types of capital does not help explain slow growth in productivity, however. In fact it could make the slowdown seem worse—errors that lead to an understatement of output lead to an understatement of productivity, but errors that lead to an understatement of inputs lead to an overstatement of productivity. If there has been an acceleration of investment in nonphysical capital over the last several years, as seems likely, then multifactor productivity may show a larger slowdown than labor productivity. If we are getting so much smarter, why are we not getting richer?

Taking account of nonphysical capital could change perceptions of the slow rate of investment in the U.S. economy overall, however. Discussions of U.S. competitiveness often focus on the low rate of investment in the U.S. economy in plants and equipment in the United States relative to other countries. But perhaps the structure of the U.S. economy is simply making that kind of investment less important.

from 1948 to 1973, when productivity in the goods-producing sector grew at a rate of 3.2 percent a year and in the service-producing industries at 2.5 percent a year. Contrary to common perception, substantial growth in the productivity of the service industries was evident prior to 1973, even taking into account the various flaws in the data. Notable over this period is the strong growth of productivity in transportation, communications, utilities, trade, and the narrowly defined services sector.[13]

As Table 1.1 indicates, productivity growth in both the goods- and service-producing sectors collapsed after 1973. Productivity had actually begun to decline prior to 1973 in both the mining and the construction sectors, and this decline continued in the 1970s. Manufacturing and farming managed to sustain positive growth in productivity over this period, but at a much slower pace. Within the service-producing industries, there was substantially slower growth after 1973; only the communications industry sustained its pre-1973 performance.

Since 1979, the gap has widened between the productivity growth rates of the goods- and the service-producing sectors. The goods-producing sector has made a substantial recovery in growth, especially in manufacturing; only construction has shown continued weakness. The service-producing sector has also experienced some recovery, especially in trade, but its overall recovery has been much less than that in the goods-production sector overall and certainly very much less than the recovery in manufacturing.

One of the distinctive patterns shown in Table 1.1 is that productivity has grown extremely rapidly in the nonelectrical machinery industry, which is part of manufacturing. The computer industry is the main source of growth in this subsector, and the very rapid decline in computer prices has been captured by the price deflator for this industry and is powering its growth. The extraordinary performance of the computer industry is making a major contribution to the measured recovery of manufacturing's growth in productivity. In fact, the post-1973 recovery of the whole goods-producing sector owes a great deal to productivity in the production of computers. Among the manufacturing industries, several still had weak growth in the 1980s. The improvement in growth in the 1980s has not been uniform even within goods-producing industries.

What do the macroeconomic data say about the contribution of IT to productivity in the service-producing sector since its widespread introduction beginning in the mid-1970s? The record of productivity in this sector is highly heterogeneous. Telecommunications, for example, has long been a leader in growth in U.S. productivity and has benefited greatly from IT. Automatic switching and other developments have enabled an enormous increase in telephone service while labor input has been reduced. The telecommunications industry is one for which a good measure of output can be obtained.

IMPACT OF IMFORMATION TECHNOLOGY AT THE MACROECONOMIC LEVEL   37

Outside of communications, however, the macroeconomic data reveal scant evidence of IT's contribution to productivity. For example, there is a set of handicraft services (including teaching, health care, automotive repair, legal services, and police protection) whose costs have benefited very little from IT, even though in some cases the quality of the product has benefited greatly. Areas in which a major impact might have been expected, such as finance, insurance, and real estate (FIRE) and the narrowly defined services sector, have shown almost no growth in productivity since 1979. Data on the productivity of these services have reflected persistently slow growth (at least when the figures on productivity are not adjusted for improved quality of products), and their relative prices have consequently risen—a facet of the productivity paradox described earlier in this chapter.

The committee has noted that the data on productivity computed by BLS using output series of the NIPA are published by BLS only at a very aggregated level; BLS does not publish the data on service-sector productivity. Although these figures can be readily calculated from the Commerce Department's breakdown of GNP by industry and in fact are widely cited, the BLS itself believes that the results obtained for the service sector as a whole lack the quality to merit publication. There are several reasons for the agency's concerns.

Problems with the Data from the NIPA

The three main problems with estimating productivity from the NIPA output data are (1) the difficulty of assessing each industry's contribution to total output (discussed above), (2) the problem of accounting correctly for new products and for changes in quality, and (3) the fact that in some industries output is actually measured by inputs.

Difficulty in Accounting for New Products and Changes in Quality

An important deficiency in the data on productivity based on the NIPA is that the impacts of new products and services and of changes in the quality of existing products and services are understated or ignored.[14] This is a recognized problem with respect to goods-producing industries that introduce new products constantly. For several years after new products are introduced, their prices are not used in the calculation of the price deflators. For example, after color TVs were first introduced, the price index for televisions continued to be based solely on black and white TVs for some time. Of course the production and sale of color TVs were counted in the nominal or dollar value of output, so that color TVs did to some extent add immediately to productivity. But the price index captured neither the benefit to consumers of being able to watch in color, nor the rapid decline in price that occurs commonly with most new products in the first few years after their introduction. Overall, the impact of color TVs on productivity was understated.

Understatement of the contribution of new service products to productivity is also a serious problem. For example, measured growth in productivity has been slow in the insurance industry because the dollar value of insurance output is deflated by the price index for the activities being insured against. Income from the provision of medical insurance is deflated by the rapidly rising price deflator for medical care costs. What is not reflected in the data on productivity is that the insurance industry has in fact introduced a range of different policy options, tailoring the policies to customers' particular needs. Computer technology has provided the means for this individualized service. At the same time, according to some observers, computer and telecommunications technology has drastically reduced the length of time needed to process claims.[15] Neither the customization nor the convenience factor is reflected in the data on measured real output. Many other service industries have also provided innovative new services. For example, the financial services industry has introduced a variety of new investment securities, and the telecommunications industry can offer high-speed data transmission lines and new consumer services, such as call forwarding or caller identification. Moreover, the ability to communicate information almost instantaneously allows knowledge workers to operate in entirely new ways. Companies with operations in several countries can allow employees in the United States, for instance, to work cooperatively and concurrently with employees in London or Tokyo.

Changes in the quality of existing goods and services can be just as important as completely new products or services—sometimes more important. Although changes in quality are sometimes counted, they are often missed in measures of productivity. In manufacturing, if a newly introduced model of a product has specific additional features (e.g., an ice maker) that enable the manufacturer to charge higher prices, then this change in quality is counted as an increase in output and thus as a contributor to increased productivity. But if a new model of a refrigerator simply has a better design but takes the same inputs to manufacture, then this change in quality will generally be missed. Similarly, in services, a higher-quality (more reliable, more flexible) service that requires inputs similar to those needed for a lesser service will be ignored in measures of productivity unless the price can be increased. For example, in the supermarket industry, reported growth in productivity is low, but change in quality is a major concern. Table 1.2 shows a variety of measures of U.S. supermarket productivity and some selected measures of the quality of service being provided. Real sales per hour of labor input or per square foot of selling space have grown little over time, or have even fallen over some years. But there has been a huge increase in the variety of products offered and in the quality of other services provided.

TABLE 1.2 Indicators of Productivity and Services Provided, U.S. Supermarkets, 1948 to 1985, Selected Years

Item	1948	1957	1967	1972	1977	1982	1985
Real sales per hour	58.2	82.0	100.0	106.4	100.8	103.6	92.7
Real sales per square foot	n/a[a]	121.6	100.0	97.5	83.6	77.5	75.6
Real sales per transaction	n/a	86.0	100.0	98.4	94.0	93.3	97.0
Square feet per hour worked	n/a	67.4	100.0	109.1	120.6	133.7	122.6
Square feet per member of U.S. population, 16 and over	n/a	77.4	100.0	110.3	117.1	123.3	128.8
Items carried per store	2,200[b]	4,800	7,000	9,000	10,500	13,067	17,459
Percent stores with complete air conditioning	14	n/a	n/a	n/a	n/a	n/a	n/a
Percent with mechanical refrigeration in produce department	30	n/a	n/a	n/a	100	n/a	n/a
Percent with "extensive" delicatessen	n/a	n/a	46	n/a	n/a	n/a	n/a
Percent selling beer	29	47	55	n/a	n/a	n/a	80
Percent open Sunday	5	24	45	55	62	n/a	n/a
Percent open seven evenings	22	51	73	n/a	n/a	n/a	n/a

NOTE: Index, 1967 = 100, except as noted. Sales deflated by consumer price index (CPI) for food at home.
[a]n/a, not available.
[b]1948 figure for items carried refers to 1950.

SOURCE: Data from annual issues of Super Market Institute, *The Super Market Industry Speaks*, Super Market Institute, Chicago.

Need for Wider Use of Hedonic Price Indexes For some products, the price deflators are adjusted to capture the effects of changes in quality. For example, when a new model of computer is introduced that runs at higher speed or has more memory, these changes are reflected in what is called a hedonic price index. This price index has been in use for the computer industry for a number of years and is based on a statistical technique that estimates how much customers value speed, memory, or other characteristics of computers. The very rapid measured growth of productivity in the computer industry testifies to the impact a hedonic index can have. Estimated growth in that industry's productivity was much slower before the hedonic price index was introduced. Residential housing and automobiles are other important industries for which hedonic price indexes are used, although in neither case is the index as powerful as for the computer industry. The residential housing index adjusts mostly for the square footage of the houses built.

Hedonic price indexes are a very good tool for capturing the effects of changes in quality. They can be used to evaluate the different characteristics of a good or a service, track how these change over time, and then estimate how the market values these changing characteristics. Unfortunately, use of these indexes is very much the exception rather than the rule within the goods-producing industries, and these indexes are not used at all for price deflators for the service industries. Many people in the service industries believe that new products have proliferated to the point that conventional concepts of productivity are breaking down. It is no longer possible, for example, to talk about mail services as a homogeneous group, because overnight mail is really a different product from regular mail. Unless systematic attempts are made to capture the effects of new or different products being provided in the service sector, the quality of the data on U.S. productivity will decline.

Use of Data on Input as Measures of Output Earlier in this chapter it was noted that financial services companies have been very innovative in introducing new services and that the techniques used for measuring productivity will lead to understatement or omission of the impact of these innovations. This problem is actually much worse with respect to banks and other depository institutions, which represent about 30 percent of total employment in the finance, insurance, and real estate (FIRE) subsector, because there is no valid price deflator for this group. The deflator used is an index of compensation paid to employees in the industry, and this deflator has the effect of assuming that real output in the banking industry group rises one-for-one with the number of employees.[16] The way in which real output is computed ensures that almost no change in measured productivity will be observed in the banking industry group, regardless of what the actual increase in productivity may have been.

Industry-specific Measures of Productivity Developed by the Bureau of Labor Statistics

The Bureau of Labor Statistics (BLS) has developed another set of productivity measures for services that is not subject to the constraints imposed by adhering to the framework of the NIPA. These measures are made for a number of goods-producing industries and also for many industries classified in the Department of Commerce's Standard Industrial Classification (SIC) system as service industries.

At present, BLS publishes indexes of output per hour, that is, output per unit of labor input, for selected industries for the major service activities. These include selected industries classified at SIC code 40 and higher—transportation, communications, public utilities, trade, finance, insurance, and real estate, and business and personal services. Indexes of productivity are published for 39 service industries, covering about 42 percent of all workers in the service industries in the private business sector.

The BLS also publishes measures of productivity for the federal government with separate detail for the common functions provided by federal agencies, such as record keeping, library services, building and grounds maintenance, loans and grants, and so on. In addition, work is currently being conducted on the development of indexes of productivity for hospitals and additional wholesale trade activities.

The measures of output used in these BLS series are independently developed from data on sales, prices, and physical units whenever possible, combined with labor input weights. In some instances the data on labor input weights are not available, and approximations such as gross margins have to be used. The data on labor input cover the hours of all persons employed in a particular industry, including the self-employed, and are based on the BLS surveys of establishment employment and hours. The "hours of employees" are based on hours-paid data from the surveys of establishment employment and hours. The hours of the self-employed are derived from the household survey of employment and hours conducted for the BLS by the Bureau of the Census.

What Do the BLS Data on Selected Industries Show?

Table 1.3 shows the compound annual percentage change in output per employee-hour for selected service industries over the period from 1973 to 1990, the longest period for which continuous measures from BLS are available. Contrary to the general belief that service industries are characterized by uniformly low growth in productivity, a wide range in the rates of growth is evident. Over the most recent decade, 1980 to 1990, the rates range from a decline of 4 percent per year for gas utilities to an increase of 9 percent per year for railroads. The increase for railroads actually exceeds that for almost all manufacturing industries, in which significant rates of growth in productivity have occurred. Even over the longer period from 1973 to 1990, when the range of rates of growth was narrower, there was still considerable variation across industries.

Gaps in BLS Data and Measures of Productivity

Although BLS publishes at least one measure of productivity for each major service activity group—transportation, communications, and so on—there are major areas within each of these groups for which no measure of productivity has been developed and published.

One reason for these gaps is that it is difficult to define and develop meaningful indicators of output and/or input in many service industries. In

TABLE 1.3 Growth in Productivity in Selected U.S. Service Industries, 1973 to 1990

Service Industry	SIC[b] Codes	Period of Time and Output per Labor-Hour (average annual % change)[a]		
		1973-90	1973-80	1980-90
Transportation				
Railroad	4011	5.8	1.5	9.0
Bus carriers, class 1	411, 13, 14	-0.7[c]	-0.5	-0.7[d]
Trucking, except local	4213	3.2	2.3	3.9
Air transportation	4512, 13, 22	2.5	3.2	2.1
Petroleum pipelines	4612, 13	0.6	-0.7	1.6
Utilities				
Telephone communications	481	5.5	6.8	4.5
Electric utilities	491, 3	1.4	0.9	1.7
Gas utilities	492, 3	-2.5	-0.3	-4.0
Trade				
Scrap and waste materials	5093	n/a[e]	n/a[e]	1.4[d]
Hardware stores	5251	1.9	1.8	1.9
Department stores	5311	2.6	2.6	2.6
Variety stores	5331	-0.4	-1.6	0.5
Grocery stores	5411	-1.0	-0.1	-1.7
Retail bakeries	546	-0.7	-1.1	-0.4
New- and used-car dealers	5511	1.4	0.5	2.1
Auto and home supply stores	5531	2.2	2.4	2.0
Gasoline service stations	5541	2.9	2.9	2.9
Men's and boys' clothing stores	5611	1.7	0.5	2.6
Women's clothing stores	5621	3.2	3.3	3.2
Family clothing stores	5651	1.8	1.8	1.8
Shoe stores	5661	1.5	1.4	1.6
Home furniture stores	571	1.0	0.3	1.5
Household appliance stores	5722	2.5[c]	2.7	2.6[d]
Radio, TV, and computer stores	573	4.8[c]	4.3	5.7[d]
Eating and drinking places	581	-0.6	-0.5	-0.6
Drug stores	5912	0.5	1.4	-0.1
Liquor stores	5921	-0.4	0.2	-0.8
Business and personal services				
Commercial banks	602	1.2	-0.5	2.7
Hotels and motels	7011	-0.4	0.4	-1.0
Laundry and cleaning services	721	-0.8	-1.2	-0.5
Beauty and barber shops	7231, 41	0.8	0.0	1.4
Automotive repair shops	753	-0.2	-1.2	0.4

[a]Based on compounding formula.
[b]Standard Industrial Classification system code.
[c]1973 to 1989.
[d]1980 to 1989.
[e]n/a, not available.

SOURCE: Bureau of Labor Statistics.

most cases adequate measures have to be derived from data obtained in surveys conducted for purposes other than measuring productivity. For measuring productivity, the output indicator should be final to the activity being examined, quantifiable, and consistent in coverage with, but independent of, the input indicators; should reflect differences in the quality of the activity being evaluated; and should represent the major part of the activities of the sector. For many service activities, the available data do not meet these criteria. The major gap within communications is radio and television broadcasting; in electricity, gas, and sanitary services, it is sanitary services. In trade, the gap in coverage is in the area of wholesale trade; in finance, insurance, and real estate the gap is in the real estate component. In business and personal services, no measures are available for health, education, and legal services. Finally, in the area of government, the major gap is in state and local government.

Conclusions on Productivity Measures Developed from BLS Data

The BLS has made considerable progress in developing indexes of productivity for selected service industries. The measures of productivity for some of these industries are very accurate, clearly reflecting changes in output per unit of labor input. Because the concepts of output are relatively straightforward and appropriate data are readily available, the measures for transportation, communications, and public utilities fall into this category. The measures for some of the trade industries present some difficulties primarily because of the heterogeneity of the categories of merchandise line sales and the limited availability of adequate price deflators. However, these indexes of productivity are useful indicators of trends over time and are continually being improved as the number of detailed price indexes increases.[17]

Many difficulties remain in clarifying some of the basic conceptual problems of defining the output of certain service industries, and many inadequacies are present in the data available.[18] In particular, the BLS does not have the resources to follow the rapidly changing nature of the output in many services industries, changes that have been enabled by the use of IT in many cases. BLS's measurement of productivity is good if output over time can be captured adequately by a simple measure such as passenger-miles. It does not do so well when other characteristics are important, and in such situations it suffers from the same kinds of problems that the BEA data suffer from. For example, in the case of airlines, no account is taken of changes in the frequency of service, ease of booking or changing reservations, flying time, number of stops, on-time record, and so on. For many service industries, these aspects of service quality are crucial.

ALTERNATIVE MEASURES OF PRODUCTIVITY AND PERFORMANCE

The slowdown in the growth of measured productivity in services has been the subject of great concern among policymakers, but productivity is only one measure of economic performance. For the business manager, other measures of performance may provide a better guide to long-term profitability and success. Productivity and profitability are linked in that, other things being equal, a company that is able to raise its productivity relative to that of its competitors will be able to lower its costs and raise its margins or reduce prices to increase market share.

But other things are not always equal. For example, a company that provides a unique new product or service may be able to raise its profitability by more than a company that simply concentrates on raising productivity in its existing lines of business. Or an industry may find that its market conditions change. The deregulation of many service industries has forced them to adapt and, in many cases, to raise productivity. But the increase in competition within these industries has lowered prices, and margins and profits are hard to come by. Airlines, railroads, and trucking are all in this position.

For workers, employment may be more important than productivity, especially in the short run. In fact some people see a trade-off between jobs and increases in productivity. The U.S. economy has been very successful over the years in increasing the number of jobs it has generated, and the largest number of these have been in the service sector. The fear in some quarters is that as some labor-intensive companies in the service sector seek to boost their productivity via restructuring, the creation of full-time jobs may slow.[19]

However, downsizing is not a long-term recipe for sustained growth in productivity. Once companies have eliminated excess staff, they will need to look beyond downsizing and restructuring and embark on a path of judicious expansion that includes increases in the rate of hiring and in capacity. Recent evidence suggests that this may be starting to happen. Over the period from October 1992 to May 1993, job growth averaged 165,000 jobs per month, well in excess of the paltry gains of 18,000 per month that occurred in the first 17 months of the recovery. For example, during 1992 business spending on capital equipment has risen at an annual rate of 16 percent, with 60 percent of the increase concentrated in IT hardware.

For some purposes international competitiveness is as important or more important than productivity. Again, the two are linked, but external circumstances may change so that the two indicators of performance move differently from each other. For example, the U.S. auto industry and the U.S. textile industry have both succeeded reasonably well in raising productivity in recent years. But both industries have come under intense competition from foreign companies that have done as well or better in increasing productivity and product quality or have been able to make use of less costly labor. A recent study indicates that compared to similar industries of other countries, U.S. service industries have generally higher absolute levels of productivity (Box 1.3), although U.S. rates of growth in productivity have lagged those of many other nations.[20] Furthermore, the United States maintains a healthy $52 billion service trade surplus with foreign nations.[21]

OBSERVATIONS AND CONCLUSIONS

Many Factors Influence Productivity: IT Affects Many Aspects of Performance

As noted at the beginning of this chapter, many factors besides the application of information technology determine growth in the productivity of the U.S. service sector. This is not surprising, since output itself is a function of multiple inputs and technology, the latter affecting how inputs are combined in production. Productivity is also influenced, for example, by other kinds of capital investment, such as buildings for retailers or airplanes for airline companies. The fact that over the past 15 to 20 years slow growth in productivity has been accompanied by rapid investment in IT has suggested to some people that the use of IT has actually caused the slowdown in productivity growth. But the committee determined that it is a mistake to conclude that IT is the culprit. It surely is in some cases, but in others it has probably made a large positive contribution. The key point is that the currently available macroeconomic data cannot precisely measure how investments in IT alone are influencing productivity in the services. As documented and discussed above in this chapter, the committee's findings have led it to make the following observations about current macroeconomic data on service-sector productivity and how investments in and the use of IT have influenced these data:

- The BEA macroeconomic data do not deal adequately with changes in the quality of the services provided. And IT is often used to improve the quality of services. The development and use of better measures of output might show a very different picture of growth in productivity.
- The BEA macroeconomic data do not adequately allow for the effects of new services, and IT is often used to provide new services. Again, the development and use of better measures of output that account for new services could show a radically different picture of growth in productivity.
- Existing data on the capital input to production do not take account of the knowledge capital (see Box 1.2) that is considered by many to be the

BOX 1.3 A Recent Study of Service-Sector Productivity in the United States and Other Countries

The Global Institute of McKinsey & Co., assisted by economists Martin Baily, Francis Bator, and Robert Solow, completed in 1992 a comparison of the productivity of the airline, banking, general merchandise retailing, telecommunications, and restaurant industries in the United States relative to the comparable industries in European countries and Japan.

For three of the industries—airlines, banking, and telecommunications—the study used quantitative output measures of the type used by the Bureau of Labor Statistics in its analysis of specific industries. For example, in airlines, different output measures were combined, such as passenger-miles, number of aircraft maintained, and number of passengers served. Adjustments were made to allow for such factors as different route lengths and fleet structures. For the other two industries value added was the measure of output, with the international comparisons made using what are called purchasing power parity exchange rates.

Except in the restaurant industry, where productivity was comparable in the countries studied, the findings indicated that the U.S. industries had a lead in productivity, usually in the range of 20 to 40 percent. Several explanations for this productivity lead were examined. For example, it was found that U.S. airlines' larger average size gave them some advantage over European airlines. Differences in the mix of output and in capital intensity were also significant in some cases. The most important difference overall, however, was found to be differences in how the work force is organized and managed. There is greater competitive pressure and less restrictive regulation in the U.S. industries than in those of other countries studied.

The McKinsey study is based on an analysis in a single year (1989) of productivity levels and therefore does not directly contradict the Bureau of Economic Analysis macroeconomic data that show a slow rate of growth of productivity in the service sector in the United States. But the finding that U.S. services have a substantial lead over other countries could reinforce the concerns about the BEA data that are presented in this chapter.

In general the McKinsey study concluded that differences in technology were not the most important factor in the productivity differences that they found, since the technology is available to enterprises in all of the countries studied if they wish to use it. For telecommunications and banking, the study did conclude that a failure to adopt the most advanced information technology had hurt productivity in other countries. The telecommunications industry in Germany, for example, had not introduced electronic switching and could not offer business customers high-speed data transmission. And in the banking industry, both Germany and

> the United Kingdom suffered a productivity disadvantage because fewer automatic teller machines had been deployed. U.S. banks had invested more heavily in terminals, allowing many activities to be centralized that were still carried out less productively in branches overseas, particularly so in the United Kingdom.

most important part of the capital base of the service industries. The use of any improved measure of capital input could also drastically change the estimates of growth in productivity.
- In some service industries, the BEA data exclude, by definition, any changes in measured productivity because real output is measured by the number of employees working in the industry. Banking and financial services are the most important examples.

For the business decision maker, productivity may be an important consideration but will often not be the most important one. Productivity is important for business because a company that has weak productivity in its core business activities, relative to other companies, is tying one hand behind its back in its competitive struggle. But productivity is rarely sufficient for business success and should not be the sole or even the primary basis for most companies' decisions about investment in IT. Providing value to the consumer is often more important than increasing productivity, and such circumstances will require that measures of performance be used to track growth in the economy and to evaluate the part played by IT. Making better business and policy decisions about investing in IT requires having more information about what IT is being used for than can be provided by the standard data on productivity. In Chapters 2 through 4, the committee discusses how IT has been used to improve performance at the industry, enterprise, and activity levels of the U.S. service sector.

ORGANIZATION AND SCOPE OF THIS REPORT

In refining its approach in response to its initial findings, the committee chose to investigate the full range of impacts of the use of IT on performance in the service sector. Thus the committee examined the nature and measurement of performance in services at progressively less aggregated levels of analysis: the industry level (Chapter 2), the enterprise level (Chapter 3), and the activity level (Chapter 4). These chapters are supplemented by appendixes that provide more methodological detail and supporting data: Appendix A describes selected research on economic and strategic impacts of IT; Appendix B describes methods used by the Bureau of Economic Analysis to derive measures of output; Appendix C describes methods used by the Bureau of Labor Statistics for deriving measures of productivity; Appendix D describes how the committee conducted its study, including the interview process used by the committee to inform its deliberations and a summary of its results.

Chapters 2 through 4 culminate in Chapter 5, which discusses implications for managers in organizations wishing to improve their management of information technology, and Chapter 6, which presents issues and recommendations for public policy.

To put this report in perspective, some observations on the committee's operation and scope of concern are appropriate. First, this report was shaped by interactions within a multidisciplinary committee that included business executives, economists, behavioral scientists, management theorists, and technologists. Second, the committee considered the context of international competitiveness in conducting its analysis, but detailed investigation of international conditions was beyond its scope. Third, although smaller companies were represented in the data that support industry- and national-level analyses, the committee's resources did not permit a systematic examination of the distinguishing characteristics of smaller enterprises.

In addition to using the standard macroeconomic data collected and developed by government agencies, the committee drew on observations from managers and executives in industry (a group including some of the committee's own members, as well as numerous others). These observations were obtained through interviews that were used to develop and check insights, not to generate quantitative data. Appendixes provide methodological and supporting details about the committee's sources of information and its approach. Appendix E lists the interviewed executives, whose observations helped the committee to understand the processes by which IT projects are planned, implemented, and evaluated.

At the macroeconomic level, the committee was concerned about the constraining effects of looking at services from the traditional perspectives of goods-production (Chapter 1). At present, most of the terminology, methodology, and data for analyzing productivity (and performance) derive from earlier studies in the goods-producing industries, but to the committee, most of these seemed inadequate for understanding trends in the service sector. For example, whereas productivity in goods-producing activities is measured in terms that refer to relatively concrete units of output, dollar sales, or profits, performance in services may relate to more subjective quantities such as timing, quality, comfort, or convenience. Measurement difficulties are a theme that runs through the report.

NOTES AND REFERENCES

[1] This figure is for checks cleared, deposits processed, and cash distributed by human tellers. Cash distributed by automated teller machines is not included. Data reported in 1992 by The Global Institute of McKinsey and Company (see Box 1.3).

[2] See, for example, Baily, M., and R. Gordon, 1986, "The Productivity Slowdown: Measurement Issues and the Explosion of Computer Power," pp. 347-431 in *Brookings Papers on Economic Activity*, W. Brainard and G. Perry (eds.), Brookings Institution, Washington, D.C.; Roach, Stephen S., 1988, "Technology and the Services Sector: America's Hidden Competitive Challenge," in *Technology in Services*, Bruce R. Guile and James Brian Quinn (eds.), National Academy Press, Washington, D.C.; Roach, Stephen S., 1991, "Services Under Siege: The Restructuring Imperative," *Harvard Business Review*, September-October, pp. 82-91; and Strassmann, P., 1990, *The Business Value of Computers*, Information Economics Press, New Canaan, Conn.

[3] A paper by Paul Attewell that was brought to the attention of the committee while this report was in press addresses some of these issues. See Attewell, Paul. 1994. "Information Technology and the Productivity Paradox," in *Understanding the Productivity Paradox: Organizational Linkages*, Douglas H. Harris (ed.), National Academy Press, Washington, D.C., in preparation.

[4] One variant of this idea suggests that IT has transformed the way business is conducted and is essential to competitive success, but the changes it has facilitated do not raise the overall output of the economy. For example, individual companies can use IT to target their marketing campaigns more effectively, but overall industry sales are not affected and so neither is productivity measured at the industry level.

[5] For a discussion of the slowdown in the United States and other countries, see Baumol, William J., Sue Anne Batey Blackman, and Edward N. Wolff, 1989, *Productivity and American Leadership: The Long View*, MIT Press, Cambridge, Mass.; and Baily, Martin N., and Alok K. Chakrabarti, 1988, *Innovation and the Productivity Crisis*, Brookings Institution, Washington, D.C. However, note that U.S. productivity growth rates that lag behind those of its international competitors are a distinct concern for U.S. policymakers, even though U.S. base productivity levels may still be higher than those of its competitors.

[6] See, for example, Kendrick, J.W., 1987, "Service Sector Productivity," *Business Economics*, April, pp. 18-24.

[7] David, Paul A. 1990. "The Dynamo and the Computer: An Historical Perspective on the Modern Productivity Paradox," *American Economic Review*, May, pp. 355-361.

[8] Brynjolfsson, Erik, and Lorin Hitt. 1993. "Is Information Systems Spending Productive? New Evidence and New Results," MIT Sloan School of Management, Working Paper 3571-93, September 24. (To appear in *Proceedings of the 14th International Conference on Information Systems*.)

[9] The part of the government sector that is subtracted is "general government." This includes the salaries of government workers in the various federal, state, and local agencies. The output of "government enterprises," such as the Postal Service and the Tennessee Valley Authority, are included in the business sector of the economy.

[10] The capital goods purchased by an industry are not subtracted from the gross output of the industry. Value added in an industry reflects the payments to both labor and capital inputs to the industry.

[11] One difficulty is that there is not a direct match between products and industries. Plants in several industries cast their own steel products, for example. An industry deflator should be based on the prices of the products that are produced by the plants that are classified within that industry.

[12] Also included in Table 1.1 is productivity for the government sector, although any productivity that shows up in the data is purely the result of shifts in the composition of government activities. By assumption there is no productivity growth within government activities.

[13] The narrowly defined services sector consists of hotels and other lodging places, personal services, business services, auto repair and similar services, motion pictures, amusement and recreation services, health care, legal services, education, and social services. By contrast, the term *service sector* is used throughout this report to denote the entire range of service industries, as noted on the opening page of this chapter.

[14] Though important when productivity is used as an indicator of living standards, adjustments for changes in product quality can be misleading if the issue at hand is product cost analysis. For example, if the number of teaching hours per student does not decline, college costs must rise as quickly as faculty salaries, whether or not the quality of teaching changes.

[15] Not everyone agrees that claims processing has speeded up. There have been complaints that some insurance companies have delayed payments.

[16] For example, the GDP originating in the commercial banking industry per full-time employee in 1980 ($37,600 in 1982 dollars) was virtually identical to that in 1988 ($37,900 in 1982 dollars). This small change was due entirely to a different structure in the commercial banking industry.

[17] The use of gross margin weighting as an approximation of labor input weighting is appropriate as long as labor costs represent a significant portion of gross margins and the elements of margins do not change over time.

[18] The difficulties that remain involve clarifying some basic conceptual problems of defining output for some service industries and filling gaps in data available. With regard to data, more and improved data are needed on prices, value of output, capital, and material input. The BLS and other government statistical agencies have undertaken initiatives to expand the coverage in the service sector, and the results of these efforts should lead to better and more comprehensive industry measures. Collection of more measures of service industry prices, expanded data on hours worked that provide more disaggregation, and continued work on public-sector productivity by BLS are but a few examples. However, some areas—e.g., education, entertainment, legal and social services, and many segments of medical services—present such severe conceptual and data problems that appropriate solutions may be a long time in coming. Additional resources may have only a limited effect until the conceptual problems can be dealt with.

In expanding the number of industries for which measures are prepared, the BLS has had to take these problems, among others, into consideration, and this has limited the number of service industries for which measures have been developed. Nevertheless, adequate measures of productivity have been developed for many service industries. The problems of measuring productivity are different for each of the various service industries, and the approaches followed vary.

[19] The recovery of 1993 is widely believed to be relatively weak by historical standards. For example, unpublished data from the Bureau of Labor Statistics, U.S. Department of Labor, indicate that jobs in the ninth quarter of this recovery rose by 0.3 percent as compared to their nadir in the first quarter of 1991. By comparison, the corresponding figure for the eight previous recessions is 6.8 percent. In this recovery, manufacturing firms seem to be relying more on overtime than on new hiring to meet expanding demand for goods, while service firms seem to be relying more on hiring part-time workers with few benefits (for one example, see Swoboda, Frank, 1992, "In Omaha, the Underside of a Jobs Promise," *Washington Post*, October 25, p. H-1). The result in manufacturing has been fewer jobs with longer work weeks, and in services more jobs with shorter work weeks (see Uchitelle, Louis, 1993, "Fewer Jobs Filled As Factories Rely on Overtime Pay," *New York Times*, May 16, p. 1). Even strong companies are cutting labor costs to maintain or increase profit margins (see Uchitelle, Louis, 1993, "Strong Companies Are Joining Trend to Eliminate Jobs," *New York Times*, July 26).

[20] Recent data suggest that the slowdown in growth of U.S. productivity has been accompanied by a slowdown in that of the other leading industrial countries, and that the percentage

decline in Japan has been almost exactly as great as that in the United States. Further, all industrial countries have moved closer to the United States in levels of productivity and GDP per capita, although they have not caught up with this country in real terms (i.e., in terms of purchasing power parity exchange rates). With the race narrowing, it is a tautology that the laggards must be running faster than the leader, thus explaining how the United States can be ahead of everyone else in productivity level, although its productivity growth rate lags behind those of many of the other countries.

[21]U.S. Department of Commerce, Bureau of Economic Analysis. 1992. *Survey of Current Business*, June, Table 3, "Selected Services Transactions," p. 96.

BIBLIOGRAPHY FOR CHAPTER 1

Brand, Horst, and John Duke. 1982. "Productivity in Commercial Banking: Computers Spur the Advance," *Monthly Labor Review*, Vol. 105 (December), pp. 19-27.

Brand, Horst, and Zaul Ahmed. 1986. "Productivity in Beauty and Barber Shops," *Monthly Labor Review*, Vol. 109.

Carnes, Richard B. 1978. "Laundry and Cleaning Services Pressed to Post Productivity Gains." *Monthly Labor Review*, Vol. 101 (February), pp. 38-42.

Carnes, Richard B., and Horst Brand. 1977. "Productivity and New Technology in Eating and Drinking Places," *Monthly Labor Review*, Vol. 100 (September), pp. 9-15.

Dean, Edwin, and Kent Kunze. 1990. "Productivity Measurement in Service Industries," *Output Measurement in the Services Sector*, National Bureau of Economic Research, Cambridge, Mass.

Duke, John. 1977. "New-Car Dealers Experience Long-Term Gains in Productivity," *Monthly Labor Review*, Vol. 100 (March), pp. 29-33.

Friedman, Brian. 1984. "Productivity in the Apparel and Accessories Stores Industries," *Monthly Labor Review*, Vol. 107 (October), pp. 37-42.

Friedman, Brian, and John L. Carey. 1975. "Productivity in Gasoline Stations, 1958-1973," *Monthly Labor Review*, Vol. 98 (February), pp. 32-36.

Kutscher, Ronald, and Jerome A. Mark. 1983. "The Service-Producing Sector: Some Common Perceptions Reviewed," *Monthly Labor Review*, Vol. 106 (April), pp. 21-24.

Mark, Jerome A. 1982. "Measuring Productivity in the Services," *Monthly Labor Review*, Vol. 105 (June), pp. 3-8.

Mark, Jerome A. 1988. "Measuring Productivity in Service Industries," in *Technology in Services: Policies for Growth, Trade, and Employment*, Bruce R. Guile and James Brian Quinn (eds.), National Academy Press, Washington, D.C.

Mincer, Jacob. 1974. *Schooling, Experience and Earnings*, Columbia University Press, New York.

Roach, Stephen S. 1991. "Services Under Siege: The Restructuring Imperative," *Harvard Business Review*, September-October, pp. 82-91.

Smith, Anthony D. 1972. *The Measurement and Interpretation of Service Output Changes*, National Economic Development Office, London.

Waldorf, William H., Kent Kunze, Lawrence S. Rosenblum, and Michael B. Tannen. 1986. "New Measures of the Contribution of Education and Experience to U.S. Productivity Growth," paper presented at annual meetings of American Economic Association, Dec. 28-30, New Orleans, La.

2
Impacts of Information Technology at the Industry Level

As discussed in Chapter 1, it is difficult to generalize about the impacts of information technology (IT) on productivity or performance in the service sector, because the effects of using IT cannot be isolated from the effects of other factors and because the service sector is highly heterogeneous. A better picture of IT's impact can therefore be obtained by focusing on individual industries. Although firms differ within a given industry, they must generally share a common environment whose factors are relevant to their performance—for example, an industry's requirements for particular kinds of workers and skills, the quality of its labor-management relations, the presence or absence of regulation, how capital- or labor-intensive the industry is, and the kinds of technology applications associated with it all influence the performance of the firms within that industry.

Likewise, an industry's environment affects the nature of the benefits that companies can realize from use of IT. Although the dimensions on which performance may be evaluated—such as the nature of improvements in product quality, increases in product variety, and product innovations—will therefore vary across industries, industry context is important for understanding both how and how much the use of IT has affected an industry's performance in providing services. In addition, the experience of one industry may provide insights relevant to understanding or anticipating effects in another.

To explore how industry context affects the use of IT and performance, the committee focused on six industries: air transport, telecommunications, retail and wholesale trade, health care, banking, and insurance. Together the industries chosen accounted for about 27 percent of the gross domestic product and 35 percent of U.S. employment in 1989; they are also proportionately much higher users of IT than are some other industries (Tables 2.1 and 2.2).[1] The sectors to which some of these industries belong are relatively capital-intensive; for example, the ratio of capital investment to value added in 1991 for transportation and telecommunications exceeded the comparable

TABLE 2.1 Six Selected Service Industries Compared to All U.S. Industry and All U.S. Service Industries, 1989 (figures in billions of 1982 dollars)

	GPO in 1989	Investment in IT in 1989 (as % of GPO)	Value of IT Capital Stock in 1989
GNP	4117.7		
GDP	4087.6		
All industry (manufacturing, construction, mining, and non-goods-producing)	3610.5	128.4(3.6)	513.3
Mining	127.2	1.2(0.9)	8.8
Construction	179.0	0.7(0.3)	3.2
Manufacturing	929.0	24.3(2.6)	78.0
All services (non-goods-producing industries)	2375.3	102.3(4.3)	456.1
Transportation	156.3	5.5(3.5)	20.6
Communications	109.4	17.6(16.1)	124.7
Utilities	136.6	6.3(4.6)	26.0
Wholesale	304.7	11.6(3.8)	54.0
Retail	412.0	10.6(2.6)	44.8
Financial, insurance, real estate	604.0	33.7(5.6)	123.2
Business, personal, professional services	652.3	16.9(2.6)	62.8
Six selected service industries (air transport, telecommunications, retail and wholesale trade, health care, banking, insurance)	1119.7	62.5(5.6)	291.1
Six industries as fraction of "all services"	47%	61%	64%
Six industries as fraction of "all industry"	31%	49%	57%
Six industries as fraction of GDP and GNP	27%		

SUMMARY: In 1989, six service industries (air transport, telecommunications, retail and wholesale trade, health care, banking, insurance) accounted for 27% of GNP, 31% of the 1989 GPO of "all industry," and 47% of the 1989 GPO of "all services." However, they accounted for 49% of 1989 IT expenditures by "all industry" and 61% of 1989 IT expenditures by "all services." Similarly, they accounted for 57% of the 1989 IT capital stock value of "all industry" and 64% of the 1989 IT capital stock value of "all services." In addition, these six industries averaged 5.6% in their 1989 IT investment as a percentage of GPO, while for all industries the comparable percentage was 3.6% and for all service industries it was 4.3%.

TABLE 2.2 Snapshots of Selected Service Industries, 1981 and 1989

	Air Transport	Telecommunications	Retail Trade
1981			
GPO (billions of 1982 dollars)	16.8	75.7	286.4
Revenues (billions of 1982 dollars)	45.2	91.8	453.6
Number of employees (millions of jobs)	0.5	1.1	16.9
Number of hours worked (billions)	0.9	2.4	27.4
Annual investment in IT (billions of 1982 dollars)	1.0	21.0	5.1
IT capital stock (billions of 1982 dollars)	1.8	125.3	13.2
GPO per labor-hour (1982 dollars)	17.70	31.97	10.44
Annual IT/GPO	6.2%	27.8%	1.8%
Annual rate of change in GPO per labor-hour	-2.7%	5.2%	1.6%
1989 (1989 Value as Percent of 1981 Value)			
GPO (billions of 1982 dollars)	31.7(189)	98.8(131)	412.0(144)
Revenues (billions of 1982 dollars)	66.6(147)	100.6(110)	628.3(138)
Number of employees (millions of jobs)	0.7(149)	0.9(82)	21.2(125)
Number of hours worked (billions)	1.4(148)	2.0(83)	32.8(120)
Annual investment in IT (billions of 1982 dollars)	3.0(288)	13.8(66)	10.6(207)
IT capital stock (billions of 1982 dollars)	9.8(543)	113.7(91)	44.8(340)
GPO per labor-hour (1982 dollars)	22.64(128)	49.97(156)	12.54(120)
Annual IT/GPO	9.4%(153)	14.0%(50)	2.6%(144)
Annual rate of change in GPO per labor-hour	-8.0%	4.0%	1.2%

NOTE: See Box 2.1 for explanation of terms and sources of data given.

TABLE 2.2 Continued

	Wholesale Trade	Health Care	Banking	Insurance
1981				
GPO				
(billions of 1982 dollars)	212.7	138.1	64.2	35.4
Revenues				
(billions of 1982 dollars)	317.6	204.8	88.7	66.8
Number of employees				
(millions of jobs)	5.7	5.9	2.0	1.2
Number of hours worked				
(billions)	11.4	10.2	3.9	2.4
Annual investment in IT				
(billions of 1982 dollars)	5.0	1.8	1.9	0.7
IT capital stock				
(billions of 1982 dollars)	13.2	8.9	5.1	1.7
GPO per labor-hour				
(1982 dollars)	18.64	13.49	16.66	14.76
Annual IT/GPO	2.4%	1.3%	3.0%	2.0%
Annual rate of change in GPO				
per labor-hour	4.7%	-1.2%	0.0%	-9.0%
1989 (1989 Value as Percent of 1981 Value)				
GPO				
(billions of 1982 dollars)	304.7(143)	164.4(119)	71.4(111)	36.7(104)
Revenues				
(billions of 1982 dollars)	400.8(126)	286.6(140)	99.8(112)	77.5(116)
Number of employees				
(millions of jobs)	6.6(116)	7.9(134)	2.3(112)	1.4(116)
Number of hours worked				
(billions)	13.1(115)	13.5(132)	4.3(110)	2.8(116)
Annual investment in IT				
(billions of 1982 dollars)	11.6(230)	3.6(204)	13.8(715)	6.2(856)
IT capital stock				
(billions of 1982 dollars)	54.0(409)	15.7(177)	35.1(690)	17.9(1080)
GPO per labor-hour				
(1982 dollars)	23.30(125)	12.14(90)	16.80(101)	13.18(89)
Annual IT/GPO	3.8%(160)	2.2%(171)	19.3%(643)	16.8%(826)
Annual rate of change in GPO				
per labor-hour	2.3%	-3.6%	0.2%	-1.1%

BOX 2.1 Notes on Terms and Data Presented in Tables 2.1 Through 2.9

Data	Source
GPO (billions of 1982 dollars)	Measures of GPO (gross domestic product originating in the U.S. economy) output prepared by the Bureau of Economic Analysis (BEA), U.S. Department of Commerce. Major revisions covering the period from 1977 to 1988 were released by the BEA in the January 1991 *Survey of Current Business*. In April 1991, the BEA further revised GPO figures for 1986 to 1988 and released 1989 figures.
Revenues (billions of 1982 dollars)	Revenues reflect measures of gross output by industry prepared by the Bureau of Labor Statistics, U.S. Department of Labor.
Employment (millions of jobs)	Employment includes both full-time and part-time employees; unpublished data, Bureau of Labor Statistics, U.S. Department of Labor.
Number of hours worked (billions)	Total hours worked by all employees (including proprietors); unpublished data, Bureau of Labor Statistics, U.S. Department of Labor.
Annual investment in IT (billions of 1982 dollars)	Annual investment in IT derived from data of Stephen Roach of Morgan Stanley, which present IT spending in current dollars and in 1987 dollars. To obtain 1982 dollar equivalents, the 1987 dollar figures have been multiplied by the ratio of the 1982 expenditure on IT for the entire service sector in current dollars (i.e., in 1982 dollars) to the 1982 expenditure on IT for the entire service sector in 1987 dollars. This approximation omits possible adjustments due to a different technology mix in 1982 compared to that of 1987 but is the best that can be done with the available data. Figures on investment in IT for 1969 (Tables 2.3 to 2.9 of this report) not presented in Roach's data, are estimated on the basis of the 1970 figure, adjusted by the annual rate of change between 1970 and 1975.
IT capital stock (billions of 1982 dollars)	Same as annual investment in IT.
GPO per labor-hour (1982 dollars)	GPO (Row 1) divided by number of hours worked (Row 4).
Annual IT/GPO	Annual investment in IT as a percentage of GPO (Row 5 divided by Row 1).
Annual rate of change in GPO per labor-hour	Annual compounded percentage change between any year and the previous year.

ratio for durable manufacturing, while the capital expenditure per full-time employee for transportation, communications, and financial services, insurance, and real estate (FIRE) was larger than or comparable to that for durable manufacturing.[2]

The discussion of these industries was informed by a variety of sources: the individual expertise and knowledge of committee members, interviews with senior executives from the six industries, data drawn from federal and other sources, and published articles and books. However, because the data available at the industry level are limited in scope and detail, this chapter's brief vignettes of each industry are intended in part to capture the direct and intuitive observations of experienced industry executives and industry analysts. Given the multidimensional nature of performance in the service industries and the resulting difficulty of isolating the specific impact of using IT vis-à-vis other factors, these vignettes are largely anecdotal but suggest the important factors that have affected overall industry performance and the scale and impact of the use of IT in each industry.

Box 2.1 describes the origin of the data on each industry presented below.

AIR TRANSPORT

In the last two decades, the U.S. air transport industry has undergone remarkable change, expanding its equipment inventories and facilities rapidly to handle substantial increases in passenger volume. In 1989, it operated a fleet of some 4000 large jet aircraft,[3] produced 433 billion revenue passenger-miles (RPMs),[4] generated revenues of $67 billion (1982 dollars), and employed about 691,000 people[5] (Table 2.3). However, poor profitability—and even sometimes net losses—have characterized the industry for much of the last decade.[6]

The industry has also undergone considerable consolidation and today is highly concentrated. As of September 1991, four large air carriers (America West, Continental, Midway, and Pan American) had filed for bankruptcy protection, and Eastern Airlines ceased operating in January 1991. Twenty-two large carriers (out of over 200 certificated U.S. air carriers) account for 95 percent of total airline revenues for scheduled passenger operations.[7]

A major event in the last decade was the deregulation of the airline industry. Beginning in the early 1980s, there was a gradual lifting of government regulations whose effect had been to reduce the efficiency of aircraft use and to generate incentives for the acquisition of certain kinds of equipment and for the maintenance of routes that did not optimize the use of resources for the country as a whole. Deregulation has allowed airlines to employ a much more efficient "hub-and-spoke" routing system, rather than the point-to-point routing used in a more regulated environment.[8] Other

TABLE 2.3 Air Transport Industry

	1969	1980	1981	1982	1983
GPO (billions of 1982 dollars)	15.1	17.3	16.8	19.0	22.8
Revenues (billions of 1982 dollars; SIC 45[a])	34.8	52.1	45.2	41.4	44.2
Output measure (billions of RPMs[c])	132[b]	254	248	260	281
Employment (millions of jobs)	0.4	0.5	0.5	0.4	0.5
Number of hours worked (billions)	0.8	1.0	0.9	0.9	0.9
Annual investment in IT (billions of 1982 dollars)	0.0	0.7	1.0	0.9	1.2
IT capital stock (billions of 1982 dollars)	0.0	1.0	1.8	2.4	3.2
GPO per labor-hour (1982 dollars)	20.00	18.19	17.70	20.88	24.49
Annual IT/GPO	0.1%	3.8%	6.2%	4.5%	5.3%
RPM[c]/labor-hour	174[b]	267	262	285	302
Annual rate of change in GPO per labor-hour[d]		-0.9%[e]	-2.7%	17.9%	17.3%

NOTE: See Box 2.1 for explanation of terms and sources of data given.

[a]Standard Industrial Classification system code.
[b]1969 figure.

important influences on the airline industry in the last decade have included significant increases in fuel costs, the 1981 strike of air traffic controllers, expensive purchases of new airplanes owing to need or to regulations calling for greater fuel efficiency or quieter aircraft, and a recessionary economy for much of the 1980s that drove down demand for air travel.

Extensive deployment of IT has been necessary to help the air transport industry deal with larger volumes of passengers and inquiries, higher operating tempos, and more complex flight and ground operations. Indeed, the air transport industry is a major consumer of IT, having spent $3 billion in 1989 (1982 dollars) on IT. The importance of IT is suggested, though not proven, by the fact that in both the air-cargo and passenger-transport segments, air transport companies prospering in the last decade have tended to be those with strong IT systems (e.g., American Airlines, United Airlines). However, the wide range of external influences on the industry in the last decade makes it difficult to identify with confidence the impact of any single factor such as IT. Indeed, some analysts assert that the benefits of IT, substantial though they

TABLE 2.3 Continued

	1984	1985	1986	1987	1988	1989
GPO (billions of 1982 dollars)	23.4	23.2	28.4	33.0	32.4	31.7
Revenues (billions of 1982 dollars; SIC 45[a])	47.9	51.1	57.7	62.3	65.1	66.6
Output measure (billions of RPMs[c])	305	336	367	404	423	433
Employment (millions of jobs)	0.5	0.5	0.6	0.6	0.7	0.7
Number of hours worked (billions)	1.0	1.1	1.2	1.2	1.3	1.4
Annual investment in IT (billions of 1982 dollars)	1.1	1.5	3.1	1.7	1.8	3.0
IT capital stock (billions of 1982 dollars)	3.8	4.6	6.9	7.6	8.2	9.8
GPO per labor-hour (1982 dollars)	23.15	21.30	24.27	26.74	24.60	22.64
Annual IT/GPO	4.5%	6.4%	11.1%	5.2%	5.5%	9.4%
RPM[c]/labor-hour	302	308	313	328	321	309
Annual rate of change in GPO per labor-hour[d]	-5.5%	-8.0%	13.9%	10.2%	-8.0%	-8.0%

[c]RPM, revenue passenger mile.
[d]The compounded annual rate of change in GPO per labor-hour from 1981 to 1989 was 3.1 percent. Labor productivity is sometimes measured in terms of GPO per labor-hour.
[e]Average annual rate of change in GPO per labor-hour from 1969 to 1980.

may be to the leaders in the airline industry, are small compared to the general economic problems that the industry faces at present.[9]

In the air transport industry, IT has had an impact on both business and operational dimensions. In the business dimension, IT has been used to improve both the cost-efficiency and quality of performance as well as to provide services not otherwise available. Perhaps the most significant of these services is the use of computerized reservation systems (CRSs). CRSs are a classic example of IT use that has had a large-scale strategic impact on an industry. Generally owned by individual airlines, these systems contain fare and route information for both the CRS owner and other carriers, and they make it possible for agents to book passage on any carrier in the database. CRSs have enabled airlines to manage passenger loads and hub-and-spoke routings that would otherwise have been extremely cumbersome and time consuming—if possible at all—under less automated conditions.

Two CRSs, SABRE (American Airlines) and APOLLO (United Airlines), dominate the industry: in 1981, nearly 80 percent of travel agencies with connections to CRSs were tied to one or both of these systems.[10] Today, virtually all airline bookings are made through one of four airline-owned CRSs.[11] Carriers without their own CRSs pay CRS owners to have their flights and fares listed, thereby providing CRS owners with additional revenue.[12]

Initially, CRSs simply replaced manual reservation systems and did not communicate either with the systems of other companies or with other departments within the owning company. However, by making relevant information about most scheduled flights available in a single database,[13] CRSs now enable passengers to use independent travel agents as well as agents from each participating airline as one-stop points of contact to gather schedule and fare information on all carriers providing the desired service and to make complete trip reservations, rather than having to call individual airlines directly. In the future, it will be common for CRSs to provide gateways to other non-airline systems through which hotel reservations and automobile rentals can be obtained.

CRSs have played an important role in facilitating the interlinkage of major and regional carriers through a process known as cross-coding. Regional carriers operate in specialized markets, whereas major carriers provide what could be called "trunk" service on major routes. Flying between two small airports on opposite ends of the country usually requires coordination of flights operated by a major carrier and by smaller regional carriers; from listing its flights on CRSs owned by major airlines, it is a relatively small step for a regional carrier to affiliate formally with a major carrier to provide a higher degree of operational integration.

CRSs have enabled implementation of a fare structure that can be very finely tuned to maximize revenues through yield management,[14] and they have provided a mechanism for the rapid implementation of price changes and for monitoring the prices of competitors. Moreover, CRS-based IT figures prominently in marketing mechanisms that have flourished since deregulation (e.g., incentives and bonuses for travel agents) and indeed in the growth of the travel industry itself. For example, CRSs have been linked to "frequent-flyer" databases that have themselves been made operationally feasible by IT.

The potential drawback of CRSs is their ability to communicate the fares of one carrier very quickly to other carriers. As of this writing, the U.S. Department of Justice (DOJ) has alleged that carriers participating in various CRSs use postings of future fare changes to fix prices at artificially high levels. For example, the DOJ suit alleges that one airline announced on January 15 a price increase to take effect on February 1, and that other airlines noticed the posting and raised prices upward accordingly. In effect, CRSs are alleged to have replaced face-to-face meetings to set prices that are illegal under antitrust laws. In response, the airlines have argued that they provide notices of future price changes for the benefit of consumers, who may wish to know when price increases are to take effect. The DOJ is seeking to enjoin the airlines from posting changes that will occur in the future.[15]

The impact of IT on the air transport industry's operations has also been quite significant. For example, IT-based systems connected to CRSs keep track of flight arrivals and departures, and they manage the many changes in planned schedules that are inherent in complex planning operations. Some airplane maintenance crews make use of knowledge-based "maintenance advisors" that guide mechanics through certain repairs. Inventories of spare parts are maintained and supplies are replenished via IT-based systems,[16] and airline food services are also being automated.[17]

Computer-based flight simulators are used extensively to train pilots for reasons of cost and safety. An hour in a flight simulator costs far less than an hour of actual flight (hundreds of dollars vs. thousands of dollars), thereby reducing fixed costs associated with crew training. In addition, emergency situations can be simulated and pilot responses rehearsed with no real danger to life or to an airplane, enabling the pilot to obtain experience and familiarity with situations that occur only rarely in actual flight. Today's simulators are so good that pilots for some commercial airplanes can be certified entirely on the basis of their experience in flight simulators.[18]

Flight safety is critically dependent on IT. Highly automated air traffic control systems manage thousands of en route flights. Weather—an important influence on safety and flight schedules—is monitored and predicted using IT-based systems. In-flight communications and navigation depend on state-of-the-art IT.[19] Weight, and therefore fuel costs, are reduced by on-board IT that monitors every aspect of an airplane's flight performance. On-board computers complement pilots' abilities in flying airliners, thus enhancing safety.[20]

IT is becoming increasingly important to airplane design, since computer-aided design and engineering save time and design effort and reduce construction costs.[21] In some cases, airframe designs stored in digital form are tested in simulated wind tunnels, and high-fidelity results can be obtained without a single model having to be built.

The logistics planning requirements of major airlines managing hundreds of flights per day are formidable, especially with hub-and-spoke routing. Today, centrally located dispatchers that previously operated out of three or four locations use IT-based systems to assist pilots with crew scheduling, flight plans, and fuel-load and weather-change calculations, an approach resulting in significant improvements in efficiency.[22] (One estimate suggests that Delta Airlines was able to reduce the amount of unproductive crew time from 11 percent to 8 percent, thereby saving $14 million per year;[23] United Airlines saved $6 million per year by installing, at a cost of

$500,000, a computer-based planning system for scheduling shift work.[24]) Working with expert systems that take on-line variables from local sites, such as the number of bags loaded onto a plane, crew schedulers and load planners are able to balance loads and to communicate directly with pilots. Airlines also use expert systems to generate least-cost routings of flights.

The benefits of using IT to assist with operations are relatively easy to demonstrate quantitatively: for example, computer-assisted route planning provides for more optimal use of fuel and assignment of crews than would manual planning. However, specific financial bottom-line benefits of using IT are more difficult to quantify. A vice president of a major airline noted,

> We want to convert our unintelligent workstations to intelligent ones because we've developed a number of programs that we believe are going to be significant in terms of their support and enhancement of customer service activities and other types of activities at the airports. Though the benefits are there, we cannot quantify them specifically. We're doing this to enhance the overall environment for the passenger.

U.S. air transport companies have consistently led the worldwide industry in major innovations such as customer reservation systems, overnight package handling, special customer services (e.g., frequent-flyer programs and package tracking), and differential pricing systems to maintain load factors. Well-automated major U.S. airlines have maintained their relative competitiveness with other international carriers and have extended their penetration of U.S. and foreign markets. Indeed, none of the several senior executives from major airlines interviewed by the committee believed they could operate without extensive IT systems, and all pointed to important cost and quality improvements enabled by IT. Given the relatively poor financial performance of the industry as a whole,[25] the ability to make necessary investments in IT may have been an important element in the survival of current industry leaders.

In the future, IT may be used by the airline industry to create a variety of additional benefits. For example, airport operations and procedures could be greatly streamlined if the current manual system of check-in were automated to link CRSs and airport systems.[26] In-flight time could be used to entertain travelers or to help them be more productive; a number of pilot projects to provide relevant services have been launched or planned.[27] IT could also be used in customized, proactive marketing—for example, potential customers could be alerted to the existence of inexpensive fares.

TELECOMMUNICATIONS

Over the last decade, the telecommunications industry has undergone dramatic structural change. It has also been highly successful in financial terms, although whether this success is despite or because of these changes is open to debate. Revenues and contributions to the gross domestic product have grown substantially for telecommunications (Table 2.4), and the industry's rate of growth in productivity of 4.8 percent per year over the period from 1979 to 1989 exceeds that of manufacturing (3.3 percent per year), as indicated in Table 1.1 in Chapter 1. In 1990, the telecommunications industry supported over 136 million access lines.[28] Although data on total minutes of local calls are not available, the Federal Communications Commission reports that 308 billion minutes in interstate calls were connected in 1990 through these access lines.[29]

Two major factors have shaped contemporary telecommunications: (1) deregulation, in combination with the divestiture of AT&T, and (2) advances in technology, with concomitant reductions in cost and changes in product offerings. The divestiture of AT&T and the consequent restructuring of the regulatory environment completely changed the character of the domestic telecommunications industry. Prior to December 1983, the industry operated as a regulated monopoly. However, in August 1982 the courts approved a consent decree that required divestiture of AT&T intra-LATA service (i.e., service within local calling areas) to seven regional holding companies by January 1, 1984. This action created more direct competition in inter-LATA (long-distance) services and equipment. The combination of the breakup of the Bell system, deregulation, and the proliferation of new, technology-based businesses has fragmented the telecommunications industry; the result has been the emergence of about a half-dozen major long-distance/interexchange carriers such as AT&T, MCI, and U.S. Sprint, and several hundred smaller carriers operating via COMSAT and leased private lines.

Such competition, combined with federally regulated charges for local access, has driven long-distance calling prices down and volume up, and much of the growth in the telephone industry in the last decade has been associated with the provision of long-distance services. Moreover, the separation of long-distance service from local carriers has forced local carriers to seek additional sources of revenue, and they have responded to these pressures by using IT to improve operations (e.g., collection of revenues from unbilled calls[30]) and to provide new services (e.g., Caller ID) to supplement traditional local telephone service ("plain old" telephone service). Some have argued that today's regulatory environment, which mandates equal charges for local access to all long-distance providers and thus has reduced pricing differentials among providers, has placed an increased emphasis on quality of service and reliability. However, the growth in the number of services that are critically dependent on telecommunications and the experience of several major and highly publicized telecommunications outages have raised the question of whether current levels of reliability are as high as those that existed before the breakup of AT&T.[31]

TABLE 2.4 Telecommunications

	1969	1980	1981	1982	1983
GPO (billions of 1982 dollars)	33.2	71.4	75.7	77.3	83.2
Revenues (billions of 1982 dollars; (SIC 481,2,9[a])	36.3	87.7	91.8	92.8	92.3
Minutes of calls (billions)		1,733	1,787	1,853	1,923
Employment (millions of jobs)	0.9	1.1	1.1	1.1	1.0
Number of hours worked (billions)	1.9	2.3	2.4	2.3	2.1
Annual investment in IT (billions of 1982 dollars)	12.7	22.7	21.0	17.3	14.3
IT capital stock (billions of 1982 dollars)	54.1	115.8	125.3	126.5	124.6
GPO per labor-hour (1982 dollars)	17.17	30.40	31.97	33.02	39.49
Annual IT/GPO	38.2%	31.8%	27.8%	22.3%	17.2%
Annual rate of change in GPO per labor-hour[b]		5.3%	5.2%	3.3%	19.6%
Minutes of calls per labor-hour		737.8	754.6	791.5	912.7

NOTE: See Box 2.1 for explanation of terms and sources of data given.

The growth of telecommunications parallels advances in information technology, because the technological substrate of telecommunications is wholly dependent on IT. The telecommunications industry's investments in IT have been very large, amounting to $12 billion to $15 billion per year in the late 1980s (1982 dollars), and those figures are for hardware only; they do not include the substantial investments in software associated with the expansion and upgrading of telecommunications networks and services. Meanwhile, during the 1980s the capabilities of underlying microelectronic technologies for telecommunications were improving at average rates of 40 to 50 percent per year.

Over the years, major innovations have improved underlying service and hardware technology, including satellite, cellular, and fiber-optic communication systems. Historically, applications of IT have driven changes in long-distance telephone service, beginning with the introduction of direct dialing between 1950 and 1952. Since then, the telephone industry has witnessed the introduction of computer-based toll operator assistance sys-

TABLE 2.4 Continued

	1984	1985	1986	1987	1988	1989
GPO (billions of 1982 dollars)	80.8	81.7	85.0	93.2	97.8	98.8
Revenues (billions of 1982 dollars; (SIC 481,2,9[a])	89.2	91.5	91.1	92.8	98.4	100.6
Minutes of calls (billions)	2,045	2,145	2,207	2,267	2,385	2,460
Employment (millions of jobs)	1.0	1.0	0.9	1.0	0.9	0.9
Number of hours worked (billions)	2.1	2.1	2.0	2.0	2.0	2.0
Annual investment in IT (billions of 1982 dollars)	13.8	15.9	16.9	15.9	13.9	13.8
IT capital stock (billions of 1982 dollars)	122.0	121.2	121.1	119.9	116.7	113.7
GPO per labor-hour (1982 dollars)	37.93	39.35	42.42	45.98	48.06	49.97
Annual IT/GPO	17.1%	19.4%	19.9%	17.1%	14.2%	14.0%
Annual rate of change in GPO per labor-hour[b]	-3.9%	3.7%	7.8%	8.4%	4.5%	4.0%
Minutes of calls per labor-hour	960.1	1033	1101.3	1118.4	1172	1244.3

[a]Standard Industrial Classification system code.
[b]The compounded annual rate of change in GPO per labor-hour from 1981 to 1989 was 5.7 percent. Labor productivity is sometimes measured in terms of GPO per labor-hour.

tems, automatic credit card validation and billing, automated directory assistance systems, automatic coin recognition in pay-telephone systems, and, recently, voice-recognition systems that build on the digitization of network and voice-recognition technology.[32] Such innovations have reduced the amount of labor required to provide telecommunications services[33] and have facilitated a gradual shift in employment toward executive and staff occupations. There has also been ongoing progress relating to encoding, processing, and transmitting messages (e.g., voice and video compression), all of which provide for more efficient use of telecommunications facilities.

A substantial amount of IT is used to support the people operating and managing the network. Operations support systems monitor traffic as well as the health and condition of facilities and switches, provide telemetry, detect faults, and provide alerts. Databases record what is in the network and how it is hooked up. Operations support systems help in keeping track of circuits and reconfiguring them. IT-based systems are used to collect vast amounts of data from multiple sources to support rate filing and network planning. Today's use of test equipment often incorporates expert-system technology in applications that automatically signal when maintenance is necessary and in techniques for optimizing network routing, especially under emergency conditions.

Managing the huge volumes of billing data that are generated in providing telecommunications services would not be possible without sophisticated IT systems. Billing is complex because companies must continuously record each use of every service, and then rate it and price it based on multiple variables (distance, time, specific service, quality of service, pricing plans, and so on). For this reason, automated billing systems are built directly into central switches, and most billing systems are therefore relatively inflexible.

Enhancements to billing systems have transformed them from being simply support systems that emphasize rates, prices, invoicing, and billing, to being strategic systems that emphasize accuracy, speed, calling patterns, and other attributes of customer service. For example, MCI developed a new marketing program by using IT for sophisticated billing and data processing: Friends and Family involves accurate monthly tracking of customers and calling circles (designated groups of people who call each other) across their use of various telecommunications services. Other billing system enhancements have given rise to customer billing and usage management tools that have historically been focused on corporate users. For example, MCI has a relatively new product, Service Without Paper, that provides corporate telecommunications managers with billing and usage data on optical disk.

Telephone credit cards (calling cards) were made possible by using IT,[34] and they represent an area of current innovation. Calling cards serve as marketing tools, promoting easy access to products and services, and they are linked with proliferating services: electronic message delivery, stock quotations and weather forecasts, language interpretation, speed dialing, and teleconferencing. Long-distance carriers are now developing voice-recognition systems that can substitute for operators in handling routine interactive telephone transactions (e.g., collect calls). In the future, enhanced calling cards may be indistinguishable from automated teller machine cards.[35]

Deregulation and technological advances have both contributed to shifts in the mix of products produced by the telecommunications industry. Falling prices for long-distance calls have contributed to a shift in the mix of local to long-distance calls. Telecommunications companies have evolved from defining the service they offer exclusively in terms of providing facilities to transmit the electrical impulses representing voices or data to redefining themselves as enterprises that help customers collect, process, and distribute data. More specifically, using IT, telecommunications companies provide more information to customers on the way infrastructure is used (e.g., billing and network management services), new information-based modes of access to information (virtual private networks, calling cards), and gateways to information services, if not information services themselves. Thus there is a blurring of the traditional categories of telecommunications and information processing, as well as a convergence of public and private networking.[36]

In recent years, much of the capital investment in the telecommunications industry has been driven by the enhancement of the communications infrastructures installed by both regional and national carriers. Today, the infrastructure of modern telecommunications makes increasing use of broadband transmission and digital switching.

Compared to analog transmissions, digitized communications improve signal fidelity and, through signal processing, use available bandwidth more efficiently. Digitized communications also facilitate data transmission (although voice signals are increasingly digitized), thereby changing the mix of voice and data traffic, and enable as well the use of companion overlay networks for network management functions (e.g., call setup) and for new services (e.g., automatic number identification—Box 2.2). The entire AT&T interchange network is digital today, as are about 40 to 50 percent of central office switching facilities in local exchanges.[37]

Broad-band transmission is associated primarily with optical fiber cable, which offers huge gains in capacity over that provided by copper cable. The bandwidth provided by fiber will greatly exceed what is needed to handle the expected traffic volume upon installation and will thus be able to accommodate increased traffic or new services. (At the same time, the prospect of "dark fiber" or unused capacity contributes to the controversy over how fast to increase network bandwidth.)

Thanks in part to deregulation, new telephone services are now introduced much more rapidly than before. IT—in particular, programmable digital switches—has been integral to the rapid development of such innovative services as call waiting, caller identification, and call forwarding. By extending the traditional notion of plain old telephone service, such services increase the number of options for local customers and generate substantial revenue for local telephone companies today.

IT has also been used in the telecommunications industry to enhance and improve corporate image and the quality of customer service, even when these considerations do not relate directly to calling volume. MCI's Richard Liebhaber described a $35 million investment to provide the capability for customer service representatives to display customer invoices and correspondence on graphics terminals, saying, "It is an opportunity to improve the image, the feel, the touch of MCI. Intuitively, I would tell you it's going to provide market share, customer satisfaction, bottom line. I can't prove it. I'm not going to waste my time trying."

> **BOX 2.2 Applications for Automatic Number Identification**
>
> Automatic Number Identification (ANI) is a service usually (though not always) provided through an integrated services digital network (ISDN) that enables the telephone number of the calling party to be transmitted along with the signal that carries the call itself.
>
> Telemarketing organizations initially used ANI to identify callers; the calling number would trigger a database inquiry, enabling the marketer to identify the caller and his or her previous history. However, many callers were disconcerted by the fact that their identities were known to the marketer without their providing any identification.
>
> New applications of ANI are being used to provide different levels of service. For example, if a caller is known from previous interactions to speak Spanish, ANI can be used to route calls from that party to Spanish-speaking operators. Credit card holders can be routed to different service staffs depending on the type of card they hold. Equipment service organizations can route calls to the appropriate staffs based on databases that coordinate telephone numbers with equipment present at given sites.
>
> SOURCE: Sweeney, Terry. 1993. "Carriers, Users Discover New Applications for Automatic Number ID," *Communications Week*, January 4, p. 27.

Future advances in telecommunications are likely to include multimedia transmission (e.g., combined two-way video and audio) made possible with the wide availability of digital networks, the assignment of telephone numbers to individuals rather than locations (resulting in a single telephone number for an individual regardless of where he or she is), and automatic translation services (giving, e.g., an American and a Japanese businessperson the opportunity to converse through a telephone, but both in their native tongues). Broad-band networking technologies supporting transmission speeds in excess of 45 megabits per second will be deployed widely in the next decade; by contrast, the technology that supports most home telephones today is limited to transmission speeds measured in tens of kilobits per second. Broad-band networking technologies will require substantial deployment of fiber optics to end users (initially commercial ones). Wireless communications (cellular telephone, personal communications services) is a market in which considerable growth is expected (subject to availability of spectrum bandwidth). Advanced intelligent network technology is expected to continue facilitating the development of additional customized communications services.

Implementing these advances is likely to have a substantial impact both on users and providers of telecommunications technology. Using sophisticated telecommunications technology most effectively will most probably require substantial learning of new skills comparable to the new skills demanded of those using increasingly powerful software packages on personal computers. As importantly, sophisticated telecommunications technology will depend increasingly on the capability to develop complex software, a task that routinely pushes the state of the art of current knowledge in computer science and software engineering.

While both financial performance and growth in productivity in the telecommunications industry have been strong, the benefits of technological innovation and investments have sometimes appeared in other segments of the economy. Private companies, whether manufacturing or service firms, may realize improvements in productivity from the installation of their own switches and terminal equipment, but these improvements are not reflected in the data for public providers of communications services. Nonregulated companies outside the industry have been able to install their own wide-area networks and "cherrypick" profitable service opportunities by selling such systems and services to others. Returns from these activities show up in sellers' and users' books of account, rather than those of telecommunication providers. There is a substantial cross-substitution between the "product" and "service" components of the telecommunications field and an increasing merging of the telecommunications business between equipment manufacturers and service providers as currently defined.

RETAIL AND WHOLESALE TRADE

The retail and wholesale trade industries are responsible for the ordering, collection, distribution, and sale of goods. Both industries have been growing. Retail revenues increased from $447 billion in 1980 to $628 billion in 1989 (1982 dollars; Table 2.5). Wholesale revenues grew from $310 billion in 1980 to $401 billion in 1989 (1982 dollars; Table 2.6). For wholesale and retail trade taken together, the 1989 investment in IT in constant dollars was 2.6 times the amount invested in IT in 1980.

The retail industry consists of a broad collection of segments with rather different businesses (department stores, restaurants, specialty stores, grocery stores, and so on) that vary greatly in terms of the categories of the items they sell, the range of prices of the items, the market size for the items, and profit margins. Retail trade is dominated by relatively few, large, national or regional chain operations specializing in merchandise trade, food, and pharmaceuticals.[38] A much larger number of smaller "mom-and-pop" retail operations are locally based; such operations are relatively easy to start (compared to ventures in telecommunications or air transport) be-

TABLE 2.5 Retail Trade

	1969	1980	1981	1982	1983
GPO (billions of 1982 dollars)	212.7	281.7	286.4	287.5	307.8
Revenues (billions of 1982 dollars; SIC 52-59[a])	326.5	446.5	453.6	459.9	485.4
Employment (millions of jobs)	12.3	16.8	16.9	16.9	17.4
Number of hours worked (billions)	22.9	27.4	27.4	27.2	27.8
Annual investment in IT (billions of 1982 dollars)	0.1	4.6	5.1	5.8	7.0
IT capital stock (billions of 1982 dollars)	0.4	10.0	13.2	16.6	20.7
GPO per labor-hour (1982 dollars)	9.31	10.28	10.44	10.56	11.06
Annual IT/GPO	0.1%	1.6%	1.8%	2.0%	2.3%
Annual rate of change in GPO per labor-hour[b]		0.9%	1.6%	1.2%	4.7%

NOTE: See Box 2.1 for explanation of terms and sources of data given.

cause their requirements for capital and technology infrastructure are relatively small. For example, a means for displaying merchandise is often the minimum capital requirement, a task that can in some cases be accomplished by publishing a catalog.

Wholesalers provide all activities involved in selling goods or services to those who buy for resale or business use. They exist as an industry because they provide efficiencies that manufacturers often are unable to support themselves.[39]

Given the heterogeneity of the products sold by retailers and wholesalers, aggregate trade output is best measured in terms of financial value. (Output measures for trade are discussed in greater detail in Appendixes B and C.) However, measured productivity varies greatly among such different elements of the retail trade industry as supermarkets and other food stores, restaurants, apparel and accessory stores, new-car dealers, gas stations, home furnishings and equipment stores, and drug stores.

Moreover, financial measures do not necessarily capture other important elements of performance. For example, the 1980s saw improvement in measures of quality such as the variety of products, geographic dispersion, demographic specialization within stores, fashion responsiveness, and hours

TABLE 2.5 Continued

	1984	1985	1986	1987	1988	1989
GPO						
(billions of 1982 dollars)	334.0	354.4	377.5	371.6	399.2	412.0
Revenues						
(billions of 1982 dollars;						
SIC 52-59[a])	521.7	549.5	574.9	595.6	623.5	628.3
Employment						
(millions of jobs)	18.3	18.9	19.5	20.1	20.6	21.2
Number of hours worked						
(billions)	29.3	29.9	30.6	31.5	32.2	32.8
Annual investment in IT						
(billions of 1982 dollars)	8.9	8.5	9.0	8.0	10.5	10.6
IT capital stock						
(billions of 1982 dollars)	25.9	30.2	34.2	36.8	41.1	44.8
GPO per labor-hour						
(1982 dollars)	11.40	11.86	12.35	11.79	12.39	12.54
Annual IT/GPO	2.7%	2.4%	2.4%	2.1%	2.6%	2.6%
Annual rate of change in GPO						
per labor-hour[b]	3.1%	4.0%	4.2%	-4.5%	5.1%	1.2%

[a]Standard Industrial Classification system code.
[b]The compounded annual rate of change in GPO per labor hour from 1981 to 1989 was 2.3 percent. Labor productivity is sometimes measured in terms of GPO per labor-hour.

open. Significant increases in the diversity of their products, the growth of chain store branches, and the proliferation of small specialty chains may have masked other elements of improvements in productivity in large chain operations. In addition, because of "overstoring" and competitive pressures, margins at both retail and wholesale levels dropped during the 1980s, despite major improvements in operational performance enabled by new IT capabilities.

Retail and wholesale enterprises seek faster receipt of goods, lower inventories and more inventory turns per year,[40] a better fit between goods offered and goods bought, and reduced labor costs. In retailing, considerable effort is made to attract customers to retail establishments, because the marginal cost of providing service to a new customer is relatively low.

In retailing, investments in IT increased from $4.6 billion in 1980 to $10.6 billion in 1989 (1982 dollars; Table 2.5). In wholesaling, investments in IT approximately tripled in the 1980s, from $4 billion in 1980 to $11.6 billion in 1989 (1982 dollars; Table 2.6). The vast bulk of these expenditures was made by large establishments, which now depend on IT for planning and control of inventories, merchandising, and logistics management. By contrast, smaller retailers use relatively little IT, except in

TABLE 2.6 Wholesale Trade

	1969	1980	1981	1982	1983
GPO (billions of 1982 dollars)	149.0	200.1	212.7	219.0	222.2
Revenues (billions of 1982 dollars; SIC 50,1[a])	210.0	310.3	317.6	318.8	315.4
Employment (millions of jobs)	4.2	5.6	5.7	5.6	5.6
Number of hours worked (billions)	8.8	11.2	11.4	11.2	11.3
Annual investment in IT (billions of 1982 dollars)	0.3	4.0	5.0	5.9	10.4
IT capital stock (billions of 1982 dollars)	0.8	10.4	13.2	16.5	23.2
GPO per labor-hour (1982 dollars)	16.97	17.81	18.64	19.62	19.70
Annual IT/GPO	0.2%	2.0%	2.4%	2.7%	4.7%
Annual rate of change in GPO per labor-hour[b]		0.4%	4.7%	5.3%	0.4%

NOTE: See Box 2.1 for explanation of terms and sources of data given.

catalog sales operations. IT has contributed to the growth observed in these two industries and also to the growing competition between them: large retail chains now use IT to provide many of the services wholesalers used to provide, and wholesalers have linked "downstream" to tie retail customers together into voluntary chains.

IT has become critically important to the retail and wholesale trade industries as a competitive tool; instead of merely providing information at greater speeds, IT can be used to help manage information that can then be coupled with strategic planning to optimize the efficiency of a business. Indeed, the National Retail Federation credits the use of IT with helping to cushion the impact of the recent recession: "Technology helped to cushion the blow. Many retailers had better information about their sales and inventories than in the last recession and were thus able to more selectively promote merchandise."[41] By enabling better and faster matching of inventories and customer needs, IT can decrease the need for retail markdowns, a major cost in retailing.

In the 1980s, wholesalers often installed direct links to suppliers through electronic data interchange and support systems for retailers to deal with stock management, merchandising, and price marking. Wholesalers for

TABLE 2.6 Continued

	1984	1985	1986	1987	1988	1989
GPO (billions of 1982 dollars)	254.9	267.1	284.7	284.3	290.6	304.7
Revenues (billions of 1982 dollars; SIC 50,1[a])	347.2	362.2	371.8	373.4	386.9	400.8
Employment (millions of jobs)	5.9	6.1	6.1	6.2	6.4	6.6
Number of hours worked (billions)	11.9	12.1	12.2	12.3	12.8	13.1
Annual investment in IT (billions of 1982 dollars)	13.9	12.3	13.7	9.6	12.6	11.6
IT capital stock (billions of 1982 dollars)	32.3	38.8	45.5	47.6	51.7	54.0
GPO per labor-hour (1982 dollars)	21.45	22.00	23.40	23.05	22.78	23.30
Annual IT/GPO	5.5%	4.6%	4.8%	3.4%	4.3%	3.8%
Annual rate of change in GPO per labor-hour[b]	8.9%	2.6%	6.4%	-1.5%	-1.2%	2.3%

[a]Standard Industrial Classification system code.
[b]The compounded annual rate of change in GPO per labor hour from 1981 to 1989 was 2.8 percent. Labor productivity is sometimes measured in terms of GPO per labor-hour.

foods, pharmaceuticals, and hospital supplies placed computerized ordering systems directly on customers' premises to great effect. These investments tended to shift shares of the market among wholesalers (or between wholesalers and retailers) rather than increase the total volume of products, so that benefits were frequently not captured in measures of output. Although volume grew during the 1980s without proportionate increases in employment, competitive pressures kept wholesalers from realizing significant gains in profitability. The number of products and the complexity of services offered by wholesalers expanded enormously during this period. Consequently, the data on profits suggest that wholesalers were passing benefits from their investments in IT through to their customers and suppliers.

A current trend is for large retailers to develop their own direct connections to suppliers and manufacturers; both Kmart and Wal-Mart have direct links to over 2000 vendors. IT is an enabling element of such connections. In one case, point-of-sale data from the retailer have been used to adjust the mix of sizes of a manufactured product based on how frequently various sizes are sold.[42]

The fact that the trade industries are very labor-intensive has led to interest in technologies and processes that reduce labor costs. For example, a top executive of a major supermarket chain noted that "scanning [has] had the highest impact of any technological advancement from IT in this business because of its improvement on productivity at the front end and through improved [e.g., faster] checkout and price removal, taking the prices off the products and not having to do price changes." Similarly, retailers have used IT to improve labor scheduling and to minimize costs.

Scanning systems are used to read a product's universal pricing code label at the cash register, look up the product's price and the applicable tax, and record this information at the register as part of the transaction. Thus price changes can be recorded in a central database at the store rather than on each item or on the shelves. Moreover, the cashier is freed from having to enter prices on the register manually. Both attributes can improve accuracy and reduce requirements for personnel; they also change the mix of skills required of cashiers. In addition, data made available at the point of sale facilitate accurate analysis of what gets sold, when, and, sometimes, to whom, while faster access to information facilitates better ordering, marketing, and merchandising; improved management of inventory; and improved scheduling of personnel. Communications systems that link point-of-sale systems in stores to headquarters allow daily and even hourly analysis of sales and trends. A major benefit can be better insights into what sells well and poorly, thus minimizing overstocking and deep discounting.

In some cases, point-of-sale systems (whether or not using scanners) have been tied to inventory control systems. Such systems are often used to link retail stores and wholesale vendors through electronic data interchange systems and allow nearly paperless and highly automatic ordering. In some instances, these systems allow orders to be shipped from wholesalers directly to retail stores, bypassing warehouses.

The large-scale deployment of point-of-sale systems and their integration into centralized ordering and inventory control networks have been important elements in the expansion of the giants in the retail industry. For example, by using standardized ordering practices and inventory control procedures and drawing on the expertise of the entire corporation regarding sales and operations techniques, a new branch of a retailer like McDonalds can be opened more economically than a store of comparable size that lacks an existing support infrastructure. One result of this trend has been a division in the number of companies as a function of size—the retail industry now consists primarily of a handful of giants and a plethora of small institutions with one or a few stores under their control.

IT has been used effectively in specialized trade applications. In furniture retailing, video catalogs are being used to show a large variety of fabrics and to aid in room planning, special orders, and follow-up, allowing the customer to more easily visualize and compare products. Restaurants today often use IT to perform location and layout analyses; manage recipes and menus; track supplies, markets, and costs; and handle general ledger accounting (accounts receivable and payable, payroll accounting and labor scheduling, and financial reporting). Supermarkets are using IT to generate cents-off coupons at the point of sale (i.e., at the cash register) that are customized to a particular consumer's shopping patterns.[43]

In other cases, IT is applied across functional activities. An example is the use of a computer-aided design (CAD) system in the general merchandise segment. Without CAD, several individuals with three separate specialties are needed to design floor plans, determine shelving requirements, and designate specific items to be placed in exact locations. Today, through the combined use of technology, historical data, and projections, individual functions can be reengineered into one process to best achieve the final goal of shelf-space management. IT is also used to support buyers in making decisions about the mix of products for individual stores and to determine optimal item-to-store allocations.

IT can be used to extend the activities of a business. A retail store may sell to other organizations the customer information captured in its marketing database. Telemarketing, which first relied on telephones and now involves combinations of telephones and computer systems, is wholly dependent on IT for collecting information on existing customers and new prospects, for disseminating information through promotional efforts, and for conducting various other sales-related activities. In addition, computer systems are used throughout the telemarketing process, for sorting, merging, and purging lists of prospective customers; distributing leads to agents; preparing for calls; dialing contacts; delivering sales presentations; referencing information; scheduling the next contact; recording contact information; carrying out the fulfillment process; and management reporting.[44]

A most promising future application of IT is its use to track the number of people entering a store, an approach pioneered by Kmart. At present, few stores can count how many people pass through its doors; measures of success (e.g., for sales and advertising) derive from measures of sales volume (number of purchases). Yet the conversion of potential customers (those who visit the store) into actual customers (those who make a purchase) is a critical but poorly understood element of the retail business, and a small upward change in conversion ratios could have a dramatic effect on sales volume. Kmart believes that the installation of IT to count customers will enable managers to determine conversion ratios with unprecedented accuracy and will guide them in their improvement.

HEALTH CARE

In recent years, public concern over the health care industry has reached unprecedented levels. The industry provides a huge volume of service:

TABLE 2.7 Health Care

	1969	1980	1981	1982	1983
Health services GPO (billions of 1982 dollars)[a]	73.4	133.8	138.1	142.0	143.7
National health expenditures (GPO, SIC 80,[b] estimated billions of 1982 dollars)[a]	n/a	309.6	321.4	326.1	330.1
Revenues (billions of 1982 dollars; SIC 80[b])	120.1	194.5	204.8	213.6	223.2
Employment (millions of jobs)	3.2	5.7	5.9	6.2	6.3
Number of hours worked (billions)	5.6[c]	9.8	10.2	10.7	10.8
Annual investment in IT (billions of 1982 dollars)	0.9	1.9	1.8	1.5	2.8
IT capital stock (billions of 1982 dollars)	3.3	8.6	8.9	8.9	10.0
GPO per labor-hour (1982 dollars)	13.01	13.64	13.49	13.27	13.25
Annual IT/GPO	1.2%	1.4%	1.3%	1.1%	2.0%
Annual rate of change in GPO per labor-hour[d]		0.4%	-1.2%	-1.6%	-0.2%

NOTE: See Box 2.1 for explanation of terms and sources of data given.

[a]GPO figures differ substantially from figures often reported as "national health expenditures" but are presented for the sake of consistency with other industries. National health expenditures are the most comprehensive measure, including both public and private spending on health care. The national health expenditure (NHE) figures presented in constant 1982 dollars are *estimated* on the basis of NHE figures in current dollars widely available in various publi-

Americans made 1.3 billion visits to physicians for ambulatory care and 31 million visits to hospitals in 1988.[45] The health care industry absorbs a large and increasing percentage of the income of workers in all sectors: the private health care industry generated $120 billion in revenues in 1969 and $287 billion in 1989 (1982 dollars; Table 2.7).[46] It is also a large employer that in 1989 provided 7.9 million jobs. Table 2.7 describes the evolution of the health care industry over the last decade.

A key element of the U.S. health care system is the massive presence of third-party payers, both private and government, that pay for most or all of the health care received by individuals. A large number of third parties obtain the resources to pay for these services from some combination of the individual and the employer for whom the individual works, or through taxes levied on the population at large.

TABLE 2.7 Continued

	1984	1985	1986	1987	1988	1989
Health services GPO (billions of 1982 dollars)[a]	145.0	148.6	150.5	158.0	161.1	164.4
National health expenditures (GPO, SIC 80,[b] estimated billions of 1982 dollars)[a]	334.3	340.2	341.7	345.3	351.4	362.6
Revenues (billions of 1982 dollars; SIC 80[b])	230.6	239.8	252.8	266.0	279.2	286.6
Employment (millions of jobs)	6.5	6.6	6.9	7.2	7.5	7.9
Number of hours worked (billions)	11.1	11.4	11.7	12.2	12.8	13.5
Annual investment in IT (billions of 1982 dollars)	2.8	2.7	3.0	3.1	3.5	3.6
IT capital stock (billions of 1982 dollars)	11.1	11.8	12.7	13.6	14.7	15.7
GPO per labor-hour (1982 dollars)	13.08	13.07	12.85	12.97	12.59	12.14
Annual IT/GPO	2.0%	1.8%	2.0%	2.0%	2.2%	2.2%
Annual rate of change in GPO per labor-hour[d]	-1.3%	-0.1%	-1.7%	0.9%	-2.9%	-3.6%

cations. Current-dollar NHE figures are deflated by a multiplicative factor that is the ratio of the GPO for health services for a given year in 1982 dollars divided by the same quantity in current dollars for that year.
[b]Standard Industrial Classification system code.
[c]Health care hours worked in 1969 are extrapolated from 1979 ratio of jobs to hours worked.
[d]The compounded annual rate of change in GPO per labor-hour from 1981 to 1989 was -1.3 percent. Labor productivity is sometimes measured in terms of GPO per labor-hour.

Rising health care costs have been attributed to many different causes, including the prescribing of newer, more complex, and more costly medical procedures with only marginally better clinical outcomes; a litigious climate that encourages the practice of defensive medicine; the transformation of the underpaid and partly volunteer nursing force of the 1960s and early 1970s into the more professional hospital and nursing staffs of the 1980s; third-party payment of the medical expenses of large numbers of patients who are therefore not motivated to seek lower-cost care; and an aging population that can be expected to incur higher medical costs. These factors suggest that output measured by health care expenditures is problematic at best.

The physical output of the health care system is also notoriously difficult to measure. For example, using treatment outcomes as a measure in individual cases is complicated by the fact that outcomes depend on factors other than the treatments provided, such as preadmission health of the patient. Measures of public health, for example, incidences of disease, are complicated by external factors such as the increasing medical needs of an aging population. Issues such as unequal access to health care further compound the difficulties of measurement. Another key issue is measuring the quality of care that patients receive.

Against this backdrop, technology, including IT, has had an undeniable impact on the success with which many medical problems are treated, e.g., cancer as treated with computer-controlled beams of radiation. IT is today an integral part of diagnosis and therapy. Microelectronics and embedded computing are essential parts of digital thermometers and sphygmomanometers; high-speed computing is at the heart of computerized tomography scanning and magnetic resonance imaging. Laboratory tests are increasingly automated, as computer-based instrumentation is used to take readings with consistency, reliability, and speed equal to or greater than that of human technicians. Monitoring of the vital signs of hospital patients and automatic signaling of the need for clinical action are performed more effectively and reliably by IT than by human monitors.

The use of IT in the business side of the health care industry is a different matter. As a whole, the health care field has been slow to use IT in its business operations and record-keeping activities. Nevertheless, pressure on the health care industry to explore the use of IT is now being exerted by a variety of factors, including the explosion of medical knowledge, the larger volume of clinical information potentially relevant to individual patients, the increasingly cooperative nature of medicine, the need for more detailed clinical audit trails to defend against potential malpractice litigation and to ensure proper third-party payment, greater regulation, greater competition among health care institutions, and greater pressure for outcomes assessment and improvement of quality and patient satisfaction.

By far the most common use of information systems in health care is for billing, accounting, and administrative tasks, which typically include the admission, transfer, and discharge of hospital patients; materials management; and scheduling and management of human and physical resources. Increasingly, hospitals recognize the need for integrating these tasks across departments. Integrated health care data systems can pass information electronically in a common format among all departments in the system, thus reducing or eliminating the need to reenter data manually. With an integrated system, billing information from the laboratory and the pharmacy can be electronically integrated in a hospital's financial office. Billing for consumable items used by a patient can be integrated with the hospital's inventory control system. In some cases, inventory control systems themselves are tied directly to hospital supply companies, and replacement orders are generated automatically when necessary.

The actual clinical practice of medicine has not effectively used IT for cost reduction as widely as would be desirable. A recent study examined the potential of IT-based physician order entry in an Indianapolis hospital to steer physicians toward lower-cost treatments; the result was that patient bills were reduced by an average of 13 percent.[47] The networked PC-based system used software that alerted physicians to the cost of various drugs and tests, warned about potential drug interactions, and specifically discouraged the use of certain expensive drugs under particular circumstances.

In the future, computer-based patient records (CPRs) hold considerable promise for improving health care and reducing costs. Today, patient records are contained on numerous slips of paper (e.g., laboratory tests, physician notes perhaps produced by transcribing the physician's dictation using a word processor) stuffed into a folder and perhaps arranged in chronological order. However, in some institutions CPRs are beginning to supplement paper records, over which they have many potential advantages. CPRs are or can be more legible, more current, more reliable and accurate, more comprehensive, more easily accessible, and more easily searchable. CPRs could also be the basis of longitudinal databases that would allow development of "best-clinical-practice" guidelines coupling treatment to expected or likely outcomes. Outcome-based treatment is thought by many to have considerable potential for reducing health care costs.

A second growing application of IT in health care is its use in giving physicians remote access to hospital information systems through dial-up modems or leased lines, allowing them to check on the status of patients through CPRs. Physicians practicing in rural areas can thus use wide-band video to consult with specialists, who tend to reside in urban areas; one often-cited use is the transmission of x-ray images by network from rural family practitioners to urban radiologists. City-to-city teleconferencing can also be used so that the best specialists can consult together. Remote access provided by IT-based systems is also very important to emergency medical teams sent into the field. Ambulance teams or rescue squads do not typically include physicians. However, radio communications can link on-site personnel with physicians elsewhere. Voice communications provide advice and direction from the physician, and both voice and data downlinks from the field to the physician provide information about the condition of the patient.

Automated systems to support clinical decision making have been the subjects of research since the mid-1960s. Given a set of data on a patient, these systems commonly act as a consultant that advises the physician on diagnosis or treatment. Such systems attempt to capture in machine-readable form the expertise that clinical physicians have about their patients and diseases. Two relatively old examples of medical "expert" systems are MYCIN, a system designed to help physicians manage different types of infection, and INTERNIST, a system designed to support diagnosis of diseases in internal medicine.

The widespread use of IT in clinical practice will require IT that can be used to support the wide range of clinical functions for which the medical profession is responsible, taking into account the high degree of variability in clinical practice from practitioner to practitioner and the reluctance of physicians to alter their practices on the basis of outside influences. Nevertheless, if physicians are willing to use data on outcomes and to adapt clinical practice to take the best advantage of IT's potential to reduce costs and improve efficiency, there are many opportunities to use information more effectively in providing health care. Future applications may include multimedia CPRs, explicit coupling of medical and related knowledge (e.g., the medical literature, government regulations regarding practice, or guidelines for practice) to a patient's medical record and/or to a specific treatment program for the individual, and universal electronic interchange of data and information.

BANKING

As a major component of the U.S. financial system, the banking industry is vital to the U.S. and world economies and to individual financial wellbeing. Banks mediate a wide range of commercial and personal transactions involving the exchange and investment of money, providing such services as loans, deposits, and trust services to individuals, small businesses, and corporations.

The banking industry is a major factor in the economy. It generated revenues of $209 billion (current dollars) in 1990. At the end of 1989, insured commercial banks alone held about $3.3 trillion in assets, $2.0 trillion in loans and leases, and $2.5 trillion in deposits. There were 12,713 banks in this category, down from a peak of about 14,481 in 1984;[48] however, the number of commercial banking offices (central and branch) grew from 57,010 in 1984 to 61,162 in 1989.[49] The industry exhibits considerable concentration. For example, in 1989, 4.8 percent of federally insured commercial banking institutions (614 commercial banks) held 74.9 percent of all assets ($2.47 trillion); 23.4 percent of these institutions held 88.9 percent of assets.[50] Savings banks exhibit similar concentration, although not as intense; in 1989, 15.8 percent of federally insured savings banks (534) held 77.2 percent of all assets ($1.2 trillion).[51] Table 2.8 describes the evolution of depository institutions over the last decade, of which banks were by far the largest component, about 90 percent.

Although the banking industry has grown at a moderate rate over the last two decades, the most significant changes in this period concern its character rather than its size. For most of its history, banking has been subject to extensive federal and state regulation. However, partial bank deregulation in the late 1970s and early 1980s led to a sharp increase in the variety of services and products offered by commercial banks. Driven by both technology and competition from nonbank financial institutions, increasing product diversification continues today in commercial banking, although it is still constrained to some extent by current regulations.

The banking industry has experienced a variety of economic and financial problems over the past several years, including losses from bad real estate loans, a large fraction of portfolio assets tied up in borrowings for takeovers and for loans to less developed countries, the failure of a number of well-known financial institutions, the widespread implications of the savings and loan crisis, and, finally, the economic downturn of 1990-1991.[52] In large part, these problems are ultimately responsible for the considerable consolidation that the banking industry has undergone in the last decade. Bank failures, contractions, mergers, and acquisitions have reduced the number of all banks and the number of large banks, and as a result, industry employment has been shrinking. Most reductions in personnel have been concentrated in back-office jobs.

Given the magnitude of the banking industry's investments in IT over the last two decades, large increases in productivity might have been expected. One reason these have not appeared in measures of macroeconomic productivity is that such measures in the banking industry remain highly problematic. Figures on the gross domestic product originating in the U.S. economy (GPO) for the banking industry are derived by the Bureau of Economic Analysis essentially from employment data (Table B.3, Appendix B), whereas measures of gross output that are generated by the Bureau of Labor Statistics take into account commercial banks' three major services—deposits, loans, and trust services (Appendix C). Neither approach is able to account for improvements in the quality of service offered to customers or for the availability of a much wider array of banking services. For example, the speed with which the processing of a loan application is completed is an indicator of service that is important to the applicant, as is the 24-hour availability through automated teller machines (ATMs) of many deposit and withdrawal services previously accessible only during bank hours. Neither of these services is captured as higher banking output at the macroeconomic level.

A second reason for the lack of large increases in measured productivity is that early applications of IT proved to be costly and cumbersome. Software and equipment had to be updated and replaced frequently. A dizzying array of new products constantly called for new software and communication capabilities. IT systems required large amounts of tailoring,

TABLE 2.8 Banking

	1969	1980	1981	1982	1983
GPO (billions of 1982 dollars)	39.6	61.9	64.2	65.2	66.1
Revenues (billions of 1982 dollars; SIC 60[a])	56.4	90.5	88.7	96.4	100.9
Employment (millions of jobs)	n/a	2.0	2.0	2.1	2.1
Number of hours worked (billions)	n/a	3.7	3.9	3.9	3.9
Annual investment in IT (billions of 1982 dollars)	0.1	1.6	1.9	1.8	2.9
IT capital stock (billions of 1982 dollars)	0.2	4.4	5.1	5.6	6.9
GPO per labor-hour (1982 dollars)		16.67	16.66	16.77	16.77
Annual IT/GPO		2.6%	3.0%	2.8%	4.4%
Annual rate of change in GPO per labor-hour[b]			0.0%	0.6%	0.0%

NOTE: Figures include all depository institutions. Commercial banks, Federal Reserve banks, and savings and loan banks account for about 90 percent of all figures. See Box 2.1 for explanation of terms and sources of data given.

training, upgrading, and updating. Cost control, management skills, and productivity tracking systems lagged behind the new technologies in a rapidly changing competitive marketplace. Margins long protected by regulations were squeezed by inverted yield structures (i.e., financial instruments whose yield varied inversely with their time to maturity), changing markets, and cross-competition with other savings and investment instruments. Risks and opportunities for profit both increased. The result was that tangible paybacks from IT investment were delayed.

Consolidations in the industry have had the desirable effect of reducing excess IT capacity, particularly that associated with back-office processing functions, and also excessive branch network structures.[53] IT has been an enabler of consolidation. However, studies of smaller mergers in the mid-1980s suggest that the noninterest expenses of merged banks do not differ significantly from the expenses of nonmerged banks.[54] Other studies suggest that economies of scale characterize some but not all activities undertaken by banks.[55]

Today, IT is being used to support growing efficiency and greater dispersion among banks. Back-office IT systems for internal accounting and

TABLE 2.8 Continued

	1984	1985	1986	1987	1988	1989
GPO						
(billions of 1982 dollars)	67.2	68.5	70.3	71.1	70.8	71.4
Revenues						
(billions of 1982 dollars; SIC 60[a])	98.6	99.9	100.3	100.3	99.5	99.8
Employment						
(millions of jobs)	2.1	2.2	2.2	2.3	2.3	2.3
Number of hours worked						
(billions)	4.0	4.1	4.2	4.3	4.2	4.3
Annual investment in IT						
(billions of 1982 dollars)	4.1	5.9	7.9	9.8	12.6	13.8
IT capital stock						
(billions of 1982 dollars)	9.1	12.5	16.9	22.2	28.8	35.1
GPO per labor-hour						
(1982 dollars)	16.60	16.58	16.62	16.70	16.77	16.80
Annual IT/GPO	6.0%	8.7%	11.2%	13.8%	17.8%	19.3%
Annual rate of change in GPO per labor-hour[b]	-1.0%	-0.2%	0.2%	0.5%	0.4%	0.2%

[a]Standard Industrial Classification system code.
[b]The compounded annual rate of change in GPO per labor-hour from 1981 to 1989 was 0.1 percent. Labor productivity is sometimes measured in terms of GPO per labor-hour.

customer accounting were the focus of IT investment throughout the 1970s and early 1980s. Virtually all banks were interconnected to regional and national networks. A large percentage of paper-based transactions were transmitted and processed electronically. ATM services and direct electronic deposits and withdrawals by large automated users replaced many paper processes. As new products and services expanded, and as margins became less predictable, commercial banks began investing in front-office automation to provide contact people with better information and to enhance the delivery of products and services.

Initially, investment in IT was concentrated in computers, since banking involved input-output intensive processing and huge databases. Most bank work involves establishing accounts (or customer relationships) and handling transactions within those accounts; banks process an increasing number of transactions that now total many tens of billions per year, a number that would be unthinkable without automation.[56] For example, Visa's peak capacity for processing credit card transactions grew from 30,000 per day in 1978 to over 1.4 million per day in 1991, while its response time for authorizations dropped from 5 minutes in 1973 to 1.1 seconds in 1991.[57]

Banks developed the technology for magnetic ink character recognition, which enables a high degree of automation in the check-processing system. Stand-alone systems for check processing, credit applications, and savings accounts are used by a large number of banks today. More recently, new IT-based systems have helped to consolidate mainframe-based operations. For example, the Bank of Boston revamped its securities-processing business in 1989, consolidating these operations from 11 separate locations into 2. This IT-based consolidation reduced staff requirements by 17 percent while volume increased by 80 percent.[58]

In the late 1980s, the banking industry began to focus on automation of data communications. The installation of on-line terminals in the early 1970s enabled automation of the customer interface and front-office applications in such areas as corporate treasury. ATMs, first introduced in the late 1970s, have become an agent of a strategic change in banking. More than 75,000 ATMs in the United States handle about 6 billion transactions per year for cash dispensing, funds transfer, credit card payments, and obtaining credit lines.[59] The deployment of an ATM network in 1977 was a major contributor to Citibank's growth of market share from 4 percent to 13.4 percent; between 1977 and 1988 Citibank's branch staff grew by 18 percent while they served three times as many customers.[60]) Data communications also lies at the heart of bank-to-bank transactions all over the world: the Clearing House for Interbank Payments System handles daily transactions worth nearly $2 trillion.[61]

IT enables banks to provide better service to customers. For example, Mellon Bank has installed an IT-based system to help resolve credit card billing disputes; this system enables the clerk to view in one place all documents relevant to a particular disputed transaction. Using this system, which also involved considerable reengineering of its process for handling customer complaints, Mellon was able to reduce its backlog of customer complaints from 5200 to 2200, resolving them in 25 days on average (versus 45 days previously).[62]

IT has been used to support a plethora of new products, including ATM access to banking services, the ability to shift funds between multiple accounts, and overdraft privileges.[63] Many of these new products are made possible by "securitization" of mortgages and credit card portfolios. Bank products are arguably information combined in new ways; for example, variable-rate consumer loans depend on computer-generated indexes and interest-calculating algorithms,[64] while unified statement processing enables the display of information from all accounts at one bank on one statement and "sweep" services enable customers to consolidate dividends and interest from different investment funds in one central interest-paying money market account.

Changed by sophisticated IT-based systems, loan processing shifted from personal loan officers accessing branch cash reserves to automated access to credit databases and external funds acquisition with asset-backed security arrangements.[65] Trade processors have eliminated the gap between front and back offices through automated interfaces.[66] Automated credit scoring simulates the organizational structure of centralized approval; instead of branch personnel sending applications to a central site for approval, workstations connect lenders to centralized computer systems that are used to help make decisions about granting credit.[67]

Dan Schutzer, a vice president of Citibank, asserts that IT has been used to create "whole new industries in investment banking that never existed before with the growth of derivative products, mortgage-backed securities, credit card receivables, commercial paper, corporate bonds to a large extent, and so forth. Many of these things didn't even exist as sources of revenue the way they are now."

The banking industry has invested heavily in building a sophisticated information infrastructure, which now includes high-powered desktop systems, artificial intelligence applications, automated credit scoring, electronics funds transfer, and links among a wide range of services and providers. IT will be used to enable an increasingly diverse set of banking interactions. More than likely, a higher proportion of banking will be carried out via ATMs, or more broadly over wires—via telephone or screen-based transactions—as well as by mail. Thus the interaction will be more indirect. In the future, there may be more card-based interactions, as the uses of credit cards grow and as cards themselves become "smarter" (e.g., smart card-telephone services). An increasing amount can be done at little extra cost, with relatively few people, a circumstance that promotes diversification into generation of assets (e.g., mutual funds), insurance products, and so on—building blocks for the industry. There will also be a high premium on integration of products and services—that is, standardization up to some level—followed by specialization to the customer.

Lastly, the banking industry has come under considerable competition from "nonbank banks." While the relaxation of the regulatory environment in the last decade has been important, IT has enabled a variety of nonbanking institutions to take advantage of this new environment by offering services that previously only banks could offer. For example, supermarkets with ATMs are now surrogate bank branch offices for transactions such as cash withdrawal. Large corporate entities such as AT&T and General Motors now offer widely accepted credit cards similar to Mastercard and Visa. With the cooperation of local banks, investment firms offer mortgages at favorable rates across the nation. Thus the traditional boundaries of the banking industry are blurring, and the ultimate impact of new competition is uncertain.

INSURANCE

The insurance industry is divided into two large segments: (1) life and health insurance, including pensions and annuities, and (2) property and casualty insurance. Life and health insurance is divided among individual products (sold to individual consumers) and the group market (life, health, and pension insurance products sold to employee or other groups).[68] Property and casualty insurance products are divided between personal lines (individual products, mainly automobile and homeowners' insurance) and commercial lines (e.g., coverage for liability, errors and omissions, business continuation, and employee fidelity bonding, as well as fire, theft, and so on).

Total premium receipts for life and health insurance and annuities approach $300 billion annually. Life and health insurance is provided by about 2350 companies;[69] total life insurance in force (i.e., aggregate policy face value) exceeds $10 trillion, with the average U.S. household now having more than $100,000 in coverage. Net written property and casualty premiums total about $225 billion annually,[70] with about 3800 companies providing such coverage.[71] About 55 percent of this figure covers commercial liabilities, with the remainder covering personal liability. The scale of these dollar flows makes insurance companies a major element of the U.S. financial system and major institutional investors.

The several thousand companies that provide insurance coverage range from very large multiline companies that sell a broad range of products in all states, to small companies that sell particular products to fill specialized customer or product niches. Policies are sold to the public through direct writers that sell through their own agents (often known as captive agents) or directly through telemarketing, the mail, and so on, and through agency companies that sell through independent agents who offer products from several insurance companies. In 1989 about 1.4 million people worked for insurance carriers (Table 2.9). Expenditures on IT in the insurance industry have grown significantly more rapidly than those of most of the other service industries examined. Table 2.9 describes the evolution of the industry in more detail.

In recent years, major changes have taken place in the insurance industry. Life insurance carriers have relied less on traditional whole-life policies, having been pushed by market forces to offer products that compete with a wide range of other investment vehicles. In the very competitive market for pensions and annuities, life insurance companies offer a wide range of investment vehicles to individuals and corporate pension plans. In the health insurance market, traditional indemnity-based group health plans now are in a minority, as insurers more often offer and serve as administrators of managed health care plans, such as health maintenance organizations and preferred provider organizations. Insurance companies are facing increasing competition from a range of entities, including banks and other financial institutions, health insurance plan administrators, and corporations' increasing willingness to self-insure.

Understanding the impact of these changes on productivity in the insurance industry is highly problematic, and the BLS has been unable to develop a meaningful measure of output for the insurance industry. Still, certain structural features of the industry can be identified.

Much of the insurance industry, especially the property and casualty and health segments, is data-intensive, being characterized by huge volumes of accounting, analysis and statistical data, and transaction processing. Insurance companies are concerned about the quality of business generated by their agents, as measured, for example, by the level of loss payouts resulting from the mix of products offered by a company. These companies need to be able to assess the risk to which a given portfolio exposes them, and thus they are large users of actuarial data that enable them to calculate statistically the likelihood of these risks with adequate levels of predictability. In addition, a large volume of data persists throughout an insurance product's life cycle, which includes underwriting (in which a substantial number of risk factors are evaluated in determining the acceptability of a risk and the premiums to be charged), maintaining policyholder and policy and coverage information, and keeping records of claims and payments.

Thus, it is not surprising that insurers were among the first in the commercial and corporate community to invest heavily in computers of all sizes, to develop their own extensive software and to use packaged software, and to install major telecommunications networks. For example, the insurance industry was quick to automate claims processing, which involves verifying that a claim has been submitted by a current policy holder, validating the consistency between the particular claim made and the policy's coverage (perhaps checking other policies held to coordinate benefits), and generating a check for the appropriate amount along with an explanation for how that amount was derived. All of these functions are performed today in a highly automated fashion. Automation has enabled the volume of claims processed to grow enormously with a minimal increase in personnel requirements, clearly an increase in productivity. As importantly, such systems enable claims processing to be carried out more quickly on a decentralized basis by employees (or agents) in the field who can access the necessary databases remotely.

Beyond reducing labor requirements and increasing processing speed in back-room operations such as accounting and records, insurance companies are using IT to do qualitatively different things. For example, portable computers are being used increasingly in field operations to communicate with the home office for a variety of functions. An agent tied by modem to the home office can serve a customer much more effectively now, by pro-

TABLE 2.9 Insurance

	1969	1980	1981	1982	1983
GPO					
(billions of 1982 dollars)	20.2	38.7	35.4	29.8	33.2
Revenues					
(billions of 1982 dollars;					
SIC 63[a])	44.1	67.8	66.8	67.8	67.3
Employment					
(millions of jobs)	1.0	1.2	1.2	1.2	1.2
Number of hours worked					
(billions)	1.9	2.4	2.4	2.4	2.4
Annual investment in IT					
(billions of 1982 dollars)	0.0	0.6	0.7	0.8	1.8
IT capital stock					
(billions of 1982 dollars)	0.1	1.3	1.7	2.0	3.1
GPO per labor-hour					
(1982 dollars)	10.54	16.21	14.76	12.45	13.97
Annual IT/GPO	0.2%	1.6%	2.0%	2.5%	5.3%
Annual rate of change in GPO					
per labor-hour[b]		4.0%	-9.0%	-15.6%	12.2%

NOTE: See Box 2.1 for explanation of terms and sources of data given.

viding customized quotes or claims payments instantaneously, than in the past. Insurance companies have connected their own agents and independents through networks they have designed and built themselves, or through systems such as the Insurance Value Added Network System (IVANS) developed by IBM.

Development of insurance policies for different corporate clients has also benefited from the use of IT. For example, the Aetna Life and Casualty Company used IT to revamp its "case installation" process for developing health plans for new clients.[72] The networked PC-based system now used by Aetna's Health Plan business unit for case installation was based on reengineering Aetna's installation process to homogenize case installations across regional offices and to reduce the volume of paperwork associated with each new installation and its different requirements.

Knowledge-based expert systems are being used increasingly by underwriters to help decide acceptance of applicants for coverage. Such systems facilitate the rapid comparison of a particular individual's risk profile with those in the community at large and make it easier to customize a policy based on the risks faced by that individual. They also provide the capability, based on quite sophisticated and elaborate data analysis developed by

TABLE 2.9 Continued

	1984	1985	1986	1987	1988	1989
GPO (billions of 1982 dollars)	35.9	39.5	36.0	34.4	37.0	36.7
Revenues (billions of 1982 dollars; SIC 63[a])	70.2	74.2	73.7	73.5	76.9	77.5
Employment (millions of jobs)	1.2	1.3	1.4	1.4	1.4	1.4
Number of hours worked (billions)	2.4	2.5	2.7	2.7	2.8	2.8
Annual investment in IT (billions of 1982 dollars)	3.3	3.6	4.6	5.6	6.4	6.2
IT capital stock (billions of 1982 dollars)	5.4	7.5	10.0	12.9	15.8	17.9
GPO per labor-hour (1982 dollars)	14.93	15.72	13.52	12.53	13.32	13.18
Annual IT/GPO	9.2%	9.1%	12.8%	16.4%	17.3%	16.8%
Annual rate of change in GPO per labor-hour[b]	6.9%	5.3%	-14.0%	-7.4%	6.3%	-1.1%

[a]Standard Industrial Classification system code.
[b]The compounded annual rate of change in GPO per labor-hour from 1981 to 1989 was -1.4 percent. Labor productivity is sometimes measured in terms of GPO per labor-hour.

the insurance industry, to implement widespread and varied cost-containment techniques in paying group health claims.

Quality in the insurance industry can be reflected in the extent to which insurance products can be tailored to meet the needs of individuals and in the manner in which customers are served. As is the case with many other service-providing activities, measuring the quality of the service delivered in the insurance industry is problematic. Although in some cases quality does have quantitative indicators (e.g., the average number of days needed to issue a policy or settle a claim), often the value of quality is subjective; i.e., it is in the minds of customers.

Today, many companies are using customer surveys and focus group sessions to find out what is important to their customers. Many insurers are focusing their initial reengineering efforts in areas that will affect customer service, seeking ways to further differentiate themselves in what is being viewed increasingly by many customers as a commodity market. The ultimate goal is to sell insurance to a market of one—single clients to whose individual circumstances a policy's payments and benefits are specifically tailored. The way each company uses IT will help determine whether and how it meets this goal.

Selling customized insurance to markets of one may change the traditional notion of insurance as the sharing of risk among large groups of individuals. Insurance companies have always differentiated among some risk groups (e.g., male drivers under the age of 25 usually pay more than others for auto insurance). But prior to the widespread availability of IT, data to differentiate more finely among individuals were simply unavailable. Today, the use of IT enables insurance companies to collect data on individuals from multiple sources and thereby define risk groups consisting of relatively small numbers of individuals, individuals with AIDS or cancer. Insurance may not be available to such groups at all, or only at a very high price—a possibility that poses significant questions for social policy.

IT has also been used effectively by insurance companies attempting to compete in new markets. For example, James Stewart, executive vice president and chief financial officer, noted that CIGNA invested in IT "to significantly improve and enhance the ability to deal with an individual participant's statements and a whole bunch of other services that we felt were responsive, both to the competition and to the customer's needs. That decision was made, not on a cost-benefit basis, but rather [to answer such questions as], What markets do we want to compete in? What do we need to do to position ourselves against both the insurance company and non-insurance company competition?"

Insurance agencies that provide coverage to individuals have followed a similar path with respect to using IT. A recent survey of independent agents found that 85 percent of independent agencies have some automation and that a growing number are using integrated, comprehensive full-function agency systems for back-office work (e.g., commission analyses, accounts receivable and payable). Regardless of whether they have agency systems, 90 percent have word processing, 85 percent have automated insurance rating, 76 percent have automated accounting, and 72 percent have automated billing. Somewhat fewer have automated underwriting (33 percent) and automated interfaces to multiple companies (44 percent, up from 23 percent in 1987). Seventy-two percent of these systems were installed before 1989.[73]

Agency systems, like corporate systems, have been used largely to automate what were previously manual processes (accounting, billing, marketing, and customer service). Although such systems enable the same number of people to handle a larger volume of work (and thus hold down labor costs), independent agents' desires and expectations for agency automation are, according to some observers, largely unfilled. Early agency users of IT experienced more difficulties than they had expected, partly as a result of their failure to understand the new systems, plan appropriately for their use, and train employees accordingly.

J. Raymond Caron of CIGNA Systems argues that

> There is a big evolution of IS (information systems) in an insurance environment. We went through an era with massive tab card sorting. We left that era and went into mainframe computers, data centers, and batch processing. We left that era and went into on-line applications, networks, and all that stuff. I think we're on the verge of a significant change in what IS organizations are all about, and I think that change is going to be radical. Reengineering, how we build applications, and how we work on solutions will be the new drivers.
>
> CIGNA's systems organization is going through the process of reengineering along with every other division within the company. What we are striving for in our reengineered systems organization is to be an integrated part of the business strategy. To accomplish this, we have had to help our people change their mind-set from a narrow technology perspective to a more global business perspective. Today, CIGNA systems professionals use their skills to solve business problems, not technology problems. And they understand that their performance will now be measured by customer satisfaction and business results.
>
> One of the things I'm planning is changing the way IS people think. If you get them to think about it right they can provide solutions that have nothing to do with technology. We need to get them to think that way because those might be the most powerful solutions rather than thinking the only thing IS can bring is technology. So we're restructuring IS, and I think the difference will be dramatic.

Put differently, IT may be used to drive restructurings that might not happen in the absence of technology. Developing better ways to use IT is already an integral part of many insurance companies' strategic planning and is a key factor in the industry's growth and in the successes of individual companies.

OBSERVATIONS AND CONCLUSIONS

In both scale and nature, the use of IT is highly varied within and among the industries the committee examined. That is, IT has been used by companies for many different purposes, both operational (e.g., accounting, logistics scheduling) and strategic (e.g., changing competitive positioning or providing totally new services). Although IT has been used primarily to improve the efficiency and effectiveness of specific activities, the impact of IT in these individual instances has sometimes had a large influence on the structure of the industry as a whole. Because of the effects of other non-IT forces, the significance of IT's use for an industry may be observable in aggregate industry data only when its impact is truly overwhelming or revolutionary. A good example is the telecommunications industry, which literally has been built on IT and which is now pervaded by IT. In other instances that are more likely the norm, IT's impact may be measurable only at the level of individual enterprises (e.g., in shifts of share or profit) or in activities within various companies.

At the same time, it is clear that the use of IT can bring about changes in the boundaries and definition of an industry. For example, deregulation and new technologies have allowed new players to provide services that were once the exclusive domain of traditional telephone carriers; today, private carriers and value-added carriers handle voice and data long-distance traffic for paying customers, and even some corporate networks have spare capacity that can be sold to other outside users. IT has been used to alter existing relationships among wholesalers, retailers, manufacturers, and end users (e.g., to eliminate intermediaries and enable direct sales from manufacturers to end users). Insurance companies are moving ever deeper into the business of health care management, and the lines between the two are already blurring. Through the use of IT, different industries are moving into banking, thus threatening the traditional understanding of what constitutes the banking system. IT (in the form of CRSs) has been part of what one airline executive suggested has been the transformation of the airline industry into one of the largest retailers of perishable goods (i.e., empty seats that disappear when the flight takes off). Further examples and amplifications of this point are contained in Chapter 3.

Lastly, IT may well create entirely new sectors for business that will encompass a variety of new and different industries. For example, a powerful telecommunications and information infrastructure has the potential to open the private home to a host of new information-related services. Although most network-based services have been aimed at businesses and other organizations, many now envision the creation of large home-based markets for new products combining computing and communications devices and services (e.g., multimedia technology). Although past attempts to develop services for the home such as videotext information delivery or computer-based teleshopping were largely unsuccessful, greater potential is seen in the more sophisticated offerings promised by recent and announced efforts to blend telephone, cable television, software, video, audio, text, and image database services. Better services for the home imply changes in the existing communications, information services, and entertainment industries; new markets for services; and new possibilities for home-based work. Consistent with the benefits-pass-through phenomenon discussed in Chapter 5, these new markets will likely generate public or private financial gains that far exceed those realized by the first companies entering these new markets.

Although an industry perspective offers particular insights about the actual performance of IT-based systems versus IT's measurable effects on productivity, further analysis at the enterprise and activity levels is necessary to understand where and how deployment of IT can be most effective and how IT's use is changing the basic structure of the economy, individual organizations, and most jobs.

NOTES AND REFERENCES

[1] In 1989, the United States employed 116.6 million workers in full-time and part-time jobs. See U.S. Department of Commerce, Bureau of Economic Analysis. 1990. *Survey of Current Business*, July, Table 6.6B, Government Printing Office, Washington, D.C.

[2] U.S. Department of Commerce, Bureau of Economic Analysis. 1992. *Survey of Current Business*, July, Government Printing Office, Washington, D.C. Table 6.22C (p. 91) provides corporate capital consumption allowances by industry, Table 6.1C (p. 82) provides national income by industry, and Table 6.5C (p. 84) gives full-time-equivalent employees by industry.

[3] U.S. Department of Commerce. 1992. *U.S. Industrial Outlook*, Government Printing Office, Washington, D.C., p. 40-1.

[4] The revenue passenger-mile (RPM) is the principal measure of output for the air transport industry: a single paying passenger carried for a 1000-mile airplane flight counts as 1000 revenue passenger-miles. The RPM is thus a direct measure of the service being delivered: the movement of passengers between different points.

[5] U.S. Department of Commerce, Bureau of the Census. 1991. *U.S. Statistical Abstract*, Table 1072, p. 627, Government Printing Office, Washington, D.C.

[6] Scheduled passenger carriers suffered losses from 1981 to 1983, in large part due to the recession and high fuel prices. From 1984 to 1989, the industry earned positive net income in four of the six years and reported a minimal loss in another. However, the industry's financial losses were so severe in 1990 (an operating loss of $3.95 billion in 1990-1991) that any gains in the 1980s were wiped out; scheduled passenger carriers lost about $2 billion from 1981 to 1990. (U.S. Department of Commerce, 1992, *U.S. Industrial Outlook*, p. 40-2.)

[7] U.S. Department of Commerce, 1992, *U.S. Industrial Outlook*, p. 40-1.

[8] Recent trends suggest that hub-and-spoke routing systems are most profitable under conditions of relatively high demand. Lower demand reduces the revenues that airlines can generate, while the costs of maintaining a hub are considerably less elastic. As recessionary pressures have driven down the demand for air travel, many airlines are starting to scale back the number of hubs they maintain. See Hirsch, James. 1993. "Big Airlines Scale Back Hub-Airport System to Curb Rising Costs," *Wall Street Journal*, January 12, p. A1.

[9] See Margolis, Nell. 1992. "AMR Cuts Costs, Jobs," *Computerworld*, December 21, p. 2.

[10] Transportation Research Board, National Research Council. 1991. *Winds of Change: Domestic Air Transport Since Deregulation*, Special Report 230, National Academy Press, Washington, D.C., p. 54.

[11] U.S. Department of Commerce, 1992, *U.S. Industrial Outlook*, p. 40-4.

[12] For example, this revenue stream is worth $100 million per year to American Airlines (Quinn, James Brian. 1988. "Technology in Services: Past Myths and Future Challenges," p. 37 in *Technology in Services: Policies for Growth, Trade, and Employment*, Bruce R. Guile and James Brian Quinn (eds.), National Academy Press, Washington, D.C.).

[13] The CRS is conceptually a single database, although in fact the data it contains may be physically distributed over many different computer systems. Technologically, the CRS provides a single standard interface to the human user (e.g., the travel agent) for access to multiple heterogeneous databases.

[14] The term *yield management* refers to the practice of continuously managing the number and fare class of seats on a given flight. By combining knowledge of how quickly seats of a given fare are selling with knowledge of competitors' pricing, yield management minimizes the number of empty or low-paying seats on any given flight, thus increasing revenues.

[15] See Tolchin, Martin. 1992. "U.S. Sues 8 Airlines Over Fares," *New York Times*, December 22, p. D1.

[16] *Air Transport World.* 1991. "Ryder Automates Parts Location," September, p. 106.

[17] *Air Transport World.* 1991. "Recipes by VideoSpecs," August, pp. 78-81.

[18] The A320 Airbus is a case in point. See Stix, Gary. 1991. "Along for the Ride," *Scientific American*, July, p. 97.

[19] *Air Transport World.* 1991. "ICAO Looks to Space," December, pp. 96-98.

[20] *Science.* 1989. "Flying the Electric Skies," Vol. 244(June 30):1532-1534.

[21] *Aviation Week and Space Technology.* 1991. "Airbus Employs Advanced Procedures in A330/A340 Manufacturing, Assembly," November 4, p. 48.

[22] *Air Transport World.* 1991. "Command Center on the Prairie," May, pp. 38-39.

[23] Kindel, Sharen. 1991. "The Route Cause," *Financial World*, August 20, pp. 70-72.

[24] Larson, Richard. 1988. "Operations Research and the Services Industries," in *Managing Innovation: Cases from the Services Industries*, Bruce R. Guile and James Brian Quinn (eds.), National Academy Press, Washington, D.C.

[25] From 1990 to 1992, the U.S. airline industry lost $9 billion to $10 billion dollars, wiping out all that it had earned, and more, in the 1980s. See Lenorovitz, Jeffrey. 1993. "Panel Issues Guidelines for Airline Recovery," *Aviation Week and Space Technology*, August 9, p. 31.

[26] See O'Leary, Meghan, 1991, "Airport '91," *CIO*, June, pp. 40-52; *Air Transport World*, 1991, "Ionworks," May, pp. 62-66; and *Air Transport World*, 1991, "Automation Picks Up Speed," September, pp. 51-56.

[27] *Air Transport World.* 1992. "New Cabins in the Sky," April, pp. 75-80.

[28] U.S. Telephone Association. 1992. *Statistics of the Local Exchange Carriers: 1992 for the Year 1991*, U.S. Telephone Association, Washington, D.C., p. 2.

[29] Federal Communications Commission. 1991. "FCC Releases Report on Long-Distance Market," news release, October 2, FCC, Washington, D.C.

[30] Schatz, Willie. 1992. "Who's Calling, Please?" *Computerworld*, November 23, p. 69.

[31] U.S. Department of Commerce, 1992, *U.S. Industrial Outlook*, p. 28-3.

[32] In some countries, long-distance calls are still logged by operators with hand-written tickets.

[33] According to Peter Chinloy, labor costs constituted approximately 75 percent of the operating costs for the Bell system in the early 1980s. (See Chinloy, Peter. 1981. "Implications for the Communications Workers of America of Technological Change at the Bell System," reproduced in *Productivity in the American Economy*, 1982, Hearings before the Subcommittee on Employment and Productivity of the Committee on Labor and Human Resources, U.S. Senate, March 19 and 26 and April 2 and 16, Government Printing Office, Washington, D.C.) This study of the Bell system from 1947 to 1978 also found that labor input grew more slowly than output, resulting in a steady increase in labor productivity. However, note that "labor" costs refer only to the costs incurred by telecommunications service providers; customer-provided labor (e.g., the keying by customers of telephone and credit card numbers) is not included in such costs. In other words, "reductions" in the labor required are at times more accurately characterized as shifting labor costs from provider to customer. Customers can also benefit from such shifts, as they can complete their calls more quickly, more securely, and less expensively by keying numbers themselves.

[34] Calling cards were invented in the 1950s but became especially popular after 1982, when AT&T automated the calling and billing processes, eliminating the need for operator intervention. See Ramirez, Anthony. 1992. "Plastic Keys to Phone Wizardry," *New York Times*, May 30, p. 48.

[35] See *Wall Street Journal.* 1992. "AT&T Unveils Card for ATMs That Has Wider Range of Uses," December 8, p. A6.

[36] Today, with a few exceptions (notably cable TV companies), telecommunications companies provide their customers with the ability to move and manage data and information that

the customer generates and/or owns. Local telephone companies, especially the regional Bell holding companies, are actively interested in providing information content as well as delivery. Legislative action may be taken in the future to remove the constraints placed by the 1982 consent decree on providing such services.

[37] Personal communication, Joseph Timko, vice president, AT&T Architecture, June 1992.

[38] See *Business Week.* 1992. "Clout! More and More, Retail Giants Rule the Marketplace," December 21, pp. 66-73.

[39] For example, small manufacturers often have limited financial resources that prevent them from creating a direct-selling organization. To the retailer the wholesaler offers multiple lines of merchandise and a larger assortment than is available from an individual manufacturer; wholesalers also obviate the need to work with multiple manufacturers. The wholesaler has the ability to buy in huge bulk portions that can be broken down into smaller units for the retailer. Some manufacturers are engaged in the wholesale business through the use of their sales branches. Retailers may also choose to buy directly from the manufacturer through chain-store warehouses; however, this activity does not fall within the wholesale classification.

[40] Inventory can represent as much as 70 percent of a retailer's assets. See, for example, Standard & Poor's Corp., 1992, "Retailing: Current Analysis," *Industry Surveys* 160(2), sec. 1, January 9; and Standard & Poor's Corp., 1991, "Retailing: Basic Analysis," *Industry Surveys* 159(17), sec. 1, May 2.

[41] National Retail Federation, Financial Executives Division. 1991. *Merchandising & Operating Results of Retail Stores in 1990,* National Retail Federation, New York.

[42] *Business Week.* 1992. "Clout! More and More, Retail Giants Rule the Marketplace," December 21, pp. 66-73.

[43] See Elliot, Stuart. 1993. "A Last Hurdle for Shoppers: The Checkout-Counter Pitch," *New York Times,* January 11, p. D-7.

[44] Bencin, Richard L., and Donald J. Jonovic. 1989. *Encyclopedia of Telemarketing,* Prentice Hall, Englewood Cliffs, New Jersey, p. 276.

[45] U.S. Department of Commerce, *U.S. Statistical Abstract,* 1991, Table 162, p. 104, for ambulatory care and Table 173, p. 109, for hospital usage.

[46] But see also explanatory note in Table 2.7.

[47] Tierney, W.M., M.E. Miller, J.M. Overhage, and C.J. McDonald. 1993. "Physician Inpatient Order Writing on Microcomputer Workstations: Effects on Resource Utilization," *JAMA* 269(January 20):379-383.

[48] U.S. Department of Commerce, 1991, *U.S. Statistical Abstract,* Table 807, p. 501.

[49] U.S. Department of Commerce, 1991, *U.S. Statistical Abstract,* Table 804, p. 500.

[50] U.S. Department of Commerce, 1991, *U.S. Statistical Abstract,* Table 802, p. 499.

[51] U.S. Department of Commerce, 1991, *U.S. Statistical Abstract,* Table 802, p. 499.

[52] U.S. Department of Commerce, 1992, *U.S. Industrial Outlook,* p. 46-1.

[53] Humphrey, David B. 1991. "Productivity in Banking and Effects from Deregulation," Federal Reserve Bank of Richmond, *Economic Review* 77(March/April):16-28.

[54] Srinivasan, Aruna. 1992. "Are There Cost Savings from Bank Mergers?," Federal Reserve Bank of Atlanta, *Economic Review* 77(March/April):17-28.

[55] Andersen Consulting. 1991. *Strategies for High Performance,* Arthur Andersen, Chicago.

[56] Steiner, Thomas D., and Diogo B. Teixeira. 1990. *Technology in Banking: Creating Value and Destroying Profits,* Dow Jones-Irwin, Homewood, Illinois, p. 29.

[57] Ganley, Oswald, and Gladys Ganley. 1992. "To Inform or to Control?," *The New Communications Networks,* Second Edition, Ablex Publishing, Norwood, New Jersey, p. 223. Also personal communication with Visa, 1992, cited in "Rewards and Risks: Communications and Information in the Global Financial Services Industries," PIRP, Harvard University, Cambridge, Mass., June 1992.

[58] Stewart, Thomas. 1992. "U.S. Productivity: First But Fading," *Fortune,* October 19, p. 56.

[59]Bove, Richard X. 1991. "Bank Technology Reshapes Industry," *The Bankers Magazine*, May/June, pp. 17-20.

[60]Glaser, Paul. 1988. "Using Technology for Competitive Advantage: The ATM Experience at Citicorp," in *Managing Innovation: Cases from the Services Industries*, Bruce R. Guile and James Brian Quinn (eds.), National Academy Press, Washington, D.C.

[61]Passell, Peter. 1992. "Fast Money," *New York Times Sunday Magazine*, October 18, p. 42.

[62]*Fortune*. 1992. "How to Steal the Best Ideas Around," October 19, p. 106.

[63]Steiner and Teixeira, 1990, *Technology in Banking: Creating Value and Destroying Profits*, p. 23.

[64]Steiner and Teixeira, 1990, *Technology in Banking: Creating Value and Destroying Profits*, p. 49.

[65]Bove, 1991, "Bank Technology Reshapes Industry."

[66]Andersen Consulting, 1991, *Strategies for High Performance*, p. ix.

[67]Andersen Consulting, 1991, *Strategies for High Performance*, p. 5.

[68]There are two large subgroups within the group arena: Medicare (health insurance for the elderly) and Medicaid (health insurance for the poor) are government-sponsored programs that are administered by companies under contract to states. Blue Cross and Blue Shield organizations are also state organized but privately administered. Over three-quarters of life insurers' health premiums come from the group health market (usually through employer plans). See U.S. Department of Commerce. 1992. *U.S. Industrial Outlook*, p. 50-2.

[69]U.S. Department of Commerce, 1991, *U.S. Statistical Abstract*, Table 851, p. 518.

[70]The Department of Commerce estimates life and health insurance premium receipts in 1991 at $283.5 billion and net written premium receipts for property and casualty insurance at $224.9 billion (U.S. Department of Commerce, 1992, *U.S. Industrial Outlook*, pp. 50-1 and 50-6).

[71]U.S. Department of Commerce, 1992, *U.S. Industrial Outlook*, p. 50-7.

[72]Cafasso, Rosemary. 1993. "Manual No More: Aetna Unit Gets PCs, Results," *Computerworld*, January 18, p. 37.

[73]Acord Corporation. 1992. *Moving Into the 90s: The 1992 Acord Agency Automation and Interface Survey*, Acord [Agency Company Organization for Research and Development], White Plains, New York.

3
Impacts of Information Technology at the Enterprise Level

The differing structure, environment, and competitive situation in each service industry explain only some of the differences in performance relative to investments in IT. Other differences reflect the experiences of individual companies within each industry. Both performance and the use of IT can vary greatly among companies in the same field (see Appendix A for references to relevant studies). Most of the variation reflects the fact that decisions concerning IT investment programs are made at different points in time by managers with different abilities and perspectives. Since most major decisions about IT investment are made by individual executives at the enterprise level, understanding how these decisions are made and evaluated is critical if national policy initiatives are to be effective.

This chapter examines why firms invest in IT, how firms invest in IT and the categories of applications that are typical, and how firms assess the impacts of their use of IT. It also discusses cross-cutting observations on IT and examines the widespread belief among executives that IT has enhanced performance overall, regardless of what macroeconomic measurements may indicate. The chapter is based on committee discussions informed by a set of semistructured interviews (Appendix D) held with about 80 senior managers in 46 major firms drawn from each of the major service industries—transportation, communications, retailing, wholesale distribution, health care, financial services, and professional services.

The interviews sought (1) to discover what types of enterprise-level data and experience might be available, (2) to validate further or raise informed questions about the basis for industry- and macroeconomic-level data and analysis, (3) to understand what factors managers consider important in making decisions about investing in IT, (4) to obtain some useful insights into how companies manage their IT investments for greater effectiveness, and (5) to explore further the causes for and implications of the IT paradox.

This exploratory investigation was designed to yield insights, not to substitute new statistical data for data obtained in other studies. The particular firms whose managers were interviewed were chosen because they had verifiably strong reputations as leaders in the use of IT. As such they were more likely to have both positive and negative experiences to draw on, to have thought carefully about critical issues, and to be willing to discuss them. However, their response cannot be generalized beyond this sample, because these firms were clearly more likely than the average company to provide evidence of a positive relationship between use of IT and performance. Some conclusions follow.

WHY FIRMS INVEST IN IT

Executives generally invest in IT to increase expected profits, margins, or returns on capital. Some investments—those made to reduce costs, to generate new products, to make measurable improvements in quality—may be discernible as gains in productivity in standard published reports. However, executives may also invest in IT for reasons that do not show up readily in such reports but may still be vital to the success of enterprises. For example, in some endeavors (e.g., research, engineering design, or medicine), the capacity to work at the intellectual frontier or to solve advanced problems may depend on having the most current technologies. In others (e.g., accounting, consulting, legal work, credit clearance, or trust management), flexible access to the most powerful current databases and efficient data-manipulating capabilities may be essential to deliver a competitive level of quality.

Managers generally regard IT as only one of many possible investments that may benefit their firms. When they choose to invest in IT, they do so in the belief that such an investment will provide better returns as compared to other alternatives, for example, not investing or investing in other programs. But many of the factors they consider and many of the effects of their successful investments may not show up in aggregated economic measures such as productivity, return on investment (ROI), sales, or margins.[1] For example, since companies can neither calculate nor report their "alternative cost" gains or losses—where their companies would have been positioned without an investment versus where they are with it—it is impossible for more aggregated databases to reflect such gains or losses.[2] Managers, especially in professional firms, may consider the cost of overinvestment in IT as insignificant against (the potentially much larger) losses the firm might incur if it fails to attract top talent, sustain its competitive edge, or hold market share because its IT systems are inadequate.

Among the more important rational reasons for investing in IT that are not picked up in aggregate databases are the following:

- *Expanding market share or avoiding catastrophic losses.* While aggregate industry output is a key economic indicator for policymakers, managers focus more on the performance of their individual companies. A company may gain or lose share even though statistics on an industry's performance in the aggregate may indicate relative stability. For executives, market share is a key parameter of successful performance as well as a basis for marketing, purchasing, and personal power for those in the company. Investments in IT that only shift market share may indicate little or no measurable benefit at the industry or macroeconomic level. The same is true of investments that successfully prevent very large losses—like airplane crashes or environmental catastrophes. Yet both types of investment are economically rational.

- *Creating greater flexibility and adaptability for future business environments.* Changes in the business environment (e.g., greater regulation, increased market or operational complexity) often demand significant changes in the way a company operates. In some cases, investments in IT may represent essential elements of the infrastructures that allow companies to survive despite rapid and unforeseeable changes in the external environment. In other cases, companies may invest in IT to gain future flexibility for creating products that may not yet be planned or even conceived. In still other cases, IT may enable a company to maintain or reduce its costs while providing greater variety and flexibility in its services.

- *Improving the quality and stability of internal environments.* Some firms invest in IT to obtain and analyze information that can provide a greater degree of predictability or stability in their operations and that can help them to avoid undue fluctuations in sales, profitability, or employment. Other firms may invest in IT to improve employee satisfaction or to enhance worker safety. IT can help to eliminate burdensome tasks, make jobs more attractive, shorten training cycles before an employee becomes productive, and improve morale. IT is an especially powerful tool that companies with life-critical operations can use to manage large amounts of data in real time to improve the safety of employees, customers, and the general public.

- *Improving the quality of products and of a firm's interactions with customers.* For many service firms, IT is an important element in creating services that are better customized and tailored to meet the needs of individual customers. Companies increasingly compete in other aspects of customer service quality, often using IT to serve customers more rapidly, pleasantly, responsively, accurately, and completely. Such improvements help generate long-term loyalty among customers. Similarly, IT can play an important role in improving reliability by ensuring more consistent levels of performance and minimizing errors and can thus enhance customers' perceptions of a company and its products.

As indicated above, individual firms have invested in IT to achieve a variety of results that are not generally captured in aggregate databases. A recent study by Brynjolfsson and Hitt[3] provides quantitative support for these ideas. Specifically, Brynjolfsson and Hitt analyzed output data and data on IT spending from 380 large firms that generate about $2 trillion in output annually, and found that increases in output at the firm level correlate strongly with IT expenditures, even if the macroeconomic data do not demonstrate increases in productivity across the national economy or in individual service industries. These data were taken from the 1987 to 1991 time frame.

HOW COMPANIES USE AND INVEST IN IT

Types of Applications

Senior managers interviewed by the committee tended to cluster their selected uses of IT into several broad categories that they evaluated using various techniques. The uses of IT included systems to support (1) basic infrastructure for communications and data handling, (2) mandated requirements, (3) cost reduction, (4) specific new products, (5) desired improvements in quality, and (6) major strategic repositionings (perhaps including a complete reorientation of a company's business). Companies tended to evaluate investments in IT on a program-by-program basis, rather than being concerned with measures of overall productivity. In the committee's sample, the techniques used to estimate or evaluate the impacts of IT were comparable to those used for other major investments.

Basic Infrastructure for Communications and Data Handling

Information technology infrastructures consist of those basic information storage, retrieval, communications, processing, and distribution systems that provide the backbone or framework interconnecting the multiple information-generating and information-using nodes in an organization. Although definitions may differ in detail from company to company, the IT part of a firm's basic infrastructure generally includes the core voice-transmission, data-communication, record-keeping, and transaction-processing systems necessary to conduct business. What a firm regards as infrastructure may change over time as new technologies become available and customers come to expect certain basic facilities from their service providers. Interactive data communications, for example, may be essential today, although this was rarely the case a decade ago.

Basic IT infrastructure systems are often approached as a "cost of being in the business." The majority (67 percent) of companies interviewed by the committee had done preproject analyses of IT investments in this area. But they often found that it was not worthwhile to separate out and justify individually the IT component of infrastructure—any more than it would be to use ROI techniques to justify the purchase of hammers for a carpenter, the acquisition of a telephone for a lawyer, or the installation of a roof on a new building for a real-estate developer. Some items are integral to being in a certain business. Firms tend not to give serious thought to doing without such elements of infrastructure in toto, and they often do not make a formal evaluation of their overall payback. But they frequently do evaluate incremental investments in infrastructure on a cost-benefit basis relative to other means of accomplishing a particular goal. On this basis, a majority (73 percent) of interviewed companies said that they had attained acceptable to high measured returns on such investments. But 27 percent reported negative or indeterminate returns. Measurement complexities represented serious problems.

For example, a study by the Aetna Insurance Company once analyzed the impact of IT on expense-revenue ratios over a 15-year period. Although the study concluded that IT had had little impact on these ratios, it also noted that the company could never have increased its handling of health care claims from 250,000 per week to 1.3 million per week without using IT and acknowledged the fact that this business was very profitable. Back-office automation in financial services, electronic point-of-sale systems in retail and wholesale trade, computer reservation systems in travel services, communications systems in all companies, and automatic flight control systems in aircraft for air transport are examples of large IT infrastructure systems without which individual companies could not compete today—but for which specific financial impacts are difficult to calculate.

Observed Richard Liebhaber, chief strategy and technology officer at MCI,

> There is an extensive infrastructure of holes in the ground, structures on the ground, and apparatus in the sky. That is our fundamental infrastructure. We regard it as a commodity asset: the transportation mechanism of our company. We view it from the standpoint of a cost factor, and we either build it, buy it, or lease each component depending on comparative cost and performance characteristics. The real problems in evaluating

productivity for these IT applications lie in those situations where the outputs are difficult to quantify in financial terms: "If I do this I will save 2 minutes here; if I do that I will save 8 minutes there," versus another alternative, "If I do this, I will save $9 million."

As noted above, managers are not indifferent to infrastructure costs and impacts. When IT is regarded as basic infrastructure, the managerial decision is not whether to invest in IT, but rather how to obtain needed IT capabilities at the lowest cost. If a firm's IT infrastructure requires some new capability, managers may consider alternative sources of that capability (e.g., performed in-house vs. purchased from an outside source) and seek to obtain it at the lowest long-term cost. When providing new levels of service to existing customers requires that incremental power or features be added to the base structure, companies may compare the net incremental costs and benefits of each of these features, in financial terms if possible. If features cannot be evaluated directly in financial terms, many companies use other metrics such as improvements in response times, levels of customer satisfaction, market penetration, or company image.

Several of the firms interviewed by the committee suggested that the only truly rigorous way of evaluating the payoff from investments in IT infrastructure would be to calculate the opportunity costs of not being in the business, that is, the losses that would have been incurred if the investment had not been made. However, such a calculation could be highly tenuous because of difficulties in estimating what would have happened if the investment had not been made. As Roger Ballou, president of the Travel Services Group (USA), American Express, noted:

> A good example of an infrastructure investment would be our automated authorization system. To determine the benefit of that system even today, I'd have to recreate mathematically what would exist if we didn't have it and only had our old personal telephone authorization system. For that you'd have to guess how a 20-year-old system would operate in today's world. That would be a highly theoretical exercise.

The complications of evaluating the impacts of infrastructure—and the possibilities of basing some decisions about investing in IT on cost and others on factors besides cost—were illustrated by J. Raymond Caron, president of CIGNA Systems, who observed that

> there are two types of infrastructure investments. For some, specific payback and evaluation mechanisms are used; for others, they are not. For example, for our data or voice communications we have put together a program based on AT&T's Tariff 12 and network costs. We know what our costs are, and we have goals to reduce those costs per minute, per connect, to the point where there are clear measures of benefits. In this case we can show dramatic evidence of our communications facilities cost-

ing far less today than they did 5 years ago. . . . When it comes to PC platforms (our CIGNA-Link platforms, which include PCs, LANs, the software to go along with them, plus e-mail), we find it very difficult to develop a useful cost-benefit measure. We've taken a position that we shouldn't waste time trying to do it.

Caron's comments about personal computers (PCs) illustrate a special problem in measuring enterprise-level impacts of infrastructure. The falling costs of computer hardware and applications software, the greater user friendliness of many computer systems, and the increased capability to interconnect local and remote systems have started to change the very nature of business infrastructure. IT systems are used to increase the level of information and flexibility within an entire enterprise. Such generalized impacts are exceedingly difficult to measure in the short run.

However, similar PC-based hardware and software can be specifically targeted to improve the performance of a particular operation. When used in this way, PC applications (e.g., to improve order handling, purchasing, customer inquiries or complaints, truck dispatching, field repair, editor-to-printed-page cycles, and broker-to-customer interfaces) have had considerable payoff. When specific goals are set, processes are properly reengineered, organizational interfaces are redesigned, and new incentives are provided, performance gains from specific applications can be impressive. Cycle times can be cut from days or weeks to a few hours or minutes. Layers of management or entire departments can be eliminated. For example:

• At the New York Times Company and Time Inc., PCs enable editing to continue right up to the moment when a story is electronically typeset for printing. Entire intermediate hierarchies and the attendant complexity of coordinating different functional centers have been eliminated.

• At McKesson Corporation, retail customers can use PCs to interact directly with the company's computers to eliminate many delays in order processing and much of the bureaucracy that used to exist to handle this function. The number of order takers at McKesson has been reduced from more than 700 to almost zero. The size of the sales force has been cut in half, even while sales have risen by a factor of 8. The number of buyers has been reduced from 150 to 200 located at over 100 distribution centers to just 12 sitting in front of desktop computers at a central site. Levels of management have been reduced in keeping with these changes.

In other settings (e.g., universities, research laboratories, or publishing houses), professionals often prefer to write and edit directly at their own computers, thus decreasing the number of secretaries needed for these tasks and flattening and downsizing the organization. It is not clear at this point whether measured productivity improves when (often) higher-priced employees like professors or researchers undertake such tasks.[4] In other situations, built-in desktop computer controls have eliminated much of the need for personal oversight in insurance, brokerage, and accounting applications—eliminating layers of bureaucracy.

Despite the undeniable utility of PC applications in certain settings, many executives interviewed by the committee were ambivalent about the impact of across-the-board access to desktop computing in their firms. Measures of performance are unclear, and personal intuitions about the potential and real payoffs from this type of IT vary widely. For instance, a majority of managers interviewed believed that the printed appearance and visual clarity of correspondence, graphics, reports, and desktop printed matter are better because of PC use. Communication between knowledge workers (i.e., the professionals responsible for interpreting and analyzing information made available to a company), as well as the information available to such workers, may also have been improved. But the measurable value of these improvements remains unclear when compared to the significant costs of having desktop computing available throughout an organization.

- At CIGNA Corporation, James Stewart, executive vice president and chief financial officer, said, "I'm not yet convinced that dispersal and utilization of PC-based technology have proven to be efficient. The business people in our organization drive me crazy on the subject of cost and benefit. I see increasing expenditures for what I perceive occasionally as 'toys in the business world,' which don't add up to measurable output or improve our results. I think better discipline in the effectiveness of PC technology is one of our great challenges."

- At BankAmerica, Martin Stein, vice chairman, noted: "The area where I would be the first to agree is that the banking industry has not done a good job in utilizing the PC as an office automation tool. We are faced with the typical problem. Everybody's secretary must have a 486 chip in his or her PC because it's much faster. And the question becomes, So what? The metrics for measuring this kind of productivity are not very good."

Interviewees reported that, to better manage the costs of their basic IT infrastructures, some companies regarded them as a "utility" and charged divisions for their use, just as divisions would be charged for externally purchased services. To further control costs, a few companies (10 to 20 percent) had begun to benchmark the utility's costs and performance against the prices and performance available for similar services bought externally. (Benchmarking is discussed in greater detail in Chapter 5.)

Skepticism concerning the degree of payoff from general office use of desktop computers seemed widespread among interviewed executives. This may reflect the fact that PC software in its first decade was not well suited to the needs of nontechnical users and that many senior executives used comput-

> **BOX 3.1 Using Lotus Notes at Chase Manhattan Bank**
>
> Chase Manhattan is beginning a project to deliver financial information to its customers using Lotus Notes, a "groupware" application designed to facilitate transfers of information contained in large databases. Senior Vice President Craig Goldman argues that Notes creates a new attitude for the information services department, allowing managers to focus on the front office where employees interact with customers rather than on the back office. Goldman believes that Notes provides an environment that will let employees react quickly to new business opportunities.
>
> SOURCE: Vizard, Michael. 1993. "Chase Banking on Notes to Reach Customer Desktops," *Computerworld*, April 12, p. 47.

ers sparingly because of unfamiliarity or discomfort with them. However, this is clearly changing; software is improving rapidly, and upper-level managers increasingly are individuals who grew up with personal computing.

Recently, a number of companies have reported observing enhanced performance when new, specialized "groupware" communication tools (like TeamFocus, Lotus Notes, or VisionQuest) are used to capture system knowledge, make meetings more efficient, and realize some of the communications benefits sought for PCs (Box 3.1). The emergence of simpler network software, multimedia capabilities made possible by autosynchronous transfer technologies, and greater capacities for electronically connecting fixed and mobile workstations may increase the benefits derived from desktop computing.

Mandated Systems

Regulators such as the Internal Revenue Service, the Food and Drug Administration, the Securities and Exchange Commission, state and local regulatory agencies, and other constituents like the investment community now require companies to provide specific reports or to have in-line monitoring systems for operations. Most respondents to the committee's questions considered the necessary investments as costs of being in their particular business and used IT as an element in reducing the cost of complying with increasing demands from regulators and other constituents. These investments in IT are made with no possibility of showing a specific profit or gain to the company—except as compared to performing the task by more manual means. On that basis, most interviewed executives believed that the returns on investments in mandated systems were satisfactory. For many companies, mandated requirements for reporting and monitoring have escalated in recent years, perhaps because computers have made more complex reporting easier or even possible. Almost by definition, mandated investments in IT do not contribute to a company's measurable overall productivity or gains in performance.

But interviewed company executives did not manage mandated investments in IT casually. Many estimated the relative cost of achieving the desired result using system A versus system B. While no evaluations were made of direct payoffs or returns for such investments, they were carefully monitored and evaluated using benchmarks, performance metrics established on installation, and operations costs versus other alternatives.

Cost Reduction

Cost reduction is often a major goal of investing in IT. This was especially true in first-generation applications, in which IT often substituted directly for manual or clerical labor in repetitive transactions such as materials-handling activities or in large record-keeping departments such as accounting, purchasing, or personnel. Other first-generation uses allowed firms to achieve substantial gains by avoiding costs associated with excessive capital float, inventories, and billing or payment errors—and by saving on the costs of paper processing, check handling, production set-up, engineering drawings, or shipping. While the benefits of these systems were said to be substantial, independent studies and the committee's interviews suggest that large companies have begun to reach limits in automating repetitive functions and achieving what might be called the industrialization of services.[5] They are now focusing on using IT for other, more complex—and often strategic—purposes.

Second-generation cost-reducing systems are often focused on consolidating or eliminating facilities such as data centers, production-planning departments, or order-processing bureaucracies. An interesting application in this area was illustrated by Craig Goldman, senior vice president and chief information officer of Chase Manhattan Bank:

> There is a significant cost-reducing phenomenon that is not well documented in the industry. That is picking a single site [from which] to deliver an information-intensive product on a global basis. It means you have common software in one location that delivers outputs to multiple sales locations or distribution centers. Anytime you have software in multiple locations, it is never common and this lack of commonality is usually very expensive. That is where we see large potential efficiencies.

A large majority (85 percent) of the companies interviewed made formal evaluations of their cost-reducing IT projects. These firms generally found that direct financial savings and returns on investment could be calculated with relative ease. Standard formal capital planning and payback analysis techniques widely accepted in industry are applicable in this context. Although often not implemented consistently or well in the early days of IT, ROI calculations for these projects were said to be fairly straightforward now. In most cases, interviewed companies now claimed to achieve targeted results or to exceed them through secondary uses of the same IT technology. At the same time, the payoffs from cost-reducing systems often were not as high as they could have been because of inadequate reengineering of processes and inadequate reorganization of personnel. (This point is addressed further in Chapter 4.)

Specific New Products or Opportunities

IT can enable the creation and delivery of specific new information-based service products that are extensions of a company's basic repertoire. Sometimes, such extensions are relatively modest, for example, a new "shopping channel" offered by a cable TV company. In other cases, such extensions have a major impact; for example, a telecommunications company may install new software that allows differential billing rates for calls placed to special parties or at a given time of day (MCI's Friends and Family program or AT&T's Reach Out America program).

If a new product is distinctive enough, a company can measure its impact on profit and sales quite explicitly. However, many new products merely apply new applications software to flexible IT infrastructures already developed, as when a new insurance product is offered using existing systems. In such cases, it is difficult to assess the total costs of the new product, although its incremental costs may be easy to evaluate. Such joint cost situations may introduce other complexities. By further utilizing existing IT infrastructure, some particularly innovative new products may simultaneously lower average costs in the system, thus allowing greater pricing and servicing flexibility on existing products. A prime example is MCI's Friends and Family program, which lowers costs for residential customers yet uses the network's otherwise excess capacity in nonbusiness hours. In the words of Richard Liebhaber at MCI:

> The decision to do Friends and Family was a combination of retention and market share: 62.8 percent of MCI's traffic was during the day; 33 percent of the traffic (in 1990) was off shift. The percentages in residential traffic were approximately reversed. Even today much of our infrastructure is idle during the night. So when we introduce a new product for nighttime residential traffic, such as Friends and Family, it may not require much capital. Many of the key investments will be for marketing rather than technological infrastructure. Returns are going to be largely the difference between increased market volume (share) and marketing costs.

The creation and delivery of specific new service products have a more modest and often a much more predictable impact than do strategic innovations (see below), because such products can be offered within the context of a well-understood business concept. A majority (64 percent) of the companies interviewed by the committee said that IT investments used to support new service products could usually be analyzed explicitly for profitability and returns. The vast majority (90 percent) of responding companies noted that they received satisfactory to high returns on these investments.

It is important to note that the corporate financial statements that are the basis for macroeconomic statistics reflect total returns from specific products, rather than the prorated returns that might be more appropriately assigned to IT as just one component of total investment. Any bias in reported data would therefore overstate positive returns on IT at more aggregated levels. Even for investments in IT that seemed to have quite measurable results, companies whose representatives were interviewed only had an overall correlation between investments and total project returns. This is a special problem in interpreting results when—as has been noted—many new information-based products capitalize on installed infrastructure and marginal investments for the new products themselves are minimal.

Conversely, if new products do not achieve desired returns, one cannot conclude that the fault lies in the IT system. Poor planning and implementation may be the principal culprits. Further, since potential payoffs from new products are always probabilistic, multiple projects and investments in IT are often necessary—as in any other innovative field—to obtain a single payoff. Hence, average payoffs on new products will be considerably less than those on established ones. And actual returns may not appear until long after investments have been made.

Improvements in Quality

Improved quality is often a most important output of IT systems. Yet most service companies encounter major problems in appraising the impacts of IT on service quality, and especially in measuring that impact in financial terms. This is true when two services are compared simultaneously or when a service output at one time is compared to an output at an earlier date. Service quality is often an intangible whose real value exists only in the mind of a customer. Respondents to the committee's interviews noted that it was impossible to quantify how much more valuable it is to a customer to receive a monthly bank statement within 48 hours versus a week later; how much more a cleaner, neater, more professional letter is worth; how much better served a customer may be in choosing from 100 financial service products rather than from 50; or how much it benefits a customer to have a shorter wait, a more accurate sales slip, or a more relaxed clerk in a checkout line. Companies reported that it was also very difficult to define the relative worth to customers of the more precise analytical and diagnostic capabilities now available in, for example, medicine or design, versus the less powerful but sometimes cheaper techniques of the past.

Often IT allows the handling of enormous increases in complexity. Although large benefits accrue to customers, competition may prevent the service company from increasing its sales or profits. For example, travel agents must complete in minutes arrangements that they could not have handled in days—or in some cases weeks—only a decade ago. To optimize their load factors, airlines make an average of 175,000 fare adjustments a day and up to 600,000 on some days. While these may pay off in higher profits at the airline level, travel agents must often re-search and re-issue tickets multiple times for a given customer's flight. Complexity, compounded by tasks such as worldwide arrangements, has increased by orders of magnitude; however, agents' average commissions have held steady at between 7.5 and 9.5 percent on airline prices that have dropped in real terms since deregulation.

Other factors further complicate determinations of quality. First, the quality of outcomes is heavily dependent on the actions of the buyer. Superb educational, health care, consulting, or financial services can be rendered useless if the buyer does not follow up properly. Alternatively, excellent customer implementation can convert poor-quality services into astounding successes—as successful graduates from poor schooling systems so often prove. Second, final outcomes may not be known until long after the delivery of a service. The true costs and benefits of education, surgery, dentistry, or insurance, for example, may not be known to either the customer or the provider for years or decades. Even then exogenous events may largely determine outcomes. But the customer will perceive—and receive—the service's value in terms of actual outcomes, not only those over which the producer might have had reasonable control.

Measures of IT's impact on performance are essentially useless unless they adequately reflect the quality of output. While a significant majority (over 80 percent) of the responding companies had established formal metrics to measure the quality of their service, these were almost always engineering metrics (such as system response times, percentages of time computers were available, and cycle times for operations) or data from customer surveys (expressing customers' views of the services of the company) that could not be converted into financial measures of the quality of output. Even when they had elaborate engineering and survey mechanisms to monitor quality, companies could not isolate the relative contributions of IT, versus those of other factors such as management, in creating these outputs. Nor could they relate such measures directly to financial results.

American Express's $6.8 billion Travel Related Services (TRS) Group is a case in point. The TRS Group samples client satisfaction monthly on such matters as timeliness, accuracy, and problem resolution for all its transaction types. It tracks some 46 measurements—defined as important by client research—broken down into six main categories. American Express asks its clients to weigh the importance of each issue, leading to a weighted customer satisfaction index that summarizes the key metrics and aggregates the number of "dissatisfying incidents" recorded in interviews and in customer complaints. American Express uses these indexes as direct measures of the quality of its performance. These metrics are tied into a total quality management approach throughout the TRS Group division for improving the overall effectiveness (efficiency and quality) of its operations. Yet American Express cannot place a direct dollar value on improvements in quality.

Unless sales increase or capital or labor requirements decrease as a direct result of investing in IT to improve the quality of output, companies are generally unable to place a financial value on the benefits they receive from using IT. Surrogate measures of quality—engineering metrics or data from customer surveys—were used by a vast majority (90 percent) of the companies interviewed by the committee. Yet no company stated that it could reliably convert such measures into metrics of financial payoff. Intangibles such as a firm's better responsiveness to customers and increased coordination with suppliers do not always increase the total volume or the margins and prices on products a company sells or services.[6] Competitors may quickly match the new capability, and each company may merely maintain its share of a total market that has not grown in size.

Although companies often try hard to measure the impact of IT on quality, capturing such impacts and presenting them in ways that can be aggregated at higher levels of data are real problems.

Major Strategic Innovations

Strategic investments in IT are those that significantly change the positioning of a company in its markets, redefine the basic nature of the company, or are necessary to maintain the viability of the company despite unforeseen competitive incursions. Strategic systems tend to simultaneously change many different elements of customer, cost, and competitive relationships—not just revenues or costs. They affect such things as quality of customer service, flexibility, break-even points, response times, and market image, which cannot be measured in simple financial terms and hence be picked up in macroeconomic data.

Strategic changes almost always induce a competitive response whose timing, scope, and force are unpredictable. So many things happen at once in the marketplace that respondents reported that it was difficult, even post hoc, to sort out impacts precisely. As in the introduction of new products, major effects may not be felt for a long time. For example, both the retail trade and telecommunications industries are in the midst of huge transformations—involving optical-scanning, computing, and digital communication technologies—that were largely unforeseen when these innovations were first introduced.

In some cases, incremental applications of IT may ultimately restructure a company so much that they redefine the very nature of the company's business in ways that could not have been foreseen at the time of installation. For example, Bankers Trust automated its back-office functions so successfully in the early 1980s that it was able to handle many wholesale banking operations with a sophistication much greater than that of most of its competitors. As its wholesale volume grew, it sold its credit card operations and its New York retail and upstate commercial banking operations. The core of its business became proprietary trading in bulk capital market activities, and Bankers Trust reoriented itself toward wholesale banking and trust operations. Within the wholesale markets it understood well, Bankers Trust could take higher risks with newer, more complex instruments, making possible much higher margins. In terms of efficiency, automation enabled Bankers Trust to cut its staff by two-thirds, while tripling its volume. But more importantly, Bankers Trust had redefined its total business concept and its options for future growth.

When they are successful, strategic systems offer the highest potential payoffs from IT. But, by definition, strategic investments in IT systems are infrequent and the results are difficult to forecast precisely because no one has developed or exploited such systems before. Classics among systems representing strategic investments are ECONOMOST and its successor systems at McKesson, Cosmos II at Federal Express, automated teller systems at Citicorp, and AANET at Arthur Andersen & Co. Other examples include Bank of America's COIN, Levi Strauss's Levi-Link, CHIPS (Clearinghouse for Interbank Payments system), and the Depository Trust. All of these systems enabled their sponsoring companies to offer new services to clients, but it was their capacity to restructure the business in its industry that qualified the systems as strategic. In some cases, investments in IT that the sponsoring companies hoped would have strategic impact failed or yielded disappointing returns: these include videotext, the New York Times Reference Service, Federal Express's Zap-mail, and AMR-AMRIS's CONFIRM system. Systems in the latter category show up both in higher cumulative IT investment figures (until written off) and in decreased profits at the macroeconomic level.

Perhaps the best known example of an IT application with strategic impact is the SABRE system of American Airlines. In addition to providing efficient and accurate flight reservations, SABRE enables the company to handle hundreds of thousands of pricing and routing changes each day to optimize customer value and its own costs. The airline can hold Friday afternoon seats open for business travelers who are willing to pay a higher price than leisure passengers will pay. While offering discount fares early in the year for the Christmas season, the airline can ensure that seats are available for passengers who wait until later in the year, thus balancing and increasing profits over the long haul. It can also control oversales on flights and the customer unhappiness that results. By using a post-departure checkout procedure, American can also sell at later stops the seats opened up by "no-shows." And it can better control subsidiary services, such as special meals and handicapped support, as well as flight operations. American believes its greater capability in these respects and its capacity to finely segment its customer base because of the detailed information it has available have enabled it to grow steadily during the post-deregulation shakeout when many other airlines have lost control of their costs. Many credit SABRE for converting American from one of the weaker airlines in the late 1970s to one of the strongest airlines today (although, like other airlines, it faces financial challenges).

The strategic use of IT to change a company's positioning in the marketplace—and the difficulty of measuring that impact—is illustrated in telecommunications by Richard Liebhaber of MCI, who said,

> We deal with 20 million customers every month. It's the only business in the world where companies invoice every minute, every second, every line item. And people send us letters about details in their bills. Wouldn't it be powerful, as a service provision, if we could convert all our workstations in customer service to image capability and provide our representatives with the invoice and any letters about it in image form? When the customer call comes, we could answer questions immediately and better, but there would be no measurable productivity increase there. . . . It is an opportunity to improve the image, the feel, the touch of MCI. Intuitively, I would tell you it's going to provide market share, customer satisfaction, bottom line. I can't prove it. I'm not going to waste my time trying.

The strategic use of IT may also enable industries to develop additional revenue streams of considerable value. One example is the sale of mailing lists created and maintained by IT systems among mail-order retail houses; in some instances, the revenue from such sales is an important fraction of the revenue generated by actual sales. A second example is the revenue stream that goes to owners of major computerized reservation systems (CRSs); airlines unable to afford their own CRSs must buy services provided by existing CRS owners. The revenue from such sales is substantial.

IT may also help to create whole new lines of business for an entire industry, as mortgage-backed securities, swaps, and derivative securities have in investment banking. As Daniel Schutzer, vice president at Citibank, noted:

The quality of the total service we deliver and the fact that these are whole businesses now handling trillions of dollars and making hundreds of millions in profit leave no doubt in my mind that there has been productivity. But if we're talking about productivity in terms of the number of people that run branches and how much profit we're making on our old lines, we probably haven't really decreased the number of people; for years, we were building many more branches.

The use of IT has facilitated the formation of many new industries or markets, as the examples in Table 3.1 indicate. The list there is incomplete, and the data indicate only approximate scales. The full impact of creating these new industries often will not be reflected as benefits for the originating firm(s) or to the original service industries they might supplant. There can often be substantial delays before macroeconomic data are restructured to reflect such new industries. Although other forces helped to create these new markets and industries, most would have been essentially impossible to operate at their existing scales and efficiencies without IT. How much they substituted for other businesses is unknown. Even the incomplete list in Table 3.1 suggests that new service benefits to customers substantially outweigh aggregate investments in IT.

One of the most powerful strategic applications of IT is the large-scale capture, segmentation, and integration of data about both markets and operations (Box 3.2). Use of the resulting data and information has helped revolutionize the ways in which business (and even government) is conducted.[7] For example,

• Retail chains, by keeping track of product features and sales trends in detail, can help innovators design products most suited to the market. By using these data to constantly update operations, producers can access markets more quickly, shorten cycle times, and decrease their risks from innovation. Customers are presented with the products they most want. And shortening production-to-market times (as Levi Strauss's Levi-Link does) reduces inventory risks for both producers and distributors.

• Researchers in companies routinely use electronic networking to communicate internationally and with more centers of expertise than in the past, bringing together the best minds in an entire company (and the outside world) to bear on a problem. Professional service firms can quickly access their expertise anywhere in the world. The potentials for synergy and value are well recognized in research and consulting networks such as Internet or AANET.

Arthur Andersen & Co. has developed a network, AANET, that helps link over 60,000 people in some 300 offices in 70 countries. The company's cumulative experience is growing so rapidly that executives say, "Even those in the know may not have the best answer to the totality of a complex

TABLE 3.1 Scalar Estimates of New Markets and Industries Largely Facilitated by IT

Industry Type[a]	Sales Volume or Revenues (billions of dollars)[b]	Year	Source
Catalog retailing	47.2	1992	*Catalog Age*, March 1993
Computer software and services	79.8	1989	*The 5th Annual Computer Industry Almanac*, 1992
Fast-food restaurants	75.6	1992	*Frozen Food Digest*, March 1993
Wholesale clubs	33.0	1992	*Financial Times*, May 21, 1993
Discount merchandise retailers	151.5	1989	*Discount Store News*, July 2, 1990
Computerized reservation services (worldwide)	1.8	1989	*PC Week*, August 7, 1989
Public information resources (North America)	11.0	1991	*Information Week*, August 26, 1991
Cellular telephones	7.2	1992	*U.S. Industrial Outlook*, 1993
Home video sales and rental	12.2	1992	*U.S. Industrial Outlook*, 1993
Basic cable television (subscription revenue)	12.6	1992	*U.S. Industrial Outlook*, 1993
Satellite services	1.5	1992	*U.S. Industrial Outlook*, 1993
Video games (worldwide)	7.0	1992	*Forbes*, January 18, 1993
Computer animation (worldwide)	> 5.0	1994	*Computer Graphics World*, March 9, 1991
Assets Managed			
Credit card receivables	206.0	1990	*Faulkner & Gray*, 1992
Swaps (worldwide—outstanding balance)	300.0	1991	*The Bankers Magazine*, May/June 1993
Mutual funds (worldwide)	161.0	1992	*Business Week*, January 18, 1993
Credit card charge volume	464.0	1991	*Faulkner & Gray*, 1993
"Securitized" home mortgages	100.0	1991	*Business Week*, July 20, 1992
Asset-backed securities	50.9 public 8.0 private	1992	*The Bankers Magazine*, May/June 1993
Transaction Volume			
New York Federal over Fedwire	150,000 transactions/minute	1990	*Computerworld*, April 22, 1991
Automated teller machines	600 million transactions/month	1991	*American Banker*, December 7, 1992

TABLE 3.1 Continued

Industry Type[a]	Sales Volume or Revenues (billions of dollars)[b]	Year	Source
Transaction Volume (continued)			
CHIPS[c]	$250 trillion	1990	Interviews with Clearinghouse for Interbank Payments
Foreign exchange market	> $600 billion/day	1990	The Economist, July 21, 1990
Treasury bond market	$100 billion/day	1990	The Economist, July 21, 1990
Depository trust (outstanding commercial paper issues)	$555 billion	1992	American Banker, September 28, 1992

[a]U.S. only unless otherwise indicated.
[b]All figures are approximations only.
[c]Clearinghouse for Interbank Payments system.

question." AANET attempts to capture and leverage knowledge wherever it exists at Arthur Andersen. Partners say that the company's distinctive competency has become "empowering people to deliver better-quality technology-based solutions to clients in a shorter time." Auditors and consultants who find unique solutions to problems introduce the solutions to the system through specially indexed subject files maintained in the Chicago headquarters. Field professionals who encounter a new problem can query everyone on the system for solutions through an electronic bulletin board. On its audit reference and resource disk (a CD-ROM system connected to desktop microcomputers), Arthur Andersen & Co. collects and distributes as much up-to-date data as it can on taxes, customers, solutions to special problems, Financial Accounting Standards Board pronouncements, court rulings, and professional standards to guide its auditors and consultants in the field. Field personnel can both tap into the headquarters database directly through AANET and carry onto a customer's premises a CD-ROM with the power of many firms' central libraries.

The capacity of many companies to develop a knowledge-based competitive advantage depends largely on the level of detail to which they can break down their contact point data and then analyze, mix, and match these data in different ways (see Box 3.2). The company with the largest and most detailed information base can segment and target its marketing and customer service activities with a precision and unit cost that smaller com-

BOX 3.2 Comprehensive and Company-wide Databases

Properly designed systems for comprehensive data capture offer companies one of the few and most important economies of scale in the current marketplace. Just as the utility of a telephone network increases dramatically with the number of telephone subscribers connected to the network, so also do comprehensive data sets enable highly sophisticated business operations. Computerized reservation systems provided important competitive advantages for individual companies, but they had major structural impacts on the entire industry when they began to carry flight and fare information for carriers other than their owners. These more comprehensive data sets enabled much tighter integration of services provided by different companies (e.g., feeder airlines and national carriers, auxiliary services such as car rentals and hotels) and facilitated "one-stop" shopping, thereby making trip planning much less onerous for individuals or travel agents. In the telecommunications industry, detailed per-call records of telephone traffic have enabled long-distance companies to develop a wide variety of call pricing plans to suit different calling patterns. In the retail industry, detailed profiles of customer preferences have increased the efficiency of marketing by enabling focused and targeted sales campaigns. The databases of Dow Jones, Merrill Lynch, Readers Digest, The New York Times, and many other service companies are unique competitive resources individually worth billions of dollars.

A firm that has taken particular advantage of comprehensive databases is Toys "R" Us, which enjoys $5.5 billion in annual sales and three times the revenues of the world's largest toy suppliers. With its command of information about the marketplace and capacity to control the positioning, display, retail advertising, and pricing of toys, Toys "R" Us can sell products virtually year around while its competitors can afford to carry significant inventories only during the short pre-Christmas season, when over 60 percent of all toys are sold at retail. Toys "R" Us, with its high volumes and sophisticated electronic inventory and point-of-sale systems, has a powerful mechanism for pretesting which toys are likely to sell—and in what form—when the big Christmas sale season comes. In addition, with its sophisticated models of toy sales, toy production, and changing tastes, it can invest in its inventories with considerably less risk than other companies. By insisting on "just-in-time" deliveries, it can further decrease mark-down losses, which are as much as 25 percent of the toy industry's cost for other retailers.

To create such comprehensive databases, it is virtually essential to capture information at the point of its creation. For example, point-of-sale systems that capture price and item information in real time are a critical element of the foundation for the use of IT in the retailing industry. Modern telecommunications systems generate large amounts of transaction information with each call (e.g., calling number, called number, time and

> length of call), thus enabling a host of new services (e.g., Caller ID and Friends and Family, as well as very detailed billing information). Airline companies capture transactions at the source through their computerized reservations systems, enabling downstream improvements in scheduling, food preparation, maintenance, and so on. Securities companies must capture each element of a transaction instantaneously and be able to display both that transaction and market averages continuously. The most valuable resources of a brokerage firm are often its electronic database, data-tracking, and computer-tracking programs without which it could not compete. Customer expectations about the professional capture and use of this information—and legal liabilities for its non-use—have grown apace.
>
> Point-of-creation data capture, coupled with a higher degree of automation in the actual mechanics of capturing data, reduces both the time required and the error rate for data entry; bar-code scanners make many fewer errors than human cashiers. In addition, capturing data at the source means that data need not be repeatedly entered (further eliminating opportunities for error), and the availability of data at the beginning of the data-processing cycle means that the benefits of automation can be captured at any point downstream. Transactions with customers are the originating point for all work processes within an industry and the key to providing new and better customer services.

petitors cannot match. Data systems have thus become one of the most important economies of scale for service enterprises.

This fact has strategic significance in systems design. Companies that do not consider the future strategic implications of comprehensive data capture at the time they develop their systems—or that attempt to save upfront costs during early systems design and installation—often lose important data and associated opportunities, as well as incur higher costs when they try later to exploit more refined breakdowns of data. Many companies have discovered that it is much easier to aggregate overly refined data later rather than to try to introduce disaggregations to a structure not built for them. A good example is provided by MCI, whose Friends and Family program is based on flexibilities designed into its IT systems from the beginning. As Richard Liebhaber of MCI said,

> How we do this is probably the most important trade secret in our company. We didn't think about Friends and Family specifically at the time we designed our IT system. What we did was focus on what we had to be able to control from an information base viewpoint—because we are an information service business—and designed in extra flexibilities at that time.

Making quantitative judgments about the impact of investments in IT for strategic purposes, as for infrastructure, presents unique problems. Strategic IT systems are not necessarily less intensive in either labor or capital than existing operations; indeed, they may well require more of both. Precise preproject calculations of expected return are difficult because ultimate consequences are often unknown. And postproject calculations require massive assumptions about what a company's cash flows would have been with and without the chain of investments involved. For example, as noted by Liebhaber,

> To analyze payoffs of Friends and Family we would have to introduce assumptions both about what our share would have been without [the product] and about how much longer you [the customer] will be a member of the MCI family as a result of this product.

In some cases, potential payoffs from success may be so obviously high as not to warrant detailed evaluation. As Robert Elmore, partner and worldwide director of the Business Systems Consulting Group at Arthur Andersen, said,

> It is often not necessary to take a detailed look at paybacks on certain strategic investments. Strategic use of information is often dealing with a 100-to-1 return or at least a 10-to-1 return, and in these cases returns should be obvious. For example, our electronic bulletin board was installed about 4 years ago, and there is no question among our practitioners that it gives us a competitive advantage and that it has made a large direct contribution to sales growth. We expect our line of business to triple in size in the next few years. We couldn't even think about being that large if we did not have this capacity to leverage our intellectual capital across the entire division.

In other instances, broad gauges such as changes in market share, total profitability, growth rates, overall sales, and returns on investment may be relevant to judging strategic impact. When a major strategic change results from a series of incremental decisions (as in the case of Bankers Trust), it may be possible to justify each incremental step by using traditional measures. However, when the aggregate impact is considered post hoc, these detailed numerical analyses may have little meaning because of failures in some projects and unexpected synergies among others. In some cases, the risk posed by a strategic project may be unassessable by strict financial analyses. The only reason some projects succeed is that an individual entrepreneur evaluates risks differently and actually enters the field to test the assumptions underlying a project. Turner Broadcasting Company and Federal Express's overnight package service are success stories in this category.

Decision Making About Investing in IT and the Rigor of Program Evaluation

Given the multitude of reasons for investing in IT and the different ways in which firms use IT, processes for decision making about IT of course vary from firm to firm. Nevertheless, two common characteristics stood out in the committee's sample group: (1) the similarity between the practices these companies use for decision making about IT and those used for other types of corporate technology investments and (2) the difficulty of separating IT's impacts from those of other factors affecting the success or failure of a project.

The committee's sample of firms tended to use decision-making procedures for IT investments that were (1) comparable to those they use for other projects and (2) similar to those other companies use when investing in high-technology projects. A large majority of the companies interviewed by the committee (see Question Box 2 in Appendix D) reported that they routinely undertook preproject evaluations of investments in IT program by program. Depending on the nature and purpose of a given project (IT or not), preproject assessments varied greatly in the degree of quantification used. Few companies felt they had effective systems for evaluating the aggregate paybacks from all IT programs. A vice president of a major airline reflected the position that many respondents expressed. He said,

> The process that we've followed for the last 10 years—for all of the projects that have been large investments—is to put them through a very rigid justification process. The focus is on ROI justification. There are some strategic implementations or implementations which you can't justify, no matter how hard you might try, in terms of dollars and cents. But there must be the implication that implementation will be an advantage for the company from a strategic viewpoint. It's basically a system-by-system process that is very similar to our capital allocation process. As a matter of fact, all the resources that are used at the IT end of the business are allocated through a process that very similarly matches our capital allocation process within the company.

In certain cases in which the desired result is relatively easy to specify (e.g., for cost-reducing systems and certain new-product projects), companies tend to use the same rigorous ROI and financial evaluation techniques for IT investments that they would use for non-IT investments devoted to the same ends. But for many systems, data forecasts are less precise, and calculations of ROI are often not as useful as other metrics. For example, because there are no positive returns from mandated systems, companies often merely compare various IT systems to see which will give the desired effect at the lowest long-term cost. Because it is frequently impossible to measure the impacts of improvements in quality precisely in terms of sales or profit, firms often use engineering metrics like response times, error rates, or service availability times when evaluating investments in systems intended to improve quality. Similarly, the long-term effects of strategic flexibility, more refined data-handling capabilities, or more detail in databases may defy financial quantification. Hence strategic investments may be evaluated in terms of their probable effects on market share, customer satisfaction, capacity to attract or empower personnel, or potential for future flexibility, as well as their capacity to accomplish a specific current mission or major goal.

Major effects of strategic investments may not be felt for a long time, and the timing and impact of specific events, if they occur at all, are also unpredictable. The entire cost structure and cost competitiveness of a firm within its industry may be affected, also unpredictably. In some cases, so many intangibles are involved that management's judgment may be a better indicator than detailed metrics. Although many interviewed companies noted that it is often not possible to develop accurate quantitative or financial metrics to measure the potential or actual benefits of some strategic investments in IT, they tended to treat such decisions within the same framework used for other complex advanced-technology ventures.

A good analogy can be found in research and development (R&D). Both R&D and IT are often intended to provide new options for the investing company. In many cases, investments in R&D and IT are uncertain with respect to payoff. Payoff is usually not immediate, and the expected value is often not quantifiable or even estimable, let alone predictable. Executives try their best to forecast expected benefits, but success is often driven more by vision and superb implementation than by meeting accurate financial analyses. As with R&D, some IT projects succeed, and some do not. It is not surprising that the experience of firms in implementing new IT systems varies from extraordinary success to utter failure, a fact illustrated by many studies at the enterprise level.

Sometimes, the analogy goes much deeper—implementing a new IT application may in fact *be* an R&D venture. If IT has never been used in a particular application before, managers may not understand whether, how, or how well the system will function in practice. There can be large uncertainties in the amount of time it takes to develop the application, apply IT to it, and develop specific software for it. Such efforts can be very expensive. Often a functionally complete IT infrastructure must be put into place before the real pros and cons of possible applications can be reasonably tested. If the system is installed in an ongoing operation, there are additional risks of interrupting the business itself. For example, the New York Stock Exchange had to install its automated trading system successfully without any interruption of operations; otherwise losses could have been catastrophic. Similarly, in the mid-1980s, Kmart invested in an expensive relational database system to store scanner data (hundreds of gigabytes) from retailers with only the belief (not the assurance) that once such data were made available, retailers would be able to exploit that data to their advantage.

A second key characteristic of decision making for investing in IT in any complex situation is that it is virtually impossible to separate IT's contributions to success or failure from the effects of other factors such as planning, training, management, or other supporting investments—or from other important changes that may be happening in the marketplace and business environment at that time and that may make it difficult to sort out net effects, even post hoc. Against a backdrop of extensive external change, it is often impossible to discern the financial impact of entire programs, let alone the contribution of IT to those programs.

Like a milling machine or a grinder, IT is only one component of a system that enables a company to produce and deliver a good or service effectively; actual production usually requires many other components, including management, facilities, training, support, organizational factors, systems, equipment, and even materials. For example, when incremental increases in sales or levels of service require an incremental buildup of a firm's physical plant or capacity, the cost of IT may be just another component in the aggregate investment needed to bring the new business opportunity into being (e.g., the IT accompanying an extension of operations into a new geographical area). At best, it may be possible for a company to impute to the IT investment a prorated share of a project's total return based on its relative cost as one factor. In many cases, executive intuition and judgment may be as satisfactory as more complex numerical allocations of cost and benefits.

In a strict sense, the proper way to evaluate the impact of IT is to measure the effects of a total system and then to analyze IT's direct contribution to them on a factor contribution basis.[8] However, due to the inability to separate the influence of IT from that of other important factors at the enterprise level, such an approach to evaluation is rarely feasible, and no company interviewed by the committee had used it. However, this is also true for evaluating investments in fixed equipment in manufacturing industries and other, non-IT business investments in most enterprises. Although a majority of those interviewed by the committee had tried to evaluate their firm's overall payoff from IT, none felt that they had satisfactory financial metrics for this purpose.[9]

To supplement or take the place of unsatisfactory financial metrics, many companies reported using engineering metrics to determine important impacts of IT. Engineering metrics often reflect more detailed aspects of an individual firm's work process (e.g., the number of individual transactions processed per employee in the banking industry, the number of claims processed per employee in the insurance industry, the time taken per customer service request in the telecommunications industry, the time before the arrival of desired merchandise in the retail trade industry; Box 3.3 gives additional examples).[10] Engineering metrics are very useful for diagnostic purposes and to compare the performance of one company to that of another (benchmarking). For those types of investments in IT for which financial measures are ineffective (particularly for improvements in quality), managers rely heavily on engineering

> **BOX 3.3 Examples of Engineering Metrics**
>
> **Airlines**
> - Fuel cost per passenger-mile
> - Load factors (average percentage of occupied seating on scheduled flights)
> - Response time for customer inquiries on reservations lines
>
> **Telephone Companies**
> - Average repair time for service calls
> - Number of calls processed per operator-day
> - Cost per mile to install cable
> - Sources and destinations
> - Connection delays
> - Number and duration of interruptions
> - Frequency of disconnects
> - Signal variation over different intervals, signal strength and other measures of signal quality
> - System "down" times

metrics to plan and oversee performance. Often such metrics cannot be related directly to bottom-line measures of revenue or profitability. The fact that no company interviewed by the committee had been able to do so supports the contention that macroeconomic data based on financial reports cannot accurately reflect changes in quality. Data from engineering metrics on the true impacts of IT on many aspects of quality are available only at the enterprise level and are not captured at any higher level of aggregation.

CROSS-CUTTING OBSERVATIONS REGARDING ALL USES OF INFORMATION TECHNOLOGY

Despite the wide variety of IT uses described above, several observations seem to apply to all of them.

Controlling the Costs of IT

IT has become a significant element in the cost structure of many companies. From 1981 to 1989, absolute annual expenditures on IT in constant dollars grew by 86 percent nationally across the entire service sector.[11] More importantly, this figure understates by a substantial amount the total cost of IT, since it reflects only expenditures on hardware—mainframe computers, PCs, terminals, data communications networks, and the like. At least as important for an organization that wishes to make effective use of IT are several other essential elements that seriously affect profits from IT's use:

- *Software, whether custom-made, off-the-shelf, or user-developed.* Initial investments can vary from very costly domain-specific software to inexpensive "shrink wrapped" diskettes and user-developed spreadsheets, databases, and so on.
- *Training and support.* Users often require extensive training and support if they are to use a technology effectively. Even then they are unlikely to achieve the ability to use a system's full capability before the next generation of technology and customer demands require further changes.
- *Maintenance and upgrading.* Hardware and software in place must be constantly maintained—and often upgraded or replaced—long before they have reached the use life calculated at the time they were acquired. The latter two categories often represent over 60 percent of the ongoing cost for a sophisticated system.

Despite the importance of the elements listed above, the accounting rules that determine a company's book value do not treat hardware, software, and IT service (e.g., maintenance, training, support) equally. IT hardware costs (and initial software costs, if demanded by IRS) are usually carried on a company's books as depreciable assets. The costs for equally important software support, training, and IT service are generally treated as expenses (see Appendix D). Since overall IT costs are typically divided about equally among hardware, software, and service, a company's true investments in IT are rarely reflected in statements of book value.

Even for elements of IT captured on a balance sheet, the capabilities of IT improve so rapidly that any given IT investment may be obsolete before a company can obtain the full benefits for which the technology was purchased. Various studies have suggested the effects of overinvestment, duplication, and dissipation of profits that may occur.[12] Repeated replacement poses problems for all companies. But the committee's interviews confirmed studies indicating that replacement costs are a special issue in professional services, such as accounting, consulting, medicine, scientific research, architecture, engineering design, advertising, entertainment, or the law. These concerns were well captured by Marshall Carter, currently chairman and chief executive officer of State Street Bank and Trust Company, who said:

> The investment side of this poses problems. We have traditionally invested in technology on a 3- to 7-year cycle. But now the shelf life of a lot of things is 18 to 36 months. If you're not putting in tens of millions per year, you'll find you're falling behind the competition. Yet you must constantly invest even more in your capital base before you can get a complete payoff. For example, we're now installing a global treasury system. Within 18 to 36 months, there'll be a new version or modules that we'll have to rebuy.

Once a significant IT infrastructure is acquired, costs for hardware, software support, and maintenance become more fixed than variable in nature. These fixed IT costs become especially burdensome when revenues are squeezed by recessions or competitive pressures. A special problem exists because IT systems are purchased in "lumps." Because of the power of individual systems and long learning times, companies tend to purchase more capacity than warranted by average levels of demand. As a result, entire industries tend to overcapacity. In such situations where costs are mainly fixed, each producer can (up to the constraints on its capacity) gain total margin by selectively lowering prices to increase volume. The result is strong downward pressures on average prices (and thus on the percentage of margins) in services using IT,[13] even though the services provided may be much more complex and of higher absolute value to the customer.

Daniel Schutzer at Citibank expressed one strategic response to this problem:

> Today we would like to move to an architecture which is less fixed-cost based and more variable. This would let us make sure our businesses remain profitable as they're growing and as they're shrinking, without being stuck with big fixed costs just at the wrong times. We see the technology moving more toward totally network-based systems where our divisions provide services on top of an intelligent network. All of these things dictate a more open-systems approach, but we do not know now what their specific impact will be.

Enhancing Technological Sophistication and Developing Standards

Service companies have often driven the state of the art in IT software, computing algorithms, hardware, and standard setting. For example: (1) Expert system software is widely used to capture and disseminate "best practices" from one skill source to others (e.g., for paramedics, diagnosticians, maintenance personnel, or brokers). (2) Software programs for telephone switching systems (million-line programs controlling real-time operations and billing records) routinely push the software state of the art. (3) Airline scheduling problems have generated more efficient linear programming algorithms that can solve problems involving tens of thousands of variables. (4) Financial services firms' demands for analysis of huge quantities of data have driven the design and purchase of massively parallel processors.

The need to exchange data for applications extending across different organizations has driven the development of standards for electronic data interchange (EDI). Standards for document formats, communications protocols, and inter-application data transfer have enabled disparate computer systems running different software packages to communicate with each other across a variety of applications. Standards have been crucial to growth and progress in a number of industries, including travel agencies and airlines (standards for CRSs), retail-manufacturing (universal product code and EDI standards), financial services and banking (magnetic ink recognition and message security standards), and standards for asynchronous multimedia (data, voice, and video) communications. Despite such progress, meaningful standards for inter-applications data transfer have yet to be developed for important specific applications, such as standards for recording medical information, for monitoring outcomes of various procedures, or even for billing.[14]

There are, of course, important possible drawbacks to standards—notably a premature "freezing" of technology. For standards to be accepted, members of the relevant community must be willing to forego some unforeseen future opportunities and potential technological advances in favor of those created by enhanced current interoperability and electronic data interchange. When the former outweigh the latter, interested partners will resist standards, causing higher current costs but perhaps enhancing future capabilities—as did the opponents of analog standards for high-definition television.

Problems in Assessing Enterprise Performance

For companies in certain industries such as air transport and telecommunications, there are some readily quantifiable and widely accepted measures of output. Ton-miles or passenger-miles handled in transportation, packages or documents processed in overnight delivery, kilowatt-hours or cubic feet of gas delivered by utilities, and the number of calls connected, minutes connected, or access lines provided by the telecommunications industry are widely accepted examples.

In industries for which measures of physical output are available (e.g., telecommunications, transportation, electric utilities, large fast-food and merchandise chains), levels of productivity (as measured, e.g., by revenues or value added per unit of labor input) have traditionally compared favorably to those in manufacturing. However, the correlation between growth in these measures and higher profits is not always good. Fare wars in the airline industry have destroyed profits even when revenue passenger-miles have risen, and the profits of individual companies within the industry have shown even greater variations. Even a uniformly positive correlation between measures of physical output and profitability or revenues may be the result of other business practices or investments, or the result of a regulatory environment that assures operating companies a "reasonable" rate of return.

For many firms (e.g., those in financial services, health care, medicine, law, accounting, design, software, or government services), it is almost impossible to define a consistent measure of physical output that will reflect variety, complexity, quality, or value produced (see Chapter 1). In some cases, gross statistics such as the number of clients or customers served or the number of audits or medical procedures performed may be available.[15] But the qualitative nature of the output of many service companies makes its precise numerical measurement much more difficult than in goods-producing enterprises.[16] Yet it is often along these qualitative dimensions that individual service firms compete with one another.

In such cases, financial metrics such as gross revenues or profitability may be the only alternative, although even financial metrics have their limitations. A company may be a nonprofit enterprise (e.g., a nonprofit hospital). Revenues or profits may not be valid measures of output in enterprises where prices have been regulated (as in property and casualty insurance or telecommunications), where price increases are due to increased risks (as in insurance or obstetrics), or where revenues are determined by budget allocations (as in museums, foundations, or educational institutions).[17]

Assessing the performance of individual firms involves several critical difficulties, a number of which affect the usability of measures at the macroeconomic or industry levels and have been discussed from that standpoint in previous chapters.

Pass-Through of Benefits

A variety of respondents reported that the rapid advances in IT and the high levels of competition in both the IT-supplying and IT-using industries made it difficult for even innovative companies to capture benefits from their investments in IT. With rare exceptions, IT hardware and software—and supporting communication services—are available from many competing vendors. Hence it is hard to create technological barriers to entry in the service sector other than those attributable to software developed internally. Even then, since a wide variety of software approaches can (with almost equal efficiency) solve almost any given problem, there are few protectable intellectual property rights that prevent replication of results.

Fast followers can move with relative assuredness toward known results—and often at costs lower than those of the innovators because of ongoing technological advances. Technologies diffuse so rapidly that even the most innovative respondents said that, with few exceptions, IT gave them only a temporary competitive edge. When asked how long this edge might last, the usual answer was "a few months," which on further inquiry resolved into 3 to 9 months' time. Once new products or improvements in quality are copied, companies are forced to compete largely in terms of price. The same is true for each competitor, with the result that overall industry revenues may not fully reflect the benefits of an innovation—which are largely passed through to the customer instead. The innovation may proliferate so quickly that it soon becomes a routine and "commoditized" expectation of all customers. Unless the total market is growing substantially, overall industry revenues will not increase significantly despite multiple investments dedicated to innovation.

The tendency for profits from IT-based innovations to be short-lived is exacerbated by IT hardware trends. The computing power of IT has been growing so rapidly relative to unit cost (recently 35 percent per year for processors and 45 to 50 percent per year for memory) that the same dollar investment at a later time purchases substantially more power or capability. Competitors who invest later are able to buy more capacity per dollar than the original innovator, and competitors end up with either an equal capacity at less cost (reducing their fixed costs relative to those of the innovator) or a greater capacity for the same cost (resulting in a greater potential for business expansion relative to the innovator). The net result is that the ease of access to productivity-enhancing hardware (usually available to all competitors) forces many service producers to pass benefits through to others and often lowers rather than raises their prices while increasing their break-even volume.[18]

Given that the benefits of IT-enabled innovations in services are not fully realized by the innovator, who does capture them? Three beneficiaries stand out: (1) the company's direct customers, (2) its suppliers, and (3) the general public.

For example, wholesalers such as McKesson or SuperValu are linked to retail drugstores and grocery stores. As these wholesalers improved their service capabilities for customers, they actually lost percentage in margins. In the case of McKesson, currently a $7.8 billion firm, the percentage of wholesaling margins has dropped from about 7 percent to 3 percent over the last 15 years, making another 4 percentage points available for the margins of its retailers and producers. McKesson passed savings on to others by lowering prices and by providing higher levels of service to its suppliers and customers (e.g., McKesson's central maintenance of virtually all price stickers and price files for its drug retailers). As David Malmberg, vice president of McKesson's inventory management and systems services, said, "These used to be extremely time-consuming and expensive things for the retailer. They are done by our technology now. But this doesn't show up in our margins, and our competitors have to match the service. In effect, we've upped the investment ante for everyone."

The experience of SuperValu, a $9.4 billion distributor to independent grocers, is comparable. SuperValu has developed extensive inventory and product-handling technologies that allow it to manage thousands of product lines and assist suppliers and retail customers with their distribution functions, including architectural design, construction, and space management. IT systems provide services upstream, downstream, and geographically. In addition to controlling inventories in transit, SuperValu also offers extensive host-support services for the electronic point-of-sale systems of its supermarket customers, permitting them to manage their operations better through instant access to price files, shelf tag printing, and detailed reports about their products' turnover, gross profits, category profits, and so on. So effective is SuperValu at providing these services that several major supermarket chains now buy from SuperValu in order to obtain the economies of its system. No single food product manufacturer could compete with these services. This is even truer for food producers for whom SuperValu handles the complex functions of coordinating field-produce contracting and transportation, fresh-meat delivery and marking, and in-store shelf-price verification. Yet because of competitive forces, SuperValu's total aggregate margins have not changed significantly.

Firms outside the service sector that purchase services from an innovator—e.g., manufacturers buying communication services from AT&T or MCI—are often major beneficiaries. Strategic alliances—or major "outsourcing" arrangements—can present even greater potentials for pass-throughs. A large downstream partner may radically reduce its internal costs by cooperating with an efficient service provider whose own costs may not be reduced by the partnership. In these cases, the service producer may show no gain in productivity, while service users reap substantial benefits. An example is the alliance between State Street Bank and Trust Company and Ford Motor Company. State Street has had a program with Ford for several years to connect Ford's U.S. treasury and trading operations with State Street's. In the words of State Street's Marshall Carter, "Ford feels pretty strongly that they've managed to increase quality yet reduce their staff substantially as a result of this alliance and its electronic connections. You wouldn't necessarily see a productivity gain here at State Street, but you would see a dramatic productivity gain at Ford."

A third major category of beneficiary may be end users or the general public. When a transaction's marginal benefit to a customer is high and its cost drops precipitously, transaction volumes are likely to increase; this has been especially true in financial services, banking, and communications. For interstate toll calls, volume has increased since deregulation at a rate of 10.6 percent a year, while prices have decreased at a rate of 7.1 percent a year.[19] New York Stock Exchange transactions have risen from a daily average of 10 million to 12 million shares in the early 1970s to an average of 183 million shares in the third quarter of 1992.[20] Both of these service industries were deregulated during the 1980s, eliminating the monopoly profits of existing producers. Customers benefited from lower costs and subsequently a greater selection of services. Often the volume of transactions increased so rapidly that companies could not reduce the number of total employees or costs despite much more efficient transaction-level automation. In other nonregulated situations, many professional companies interviewed by the committee reported that they could not increase prices to reflect the greater value added and the lower costs enabled by their IT systems because of overcapacity, competition, industry practice, or legal constraints on pricing.

This phenomenon appears paramount in evaluating the impact of word processing and spreadsheets on report writing. The cost of making a change in a document is quite small; the result is that authors or analysts revise their manuscripts with much higher frequency (compared to pre-PC days). The customer or user of the report receives the benefit of a thoroughly massaged final product, but the total effort that went into the production of that draft may not have declined. A similar situation obtains in the use of automated teller machines (ATMs). The cost to customers of using ATMs is low; hence they engage in many more transactions than would be the case in the absence of ATMs. The ATM user thus benefits from the machine, but the expense incurred in deploying the ATM was at first generally borne by the bank. Later, banks sought to recoup some of these costs through usage fees.[21]

On the other hand, the use of IT sometimes allows companies to pass costs through to customers as well—especially in the form of personal labor or waiting times. For example, IT enables telephone customers to dial long-distance telephone calls themselves and enter their own accounting information (credit card numbers) at pay telephones; bank customers perform for themselves many of the functions of bank tellers at ATMs (e.g., checking account balances or processing deposit and withdrawal transactions). While customers may prefer to perform these activities for themselves—because doing so is more convenient or faster—the actual labor required to provide a service has not been altered much by the introduction of IT. However, it is customers who are now doing much of the work. In a similar manner, IT has enabled airlines to manage more efficient "hub-and-spoke" routing systems, and retailers to provide "retail warehouse" sales of goods in bulk. But customers also bear some of the costs from these innovations, in the form of additional waiting times or a less friendly shopping atmosphere. Very few firms—if any—track costs borne by the customer in any systematic manner, and the overall effects on society are impossible to estimate.

Time Lags and the Need for Higher Skills

Timing and implementation factors also complicate measures of IT's impact on performance at the enterprise level.[22] Various studies indicate that, as in other technology areas, there are long average time lags before highly innovative new IT systems may achieve expected payoffs.[23] Workers' productivity constantly lags behind the systems' potentials as workers learn new tasks, and there are costs associated with confusion that arises as the systems are debugged. Sometimes, workers may barely reach full capabilities before the next generation of equipment requires changes to keep up with customer demands for quality and responsiveness. One implication is that if the benefits of a system are evaluated too early in its life cycle, they are likely to be underestimated. The other is that learning effects, training requirements, backup systems, extra supervision, and delays must be provided for in any complete plan for introducing new IT systems.

The time needed for workers to learn how to interact with a new system may be compounded by concurrent changes in ways outputs are produced. Some systems may facilitate or may require the use of more expensive or more highly trained knowledge workers in the place of less skilled workers. A now familiar example is the movement away from centralized typing pools, first to distributed word processing by secretaries and then to direct preparation of texts by their professional or managerial authors. An analysis of word processing's payoffs in the early 1980s would differ considerably from today's reality. If the complexity of a business problem also increases sufficiently, both the number of workers and their skill requirements may go up[24] (Box 3.4).

In other cases, the use of IT may simplify tasks, so that the required skill levels may drop, with the effect of deterring increases in wages.[25] This pattern has been particularly evident in repetitive tasks such as product sorting, or in retail sales. A combination of lower skill requirements and wages in some cases may encourage higher staffing levels than in the past, and hence reduce measured productivity.[26] On the other hand, the capacity

---

BOX 3.4 Better Cancer Treatments May Cost More

New cancer treatment procedures (e.g., bone marrow transplants) often require more precise and expensive equipment, greater training, higher wages, more laboratory facilities, and more people to operate (per procedure) than the older chemotherapy treatments did. At the same time, the new procedures may be significantly more effective in terms of clinically measured patient outcomes, including morbidity, mortality, and long-term care costs.

However, while the costs of new procedures may well be incurred by treatment providers, none of these benefits may show up in their balance sheets or income statements. Actual outcomes may be uncertain for years, and prices established through diagnostic-related-group compensation caps may prevent prices for medical services from reflecting the higher value added.

to use less skilled people may have the benefit of increasing employment opportunities. This appears to have been the pattern in low-wage services such as retailing or fast foods. Such complexities obviate the use of any simple measures of productivity at the enterprise level.

Shifts in the Basic Nature of the Business

As noted earlier in this chapter, the use of IT may change the very nature of a firm's business. In this case, comparisons of a firm's productivity or performance in two different time periods may not be a true "apples-to-apples" comparison. It may even be the case that performance metrics designed for the old business lag in reflecting changes at the enterprise level.[27]

For example, in many large professional service organizations, tasks that used to be the very core of professional practices (e.g., doing audit checks in public accounting or preparing bubble charts for portfolio analyses in financial services or consulting firms) have become so routine and automated that they are almost loss leaders, much of whose value is passed through in order to sell clients other services that are now the professionals' core competencies. In many cases, the basic business of professional firms has become the capture, analysis, communication, and leveraging of higher-value current information for clients. Such information-intensive tasks require a high level of specialized intellectual expertise from sophisticated knowledge workers. Professional firms often obtain a competitive edge by leveraging their high-priced talent through automation of most routine tasks (e.g., literature searches, table look-ups, and routine or standardized design calculations) and development of very powerful analytical algorithms, expert systems, and extensive networking capabilities.

Investment companies provide a high-profile example. High-performance computing and electronic data systems have enabled development of complex, customized financial instruments that are difficult to create and support but that are generating totally new kinds of business. State Street Bank—managing assets of over $1 trillion and enjoying a 20 percent growth rate—is typical of those working on this complex business frontier (specifically portfolio and trust management). State Street's Carter noted:

> There are people out there all the time trying to create financial instruments that give a better yield on a portfolio. We are working on the edges of a system creating complex instruments that—right at the beginning—will be inefficient operations because of their new characteristics. Yet these are expanding the capital markets. The old instruments have become very stable, efficient, and easy to serve. The average statistics may say you're not getting "productivity" increases. If you disaggregate it you'd see more productivity on the older (lower-margin) instruments than on the newer, higher-margin ones. But as a businessman, where do you want to be?

SUMMARY AND CONCLUSIONS

Executives invest in IT programs with the intent of increasing expected returns as compared to other alternatives, for example, not investing or investing in other programs. The returns they derive from these decisions may be vital to the success of the enterprise but may not show up readily in standard measures of industry revenues or sector productivity. Information technology has enabled service firms not just to do things better in the old way (efficiency) but also to do entirely new things that provide greater benefits to outside parties (effectiveness). Many of these improvements in performance may not be reflected in increased ROI, sales, or margins, or in macroeconomic statistics. Thus, many of the difficulties in measuring the productivity and effectiveness of IT in services at the macroeconomic level have their origin at the enterprise level.

Impacts of IT that may not show up in standard financial or data reports include maintaining market share in a relatively mature marketplace, avoiding catastrophic losses due to process failures, avoiding losses of market position or profits if a competitor adopts a new technology and the firm does not, increasing flexibility to respond to unknown future market or process changes, improving employee relations or the work environment, improving the quality of customer service, handling increasing complexity, and improving the scope and responsiveness of the firm's service outputs. These are key elements of service *performance*, although they may not affect *productivity*.

In the committee's sample of companies, techniques used for decisions about investments in IT are comparable to those used for corporate decisions about investments in R&D or other complex technologies. As in R&D investments, none of the sampled companies could separate the effects of a single input (R&D or IT) from other factors that might affect the ultimate success of a given project. Nor could they always estimate or calculate financial returns accurately. For this reason many firms use engineering metrics rather than financial measures to evaluate the potential and actual impacts of an investment in IT. But these metrics also do not permit aggregation at the industry or macroeconomic levels.

Within enterprises, investments tend to fit into a few basic categories: those supporting basic infrastructure, mandated requirements, cost reduction, new products, improvements in quality, new strategic potentials, and new desktop or workstation information exchange networks. In some of these cases (e.g., cost-reducing systems, systems to support new products), financial returns are relatively easy to evaluate through the use of well-understood formal investment analyses. In others (e.g., systems like those for basic infrastructure, improvements in quality, and new strategic uses), other metrics—like engineering metrics or results of customer surveys—

may be used to estimate impacts. Even though managers may use the best techniques available, some investments in IT still are based to a large extent on the intuition or judgment of management.

Some of the more important problems in measuring impacts of IT at the firm level are (1) defining meaningful units of output that are consistent over time, (2) defining the contributions of IT as a component in the total investment package needed to create a result, (3) capturing or measuring benefits passed through to customers or suppliers, (4) establishing financial measures of the impact of intangible benefits (such as faster cycle times, greater reliability, or a broader selection of service products), (5) estimating the "opportunity costs" of what would have happened without use of a technology, (6) dealing with payoffs that are delayed due to learning factors and with (sometimes extensive) lags until actual outcomes are known, and (7) measuring changes in productivity when IT has changed the basic nature of a business and the competitive environment.

Granted all of these complications, a large majority (80 percent) of respondent companies felt that their investments in IT overall had paid off well. A majority said that they had made special studies of IT's payoff, although none had made routine measurements of overall IT returns. A large majority indicated that their special studies confirmed a positive overall payoff from IT (see Appendix D). Most expressed concern that their earlier management techniques had not been as efficient or effective as they should have been. Most were trying to improve these currently (see Chapter 5).

NOTES AND REFERENCES

[1]See, for example, Keen, P, 1988, *Competing in Time: Using Telecommunications for Competitive Advantage*, Ballinger Publishing Company, Cambridge, Mass.; U.S. Congress, Office of Technology Assessment, 1985, *Automation of America's Offices 1985-2000*, Government Printing Office, Washington, D.C.; and Watts, L., 1986, "What Price Automation?," *Northeastern University Magazine*, December.

[2]Denison, E. 1989. *Estimates of Productivity Change by Industry: An Evaluation and an Alternative*, Brookings Institution, Washington, D.C. Denison makes a strong case for the last explanation, though there is disagreement in the community on this point.

[3]Brynjolfsson, Erik, and Lorin Hitt. 1993. "Is Information Systems Spending Productive? New Evidence and New Results," MIT Sloan School of Management, Working Paper 3571-93, September 24. (To appear in *Proceedings of the 14th International Conference on Information Systems*.)

[4]The work of Sassone suggests that downsizing secretarial pools may have the unintended result that professionals end up doing many more non-IT-based support tasks that were previously done by secretaries. Thus, on balance, the result may be lower measured productivity. See Sassone, Peter. 1992. "Survey Finds Low Office Productivity Linked to Staffing Imbalances," *National Productivity Review*, Spring, pp. 147-158.

[5]Levitt, Theodore. 1976. "Industrialization of Service," *Harvard Business Review*, September-October, pp. 63-74.

[6]Brynjolfsson, Erik, and Bruce Bimber. 1991. "Information Technology and the Productivity Paradox," Working Paper, Brookings Institution, Washington, D.C., February 7.

[7] Porter, Michael E., and Victor E. Millar, 1985, "How Information Gives You Competitive Advantage," *Harvard Business Review*, July-August, pp. 149-160; Quinn, J.B., 1992, *Intelligent Enterprise*, Free Press, New York; and Wriston, Walter B., 1992, *The Twilight of Sovereignty*, Scribners, New York.

[8] Loveman, Gary, 1988, "An Assessment of the Productivity Impact of Information Technologies," MIT Management in the 1990's Program, 88-054, July.; and Kendrick, John W., 1988, "Productivity in Services," in *Technology in Services: Policies for Growth, Trade, and Employment*, Bruce R. Guile and James Brian Quinn (eds.), National Academy Press, Washington, D.C.

[9] The inadequacy of financial metrics alone for assessing the performance of a firm is discussed in Eccles, Robert, 1991, "The Performance Measurement Manifesto," *Harvard Business Review*, January-February, pp. 131-137.

[10] A Bellcore study showed that the number of employees per 1000 access lines—one of the operating company's key performance metrics—had dropped from 110 to 40 (or about a 10 percent per year compounded improvement) between 1970 and 1990.

[11] Roach, Stephen, Morgan Stanley & Co., unpublished data, April 1993.

[12] Fudenberg, Drew, and Jean Tirole. 1985. "Preemption and Rent Equalization in the Adoption of New Technology," *Review of Economic Studies* 52:383-401.

[13] Bresnahan, Timothy F. 1986. "Measuring the Spillovers from Technical Advance: Mainframe Computers in Financial Services," *American Economic Review* 76(4, September):742-755.

[14] Institute of Medicine. 1991. *The Computer-based Patient Record*, National Academy Press, Washington D.C., pp. 85-87.

[15] The meaning of aggregated statistics is also clouded by the fact that parameters such as relative unit volumes, revenues, costs, timing factors, number of clients, and so on may have little real meaning as indicators of productivity when ultimate outcomes are unknown. For a bank, the face value of loans or the number of loans handled is meaningless without knowing the quality of those loans or the creativity they represent. The number of procedures performed at a hospital compared to their cost is useless information, unless one knows their success rate and the relative health of patients at the time they were served. Even the success rate must be qualified by the subsequent quality of life or care costs patients encounter.

[16] Mark, Jerome, 1986, "Problems Encountered in Measuring Single and Multifactor Productivity," *Monthly Labor Review*, December, pp. 3-11; Baily, Martin Neill, and Robert J. Gordon, 1988, "The Productivity Slowdown: Measurement Issues and the Explosion of Computer Power," in *Brookings Papers on Economic Activity*, Vol. 2, William C. Brainard and George L. Perry (eds.), Brookings Institution, Washington, D.C., pp. 347-431; and Brynjolfsson and Bimber, 1991, "Information Technology and the Productivity Paradox."

[17] Kutscher, R., and J. Mark. 1983. "The Service Sector: Some Common Perceptions Reviewed," *Monthly Labor Review*, April, pp. 21-24.

[18] Bresnahan, 1986, "Measuring the Spillovers from Technical Advance: Mainframe Computers in Financial Services."

[19] Federal Communications Commission. 1991. *Trends in Telephone Service*, FCC, Washington, D.C., February, p. 25.

[20] Standard & Poor's Corp. 1992. *Current Statistics*, October.

[21] Both the committee's interviews and independent studies testify to the ubiquity of this phenomenon. See, for example, Brynjolfsson and Bimber, 1991, "Information Technology and the Productivity Paradox."

[22] Curley, Kathleen Foley, and Philip J. Pyburn. 1982 "'Intellectual' Technologies: The Key to Improving White-Collar Productivity," *Sloan Management Review*, Fall, pp. 31-39.

[23] Guile, Bruce R., and James Brian Quinn (eds.). 1988. *Managing Innovation: Cases from the Service Industries*, National Academy Press, Washington D.C. Also Brynjolfsson, Erik, Thomas W. Malone, and Vijay Gurbaxani. 1988. "The Impact of Information Technol-

ogy on Markets and Hierarchies," Sloan School of Management, Working Paper 2113-88, Massachusetts Institute of Technology, Cambridge, Mass.

[24]Osterman, Paul. 1986. "The Impact of Computers on the Employment of Clerks and Managers," *Industrial and Labor Relations Review* 39:175-186. Also, Krueger, A. 1993. "How Computers Have Changed the Wage Structure: Evidence from Microdata, 1984-1989," *The Quarterly Journal of Economics* 39(February):175-186.

[25]Bright, J. 1958. *Technology in Automation*, Harvard Business School Press, Boston, Mass. This is the classic statement of this argument.

[26]Baily and Gordon, 1988, "The Productivity Slowdown: Measurement Issues and the Explosion of Computer Power." Also, Hunt, H., and T. Hunt. 1986. *Clerical Employment and Technological Change*, Upjohn Institute for Labor Studies, Kalamazoo, Mich.

[27]Stalk, G., and T. Hout. 1990. *Competing Against Time: How Time-based Competition Is Reshaping Global Markets*, Free Press, New York.

4
Impacts of Information Technology at the Activity Level

INTRODUCTION

Faced with a myriad of pressures to change the way they do business, many managers in different types of firms have found it fruitful to focus on activities or major processes, rather than just on products, organizational units, specific tasks, or reporting relationships. They are attempting to redesign the work flow from beginning to end, breaking it down into component segments and asking hard questions: What should we be doing? What is the best way to do it? Which components should remain within the firm? How should the activities that continue to constitute the firm be structured into a better-functioning whole? Companies are using many of the innovative technologies and organizational methods available to answer these questions. The current attention given by researchers and corporate decision makers to "business process redesign" or reengineering is one approach to process innovation, the most recent to emerge in organizational literature.[1]

Today's information technology (IT)—which embeds the tools for specific tasks and operations within networked infrastructures whose reach can extend well beyond a firm's boundaries—provides vehicles for such changes. IT permits many of a firm's information-based tasks to be reconfigured and linked in alternative ways to generate new work flows and processes. Put differently, the use of IT permits the uncoupling and rearranging of key organizational processes to achieve much more effective organizational designs.

Past efforts to deploy IT have often focused on the level of tasks or subactivities and limited the scope of changes to existing and/or narrowly defined processes. The result has often been suboptimization (although the committee does not intend to suggest that each task or activity must be optimized), or, at best, optimization of a subset of existing tasks. By contrast, a purposive and holistic focus on the activity level—where activities are regarded as relatively complete elements of a firm's work flow that often cross functional departments (e.g., departments such as marketing, production, or research and development)—will often yield better results. Examples of activities include product design, logistics, order processing, purchasing, maintenance, and accounting. More complete redesign of processes and changing organizational relationships is possible when an activities-level view is taken.

The committee believes that the investments in IT made to date, in many instances, are on the verge of providing companies unprecedented degrees of flexibility in changing the ways activities are designed and organized. This is so for several reasons:

- A broader installed base of technologies makes new, more complex or integrated applications possible. For example, widely deployed workstations, interconnected network software, and sophisticated communications links are required for many collaborative and cross-organizational work applications to be effective.
- IT vendors are beginning to produce software that is easier to use and whose capabilities match user and customer needs more closely. As a result, relatively untutored users can do substantially more, more quickly, with the IT at their disposal.
- Early implementation experiences provide opportunities for learning about both the technology and the management of change. Thus managers are beginning to have more realistic expectations for what IT can and cannot do, and to understand better the time frames required to achieve dramatic changes.
- New technologies are being designed and introduced to increase capacities as well as integrate capabilities provided by older technologies. Resulting changes in activities in turn make possible more far-reaching changes in enterprises.

Overall, the use of IT has the effect of diminishing the parts played by place, time, and hierarchy in the structure and management of organizations.[2] Furthermore, the range of activities to which IT is being applied is still expanding.

The committee believes that activity-level analysis yields a deeper understanding of process innovation and its effects on performance. Focusing on activities means paying detailed attention to the actual work being done

> **BOX 4.1 Conceptual Frameworks for Analysis of Activities and Processes**
>
> *The value-chain model.* Work processes are sometimes understood through the use of value chains that depict the sequence in which activities typically occur and how they interact. In the simplest model, a linear one, each activity receives an input from the previous activity, adds value to that input, and passes it on to the next activity as an output. (Of course, value chains are not necessarily linear.) The value-chain model provides a useful lens for looking at how activities are linked one to another to generate the overall net benefit of an organization's procedures, and the analytical problem is the determination of how much and what kind of value is added by each activity.
>
> *The process management model.* The principles of process management can serve as a disciplined basis for analyzing how work is done at the activity level. Recently, enterprises in all types of industries have applied process management techniques to varied activities. Their goals have included both continuous or incremental improvement and radical change or—in popular terms—reengineering of their business processes.
>
> *Sociotechnical systems analysis.* From this perspective, activities are sets of tasks carried out by people whose work is united by output and by work-flow technology. The analysis treats social and technological aspects of task processes as inherently interrelated and thus suggests that social and technological issues in process redesign cannot be separately resolved. The sociotechnical systems approach affords insights into both how activities may be conceptualized and why technological change should be expected to have significant impacts on activities as well as their linkages.

or being planned, taking into account the interplay of work flows, organizational structures, staffing, and tools—including IT, both within and between firms. Interfirm effects are particularly interesting where they involve multiple firms in different industries or shifts in work among firms.

Activity-level analysis is a more refined level of analysis than has traditionally been used in assessing the aggregate outcomes of investments in IT. Activity-level insights are also not captured either in sector- or firm-level analyses. Thus, hard data are generally unavailable, and the literature suffers from a paucity of analytic models and substantial empirical research at the activity level.[3]

A number of ideas from the current organizational literature may be applied to assist with analysis at the level of activities (Box 4.1). Although these ideas do not exhaust the paradigms that might be helpful in understanding the role and influence of IT's use at the activity level in firms, they are useful as working constructs for an exploratory investigation.

Activity-level analysis may well require the development of new metrics for performance (especially ones that reflect the changing values and expectations of "customers")—in part because the output of service activities may be intangible.[4] The committee hopes that the discussion presented in this chapter can stimulate further research at the activity level that will eventually provide a more thorough empirical base and a foundation for new paradigms and concepts with which to conduct activity-level analysis.

The discussion in this report is based on material derived from the committee's interviews with senior managers as described in Appendix D, the experiences of committee members, accounts from secondary sources, conceptual models in current organizational literature (some of which have only recently appeared), and views developed in the course of the committee's deliberations.[5] Although the discussion in this chapter is more conceptual than that presented in Chapters 1 through 3, the committee believes that it is essential for completing its exploration of the relationships between investments in IT and service-sector performance.

WHAT IS AN ACTIVITY?

An activity is a structured set of tasks (work) leading to a specified output for a specified internal or external client. This report uses the term *activity* in a broad sense to refer to relatively self-contained or complete work processes regardless of level of granularity. From this broad perspective, examples of service activities include many functions performed both in manufacturing and in specialized service organizations, such as accounting, research, design, planning, marketing, advertising, or distribution firms. So viewed, service activities contribute value, in varying degrees, to an organization's major products. (Box 4.2 illustrates how one analyst relates activities to other concepts.)

Within particular enterprises and work groups, activities can be defined much more specifically in relation to tasks and outputs: writing insurance policies, opening bank accounts, selling products in a department store, routing airline tickets, and providing nursing care in a hospital may all be treated as instances of activities in the sense intended in this chapter.

Activities have several important characteristics:

- Activities operate on inputs from other activities (either internal or external to the firm).
- Activities have customers. In other words, there is a recipient for the outcomes of all activities in the work flow.
- Activities may or may not correspond to functional departments in organizations, and their linkage into the overall work flow of the organiza-

> **BOX 4.2 Process Hierarchy**
>
> Almost everything we do or are involved in is a process.... From the macroview, processes are the key activities required to manage and/or run an organization. New-product definition is a good example of a macroprocess.... A macroprocess can be subdivided into subprocesses that are logically related, sequential activities that contribute to the mission of the macroprocess.... Every macroprocess or subprocess is made up of a number of activities.... Activities are things that go on within all processes. As the name implies, they are the actions required to produce a particular result.... Each activity is made up of a number of tasks.... Normally, tasks are performed by an individual or by small teams. They make up the very smallest microview of the process.
>
> SOURCE: Harrington, H.J. 1991. *Strategy for Total Quality, Productivity, and Competitiveness*, McGraw-Hill, New York.

tion may or may not correspond to reporting structures on an organizational chart. Activities may span external organizational boundaries on either the input or output side (or both).

- To the extent that activities form relatively complete segments of a work flow (starting with an input and ending with an output to a client), they lend themselves to many forms of measurement (e.g., throughput time, client satisfaction). Activities are often the target of investments in IT, which are undertaken as projects to support changes in relatively self-contained processes.

These characteristics of activities underlie the utility of activity-level analysis for understanding service-sector performance and the potential effects of IT. Most important is the built-in customer orientation: the customer's expectations and value system can be used to set the standard against which the service activity is judged.[6] And it is at the activity level that it is possible to assess whether the customer may be better served even if measured productivity declines. For example, IT is being applied to a growing range of complex medical diagnostic procedures (such as magnetic resonance imaging or genetic testing) without apparent improvements in productivity in terms of cost but with other benefits to customers.

The independence of activities from functional and organizational boundaries is critical, since clients, whether internal or external, do not care about formal organizational boundaries nearly as much as they care about results. The measures of value added by activities (such as time to produce, time to delivery, cost, and the quality of an activity's output) enable analysts to track changes in the performance of an activity over time and to compare or "benchmark" against similar activities within the same enterprise or in other companies. (The latter measures are especially important complements to internal measures of client satisfaction in cases where performance that satisfies the short-term needs of recipients in the organization's work flow may be relatively unsatisfactory from the perspective of the ultimate customer or the firm as a whole.)

SOME OBSERVATIONS ABOUT SERVICE ACTIVITIES

The pervasiveness of service activities, their growing importance in generating value, and their generic nature make activities a critical level of analysis for understanding the impact of IT on service-sector performance.

Service Activities Are Everywhere

Service activities occur in all enterprises, not just those in so-called service industries; this is the essence of the service economy. Even within a manufacturing company, these activities often account for 60 to 75 percent of all nonmaterial costs. In fact, within most enterprises—whether in the manufacturing, services, government, or nonprofit sectors—a majority of all employment (well over 80 percent) is in service activities. Service activities thus provide units of analysis that are directly comparable between manufacturing and service firms.

Table 4.1 summarizes the employment distribution from the most recent Bureau of Labor Statistics projections.[7] Total U.S. employment is projected to grow by about 20 percent from 1990 to 2005. During this period, all blue-collar categories (agricultural workers, production and craft workers, and operators and laborers) will grow at rates substantially below the average, whereas most white-collar categories and service occupations[8] will grow substantially faster than average. These projections are fully consistent with a continuing shift of labor to service activities as applications of IT lead to organizational restructuring and job redefinition.

Service Activities Are Increasingly Important

Not only are service activities present in all enterprises, but they also now contribute most of the value added within both manufacturing and service firms. Their elevated role is especially striking in manufacturing, where more value added now derives from service-related or intellectual activities than from physical production activities. For example, research and clinical activities (rather than chemical processing, pill punching, and

TABLE 4.1 Employment Projections—Employment by Major Occupational Group, 1990 and Projected 2005 (Moderate Alternative Projection)

Major Occupational Group	Number Employed (thousands)		Percent Change	
	1990	2005	1975-1990	1990-2005
Total, all occupations	122,573	147,191	37.4	20.1
Executive, administrative, managerial	12,451	15,866	83.1	27.4
Professional specialty	15,800	20,907	59.9	32.3
Technicians, related support	4,204	5,754	75.7	36.9
Marketing, sales	14,088	17,489	55.1	24.1
Administrative support, including clerical	21,951	24,835	33.9	13.1
Service	19,204	24,806	36.1	29.2
Agricultural, forestry, fishing, and related occupations	3,506	3,665	-9.9	4.5
Precision production, craft, repair	14,124	15,909	28.9	12.6
Operators, fabricators, laborers	17,245	17,961	6.7	4.2

NOTE: The data on employment for 1990 and 2005 and the projected percentage of change from 1990 to 2005 are derived from the industry-occupation employment matrixes for each year. The data on the percentage of change from 1975 to 1990 were derived from the Current Population Survey (CPS), because a comparable industry-occupation matrix for 1975 is not available.

SOURCE: Adapted from Silvestri, G., and J. Lukasiewicz. 1991. "Occupational Employment Projections," *Monthly Labor Review* 114(November), Table 1, p. 65.

packaging) create the major value in pharmaceuticals; sophisticated customer understanding and software concepts (rather than building circuit boards and boxes) create the predominant value in computers; understanding flavorings, customer preferences, and product texturing creates value in prepared foods; and so on.

Service Activities Are Generic and Elemental

Service activities have two features that make them amenable to IT-based change. The first is that many service activities have a generic quality. That is, service activities within a given enterprise may be fundamentally similar to those performed in other, quite different enterprises. For instance, most large firms have departments that are responsible for accounting, payroll processing, legal services, and so on. Commonalities may prevail even among firms in entirely different lines of business, and so it is not surprising that Xerox (a durable-goods manufacturer) opted to compare its distribution activity against that of L.L. Bean (a catalog retailer) despite the differences in products and industries. Similarities between activities in different organizations may reflect the influence of common bodies of law, professional standards, or general practitioner knowledge.[9]

The fact that activities operate on relatively well defined inputs and generate specific products for their customers makes activities elemental. That is, they are subject to separation from each other and to recombination; they are modular components of a business or enterprise. Thus linkages between activities can be restructured, limited only by the technology and management infrastructure available to support interconnections.

The elemental and generic nature of service activities is the foundation for attempts to improve activity performance by the use of IT. If the activities that compose an organization's work flow are relatively complete components whose inputs and outputs can be received from other sources and transmitted to customers via IT-based links (and perhaps largely performed via IT as well), the IT infrastructure opens up new possibilities for designing or reorganizing processes and entire firms; even industries may be restructured as a consequence. The conceptual independence of activities from organizational boundaries assumes increasing significance given the growing perception that organizational and functional boundaries often stand in the way of opportunities for improvement.

ROLES FOR INFORMATION TECHNOLOGY IN THE EVOLUTION OF ACTIVITIES

The use of IT has been an important contributor to the prominence of service activities. For example, computer-assisted design has helped manufacturers deliver more sophisticated goods (from automobiles to integrated chips) in less time. For such goods, service activities become the vehicles for customization and differentiation—whether upstream (through design), or downstream (through marketing and post-sales service). Similarly, service products (such as loans and insurance policies) can be tailored to the needs of particular clients directly using IT; data on customers are more easily collected and analyzed; forms are more easily modified; change orders are more easily developed and communicated; and so on. As one executive in a service firm put it, "There's a sense in which we never sell the same product twice." In other words, "mass customization" is increasingly the order of the day; service firms would ideally deliver—to every customer—service products that are customized to his or her own individual needs.[10]

In general, IT is being used to play an important role in the flexible and rapid adaptation of outputs to suit the needs and expectations of clients. According to executives interviewed by the committee, new and anticipated applications rely heavily on databases, client-server systems, and local- and wide-area networking generally; as the scale and scope of databases grow and as sophisticated modeling becomes more practical, high-performance systems, such as massively parallel technology, are being contemplated. Noted a senior vice president of a major supermarket chain,

> In the 1970s and 1980s, 90 percent of the weighting given by decision makers on IT has been on hard savings, 10 percent on soft. I think the future is going to be very much oriented toward "soft savings," and it might even go to 60 to 40 on that side. The important thing is the credibility and accuracy of the information coming out of the front end. . . . In the past the drive was on the hard savings, productivity end of IT. In the future it will be in the utilization for merchandising and marketing of all that wonderful data that's coming off. In addition, the demographic information from a customer standpoint is something we're just getting into now. If the customer walks in with a magnetic-strip-reader card and identifies herself as customer X, we can track every single thing she buys and do all kinds of wonderful things with that information. . . . We can have frequent-purchaser programs, and so on.

New Tools and Tasks

As process technology, IT enables changes in the ways that the tasks that make up an activity are undertaken. Applied to information-intensive services, the use of IT can change the nature of what is delivered to clients (such as highly customized business or financial services) as well as the processes of its production. Examples of both sorts of changes abound, such as the shift from keying in data to optical scanning for data entry, the use of telephone-computer system combinations to solicit new business in lieu of "cold-call" field visits, and the use of on-line databases instead of paper files and reports to deliver customer financial data. For example, Larry Bacon, senior vice president, Information Systems Department at the Travelers Companies, described the impact of putting policy information on line.

> If you look back a few years, our personal lines operation, for example, had 80 to 100 field offices. And all of the policies . . . were in tub files and desks in those offices. So if you wanted to see all the policies you would have to go to 90 offices and read through 2 million policies in tubs and desks. Then all of a sudden a person could just issue a few commands to the computer and we'd zip through it for him. That's a huge change.

Bacon went on to enumerate such benefits as accurate and consistent calculation of premiums. Another example is provided by Merrill Lynch &

Company, which was able to substantially reduce its printing requirements by shifting to electronic delivery of information. Explained Howard Sorgen, senior vice president and chief technology officer,

> During the three-year period from 1989 through 1991, we reduced our annual output of computer-generated print from 1.3 billion to about 400 million pages. And that's not because the information provided wasn't needed by our internal and external clients. What we did was to change the way we provide that information, by shifting to downloading print files electronically to client desktops and providing the ability to view information directly from computer screens.

IT has been used to reduce the number of tasks involved in an activity, to change the nature and sequence of tasks, to change the total time involved in an activity, and so on (Box 4.3). By supporting changes in what tasks are done, as well as when, where, and how they are done, IT opens up new options for designing and structuring service activities.[11]

For example, according to Larry Bacon at the Travelers Companies, a computer-based system containing essential and optional pieces of text enables insurance sales representatives to construct group insurance policy documentation with the customer and deliver laser-printed copy the next day, in contrast to the previous approach of repeated iteration among representative, client, company lawyers, and others over a period of 3 to 9 months.

BOX 4.3 Accounts Payable at the Ford Motor Company

Prior to reengineering its accounts-payable process, Ford Motor Company employed more than 500 people. The process involved a labor-intensive matching of three documents: the purchase order (from the ordering department), the receiving document (from the materials control department), and the invoice (from the vendor). When these documents matched, payment was issued. As a result of reengineering, the ordering department now places information about the order into an on-line database. When goods are received in materials control, the database is checked to see if they correspond to an outstanding purchase order. If so, they are accepted, their receipt is logged into the database, and a check is automatically issued. Invoices are eliminated because Ford asks vendors not to send them.

The result? A reduction by 75 percent in the accounts payable work force.

SOURCE: Hammer, Michael. 1990. "Reengineering Work: Don't Automate, Obliterate," *Harvard Business Review*, July-August, pp. 104-112.

A more elaborate example is provided by Josh Weston, chairman and chief executive officer of ADP, who described the evolution of his company's payroll processing service.

> The original ADP payroll system had a lot of little vehicles going out on routes every morning, where drivers picked up paper from our clients having all the necessary information to do a payroll. Then we went into data entry—in those days it was called keypunch—and took over from there. And when everything was all done, the vehicles went back and delivered all that paper to the clients. In today's mode, just to take a few aspects of contrast, the vast bulk of our payroll input is coming from client-site PCs, where PCs dial directly into our mainframes with no people in between. And because the data is coming through a client-site PC, it's been edited and error checked before it ever gets to us, which eliminates a whole round of recycling that often used to happen. And when our mainframes are done, in a good number of cases our mainframes talk right back to those PCs, without people, communicating certain information to the client-site PCs—which they can then massage as they see fit. . . . Also, . . . previously you'd have to have hundreds of preprinted checks that had to be preregistered before you could print the checks for Client X, and then you had to change the paper for Client Y. Thanks to laser technology, now, in one single pass, the mainframes drive laser printers that absorb blank sheets on the way in, and not only does a paycheck come out with all the logos in the background and so on, but the laser printer also "signs" the checks. It makes life much simpler.

As Weston's example illustrates, the movement from relatively distinct instances of automation—such as the original ADP processing systems and the original client systems that generated the paper printout used by ADP—to far more integrated systems that involve direct computer-to-computer communication can provide a much greater degree of streamlining and other performance benefits. This movement toward greater integration over the past few years is expected by many technologists to increase the contributions of IT[12]—in ways that can be best understood by examining changes at the activity level.

One consequence of such IT-related changes in tasks is that there are many new ways to substitute goods and services for each other, enabling organizations to provide what a customer really wants by different means. For example, as discussed in Chapter 3, companies can invest in IT that allows them to use less of their own labor and invoke more labor effort by the customer—all the while providing more convenience and possibly lower costs to customers.[13] This concept is fundamental to many instances of do-it-yourself "services" provided by businesses (e.g., credit card gas pumps, long-distance dialing, machine-operated parking facilities, automated teller machines, corporate treasury systems). Further, a product itself may embody trade-offs between using goods and services to meet customer needs;

> **BOX 4.4 The Cosmos Tracking System of Federal Express**
>
> Federal Express provides guaranteed delivery of high-priority packages. However, much of its success is based on the fact that information about the status of packages in transit is often as important to the senders and receivers of those packages as the actual delivery of the package. Federal Express developed the Cosmos system to locate and track packages anywhere within the Federal Express network. This capability is based on a bar code attached to every package that is read at every package transfer point (e.g., from truck to airplane). Customers that provide a package-tracking number can thus inquire about where the package is and when it is likely to arrive; it is also possible to order rerouting of packages in transit should that be necessary.
>
> NOTE: For a good discussion of Cosmos, see Nehls, Carl, 1988, "Custodial Package Tracking at Federal Express," pp. 57-81 in *Managing Innovation: Cases from the Services Industries*, Bruce R. Guile and James Brian Quinn (eds.), National Academy Press, Washington, D.C.

for example, software such as income tax preparation packages and will-writing packages may represent a good that has service built into it as part of its "functionality."

Another consequence of IT-related changes in tasks has to do with the time value of information. Because IT can be used to make more fine-grained information available, and provide it more rapidly, new attitudes may emerge about the importance of different kinds of information at different points in business processes. These new attitudes can, in turn, lead to new services. For example, major package-delivery companies offer the service of informing people about exactly where a package in transit may be, permitting changing its destination as well as forecasting the delivery with great precision (Box 4.4).

While the initial (and still major) use of IT is the automation of routine tasks such as accounting, inventory management, handling of personnel data, and the like, IT is increasingly being applied to support knowledge-based activities (e.g., domain modeling, decision making). For example, the product management and engineering vice president of a major communications company observed that its new credit card business "was really launched out of an understanding developed through the analysis of data that's been accumulated over a number of years . . . from both internal operations as well as other, demographic databases which are commercially available and integrated with the information that the company captured routinely." The production of value in most fields now increasingly depends on the management of the knowledge that creates such new services and the coordination of these intellectual processes toward something of particular value to customers. This pattern cuts across industries, further blurring the traditional distinctions between manufacturing and service industries.[14]

The implications of tapping such uses of IT are far-reaching. For example, instead of simply providing a way to replace human effort with IT, some of the newer uses of IT are not so much replacing employees as enhancing knowledge workers. This type of application is becoming more common in finance. For example, Howard Sorgen of Merrill Lynch explained that

> in our business, the really large profits come from products and services which are heavily dependent on analysis and computation. The speed with which a particular firm can respond to a new opportunity for, say, a new derivative product depends directly on the sophistication and processing capability of the analytic software provided to the knowledge worker. Even though the technology is complex, the costs to exploit this technology are low compared to the potential gain. A good example would be the use of RISC [reduced instruction set computer]-based multiprocessors to perform the calculations necessary for derivative products such as interest rate or foreign exchange swaps or mortgage-backed securities. This is in sharp contrast to the high-volume, commodity type of technology application such as check processing—where the expenditure for equipment and staff is high relative to the profitability of the product being supported. In the latter example, enhancements to technology (better and faster check sorters) are deployed to reduce dependence on human labor, not to enhance the job of the laborer.

Further, the greater use of systems to complement knowledge workers implies a need to change the skill set that employees usually bring to their jobs. Employees must know how to construct queries, analyze data, interpret information, and draw conclusions—and do all of this using computers. Expected changes in skill demands related to new kinds of tasks, in turn, present significant challenges for an organization's human resources, as a section below, "Consequences for Employees," describes.

New Linkages and Transformations in Firms

Given that a company's activities can be linked to each other in many different ways, how should they be linked to produce the best value for the company? Prior to the advent of IT, the answer was driven by issues such as ease of management and physical proximity. However, in addition to the direct incorporation of electronic tools into many service tasks, IT provides the capability to link activities in many different ways, and it creates the basis for new organizational forms, such as cross-functional teams or processes and even cross-firm systems of linked activities.

New linkages have resulted chiefly from improvements in the variety, nature, cost, and quality of communications technologies, plus enhancements in user interfaces, database systems, and other elements of computing technology that generate and process information prepared or shared through communications links. Advances in "groupware" are expected to boost this trend by facilitating group preparation of, for instance, planning documents, project proposals, or activity reports. To date, however, most improvements of this type have come about through electronic mail (e-mail), computer networking, and related enhancements. For example, leading retailers such as Federated Department Stores have been installing and upgrading communications systems linking branches to headquarters to more quickly monitor and analyze sales data, permitting more timely changes in ordering and marketing strategies.[15] The spread of e-mail generally has been credited with increasing the pace of decision making and the scope of interactions in an enterprise, since it facilitates communication unconstrained by hierarchies. Also, as noted by Craig Goldman, senior vice president and chief information officer at Chase Manhattan Bank, e-mail tends to cut short the cycles of iteration associated with generating more formal, "letter-perfect," paper-based correspondence or memoranda. Cryptic and often poorly punctuated correspondence has become totally acceptable in the world of personal e-mail communications.

Larry Bacon of the Travelers Companies discussed the many ways that better telecommunications has fostered improvements:

> It's the ability to communicate instantly and cheaply that allows me to put workstations and people wherever they need to be but let them think that they're working with someone that is right next door, whereas they could be anywhere they need to be. So we can have a service center that's very good at doing service center-type things; it's very efficient. At a service center you have an 800 number, you have good management, you have the optimal number of people that have wonderful voices and are highly service oriented, in whatever location in the country you need to be at to get that kind of labor force and that kind of good communications economics. And they're doing their thing wherever they are. Meanwhile, we may need to have a salesman on every street corner of America or we may need to have doctors or nurses that are experts in certain fields, wherever they need to be. But we only need these people at certain times on certain pieces of business. The problem is, how do they get into the loop? Communications makes them all able to work together.

Within a firm, the potential for linking activities in different ways has an important effect on management choices regarding how centralized or decentralized activities should be. Conventional wisdom suggests that enhanced communications options are associated with greater decentralization, and recent empirical research has supported that inference. For example, distributed and, increasingly, mobile computer systems that can communicate with an office or headquarters as well as with one another will support a variety of marketing, sales, service, and analytical activities (such as order entry, market data collection, insurance policy terms and formats). Explained Roger Ferkenhoff, formerly vice president, Information Services at Sears Merchandise Group, and now retired,

> At Sears, any individual, based on authorization, can access anything he or she needs at any Sears location. . . . Our district folks are constantly on the road and on their way to the next store. They all have portable terminals. As soon as they walk into a store—we say their office is "next store, next terminal"—they have full access to any information they need. So it really has enabled us to change the structure rather dramatically.

Distributed systems obviate the necessity for all tasks to flow through an office or headquarters. In fact, continuing to route many processes through a centralized office may vitiate the speed and flexibility potentially afforded by reliance on electronic networked systems. For example, Pacific Bell has reaped benefits from a mobile terminal system developed by Bell Communications Research to support service technicians. Jack Hancock, executive vice president, Product and Technology Support, explained that

> the Technician Access Network, or TAN, . . . is a hand-held device that all technicians have. . . . [W]hereas before when technicians went out on service calls, they had to get access to a telephone pair, plug into the pair, and then call back to the maintenance center to order tests, and so forth, now the TAN device permits them to plug in directly because it is a hand-held device, a telephone. In addition it has a display so they can conduct their tests with this single handset. They can also get instructions for the next job that way, and so it has automated much of what the technician does.

Despite the many benefits being discovered for distributed systems, the advent of microcomputers has not led to the demise of centralized information systems functions. Rather, there have been changes in their size, tasks, and knowledge requirements while technical responsibilities of their client departments have grown. The kinds of distributed systems mentioned above can have significant costs for internal support services. In addition, some applications may require at least some centralization. For example, Pacific Bell's Hancock argued that telephone central office inventory systems, which track millions of items relating to the ability to establish or act on telecommunications service to a particular location, are too vast to be decentralized—although distributed access to the systems is possible. Similarly, e-mail directory services require firm-level coordination.

Thus IT-based structural change has not been in a single direction. Instances of both centralization and decentralization may be found even within the same organization. Some organizations that have already made a shift from centralization to decentralization are now considering the recentralization of selected activities (Box 4.5). The activities targeted for (re)centralization can still be dispersed, but greater central control and standardization may be asserted through links to common, central systems. The result could be called the virtually centralized (or decentralized) organization. Both kinds of choices—moves toward decentralization and moves toward virtual centralization—are made possible by advances in IT, coupled with declining telecommunications costs.

Other linkages that contribute to performance are those between firms. IT can be used to link value chains across firms and shift work involved in various functions between organizations. Marshall Carter, currently chairman and chief executive officer of State Street Bank, provided an example relating to the processing of financial information:

> Mutual fund companies each year have to do an annual report for the regulators and for other people. Prior to 1991 they prepared this report on their own with plenty of typing and all kinds of gathering of data. We've devised a way to print the report—ready for the cameras and the printing presses—with information that's stored in our databases just by pulling up the right information and arraying it, calculating exactly. It saves the mutual companies an enormous amount of money and time. But what we're doing there is adding value to the information; we're really changing the data into value-added information for the client, and he's willing to pay for that.

BOX 4.5 Recentralization of Previously Decentralized Activity

Local-area networks (LANs) are often installed on a departmental basis within an organization. As such, they are oriented toward specific needs of departments, which may not be uniform across all departments within the organization. However, data and information residing on departmental networks may have value to the entire organization, and maintenance of departmentally based LANs may be costly and distract the department from focusing on its core tasks. As a result, some organizations are beginning to recentralize control over their many distributed LANs.

SOURCE: Dostert, Michele. 1992. "LAN Control Falling to IS," *Computerworld*, December 21, p. 37.

He went on to describe how, building on technology, his business had shifted from a focus on transaction processing—providing information for the client—to a focus on strategic alliances and doing things with the client.

Considering interfirm links on a broader scale, electronic data interchange (EDI) connects companies to their suppliers, buyers, and even to their banks. Providing a shared body of information and a common set of standardized forms, EDI transforms the ordering, invoicing, shipping, tracking, and customer service functions, among others, for a growing number of enterprises.

Interfirm connectivity can both affect existing activities and at the same time make new businesses possible. For example, organizations with a well-developed in-house service activity and excess capacity may decide not only to perform the work for themselves but also to take on external clients for the service. This is what American and United Airlines have done with their computerized reservation systems, which are now dominant in the airline industry. In these cases, the technology has become the basis for a new line of business.

A different type of reconfiguration is the new business that results from an IT-based integration of complementary service activities. For example, American Airlines and CSX, a rail transport company, have developed a joint venture, Encompass, for global logistics that relies on IT. Travel agencies rely today on the availability of information concerning airlines, auto rentals, hotel reservations, and other information in comprehensive information systems. By linking these systems, customers will be able to obtain "one-stop" shopping for their travel needs.

Finally, enhanced abilities to link physically separate activities create the potential for their geographic independence (such as the remote computer-aided dispatching described for Pacific Bell above or the teleservice center described above for the Travelers Companies). Dependence on regular and reliable communication has always been fundamental to large organizations with distributed establishments. But IT is being used to support ever greater geographic dispersion of personnel, as cheaper and easier-to-use communications technology encourages more organizations to experiment with telecommuting or other modes of long-distance work for some staff. For example, companies such as insurance agencies and airlines engage in extensive telephone interactions with their customers; these companies can use nationwide toll-free numbers to route customer service calls to personnel physically located in low-wage areas, perhaps even outside the country, while networking and data communications between these customer service agents and corporate databases enable the prompt servicing of customer requests.[16]

Multinational enterprises are not new, and companies have for many decades set up operations in other countries to make use of unique facilities or capabilities, to benefit from lower-cost production labor, or to satisfy local content laws or regulations associated with selling in foreign markets. Today, however, there are signs that the global division of labor is extending to such white-collar service activities as research (Switzerland), software coding and development (programming in India), data entry (Korea), and insurance claims processing (Ireland). Among the several reasons for this pattern is IT, which can be used to connect remote parties more easily, less expensively, and very quickly. The prospect of greater globalization in turn raises questions relevant to public policy about potential reductions in local employment opportunities and changes in work force skills.

The broad distribution of capabilities to access information, solve problems, take action, and communicate has motivated new theories of organization, challenging conventional wisdom on, for example, the need for hierarchically structured bureaucracies for the coordination of complex multiperson tasks. The movement toward flatter organizations, in many instances, provides testbeds for new ideas on organization. For example, a vice president of a major communications company describes how they moved toward a more matrix-like organization because of options made possible by IT.

> IT has enabled decision making to be driven lower in the organization. It has been an aid in helping to reduce layers of management within the organization. As information becomes more readily available from the customer facing people, it has allowed us to reduce layers because we have speed of decision making and we have information that has . . . been developed by those intervening layers of the organization. . . . Thirdly, it has begun to increase the flexibility with which we can change the character of the organization. We're tending to work in more of a matrix, rather than a hierarchical, form with more teams . . . .

New and imaginative metaphors for technologically transformed organizations are beginning to appear, including the organization as network or web (versus discrete units), as jelly fish (versus dinosaur), and as intellectual holding company for electronically linked activities. It is important to note, of course, that while IT enables such forms, they are still in experimental stages in most companies, and the full capabilities of IT have not yet been fully exploited for these purposes. Thus new organizational forms should, at present, be treated essentially as possibilities. New models will ultimately be needed, or earlier paradigms for understanding organizations revised, to better understand how activities might be reorganized to exploit IT for better (or higher) performance.

Outsourcing and Industry Transformation

Perhaps the greatest impact of increased flexibility in configuring component activities is seen in a company's decision to provide a necessary service activity internally or to buy it from an outsider—the decision about whether to "outsource." The ease with which different IT operations can be coupled across institutional boundaries (e.g., through standardized electronic data interchange and networking protocols) and the external specialty service firms that are enabled by such coupling increase the range of options for redesigning overall work flow. Activities that are highly generic in nature (such as payroll) are most susceptible to being provided by external service specialists, even when rapid turnaround is required. In fact, the development of IT-service industries (contract software development and maintenance, third-party network-based services, systems integration, computing facilities management services, and so on) reflects in part a long-term trend toward outsourcing service activities (from legal work to accounting to data processing) to firms that specialize in them. To obtain faster cycle times and lower investment costs and risks, high-technology companies often outsource many specialized activities, from component design and product styling to distribution and field warehousing.

Outsourcing a given service activity may make particularly good sense when that activity involves what might be called "economies of knowledge scale." Typically, the competent provision of a service subject to economies of knowledge scale requires highly specialized (and thus costly) information tools as well as the specialized expertise required to use these tools effectively, for example, some specialized databases or knowledge systems. An individual firm that needs such a service may not find it worthwhile to use its resources to develop or provide this service in-house at truly competitive levels of cost or quality. However, an external unit might launch that activity as its core business, taking advantage of its ability to spread costs over a large number of external users and to develop specialized expertise that enables it to perform that activity particularly well. In this way, IT-enabled specialization is especially valuable for entrepreneurs seeking to focus an entire business on a given activity or set of activities.

Decisions to outsource a critical service activity can have negative consequences as well. Outsourcing may require a company to expend much more effort in establishing and maintaining stable, reliable, and high-quality interactions with external providers of services, since outsiders are by definition not conversant with the relevant corporate culture. Opportunities for synergy may be lost, since outsiders may be less motivated to look for ways to improve a client's operations, less knowledgeable about a client's operations, and less likely to seek frequent interactions between themselves and the client organization. Further, employees at the outsourcing company may lose jobs, although other jobs will be created in supplier companies.

Perhaps more serious for managers is the potential of losing control over a critical aspect of a company's operation. Reliance on external service providers may well lead to the loss of specialized skills (indeed, reducing personnel costs may have been a major reason for turning to an external provider), making it difficult for the client company to audit the quality and cost of the services being provided. Asking for changes in the nature of the services being provided may become more difficult if the external provider is large relative to the buyer—or if the company's dependence on the external service provider increases for other reasons. Unless the company has available substitute suppliers, external service providers can raise the prices they charge for their services as the cost to the client of switching to an alternative service provider increases.

IT may influence the perceived costs and benefits of a decision to outsource. The capacity to coordinate large programs has undoubtedly led to a greater number of strategic and operational alliances in recent years. Whether management decides to undertake an activity internally or to have it done by an outside source depends on many factors—such as the number of suppliers available and the criticality of the activity to the core business (this may be illuminated by value-chain analysis); an activity's synergy with or complementarity to other, critical activities; the relative costs of conducting or buying the activity; the extent to which economies of scale and scope are present; the firm's capacity to manage outsourcing; and so on.

CONSEQUENCES FOR EMPLOYEES

IT is associated with a number of direct and indirect effects on people working within organizations that use IT. Most directly, the introduction of IT can trigger redesign of jobs, restructuring of work flows, or changes in the physical location of work. These effects arise because of the nature of IT; IT consists of tools that affect what people do and how they do it. Less directly, applications in one part of an organization can alter the work and working conditions elsewhere: management systems can be used to craft reorganizations, database and communication systems that supply information at top and bottom levels can eliminate the need for certain middle levels, and so on.

The activity level is where the first effects of change will be experienced by employees, effects that will then influence performance at the firm and industry levels. Users are important stakeholders in the introduction of new information tools. Employee expectations that the benefits as well as the burdens of continued technological advance will be equitably shared may be a key factor in the successful implementation of IT. Further, although employee satisfaction with new job designs often depends upon choices that may be made for reasons unrelated to satisfying worker interests, accommodating employee concerns by explicitly dealing with them during the design phase frequently results in both improved task design and employee acceptance. Obtaining the maximum return from investments in

IT may hinge on providing avenues for employees to exercise their knowledge and skills, and it is possible to design and implement IT systems that encourage and reward extra effort and ability on the part of users.

For many employees, a first concern, naturally enough, is fear of job loss. The inherent capabilities of IT, combined with job and organization redesign permitted by the technologies, can result in substantial reduction in the demand for, or outright elimination of, particular activities. For example, a top executive of a major supermarket chain described the reduction in labor requirements associated with supermarket scanning systems.

> A large supermarket will carry 30,000 to 60,000 items. Every day, every week, there's a dynamic system of price changing and updating and deals with everything that is happening in the marketplace across all those tens of thousands of items. A typical store has some kind of pricing activity on 1500 to 2000 to 3000 of those items depending upon what inflationary, deflationary, or other outside environments it is exposed to. In the past, that meant that somebody—a person—physically had to go out there, erase every price off every one of those items, stamp a new price on it, put a new tag on it, and . . . to do that in a store took about 100 to 150 hours a week.

Thus the relative growth in jobs associated with service activities, as indicated in Table 4.1, does not guarantee substantial job growth in absolute terms. The one white-collar category showing much less than average growth is administrative support occupations, including clerical workers; this is also consistent with the observation that PCs and other office technologies are enabling professional and managerial workers to bring more of their work to completion with less need for administrative assistance. For example, Larry Bacon of the Travelers Companies described a major shift in the insurance industry from clerical to professional personnel, with workstations being manned by professional customer service representatives, underwriters, claims specialists, and nurses, for example. In addition, changes in professional, technical, and managerial jobs that are evident at the activity level suggest that growth rates in these job categories will slow (and are indeed beginning to do so).[17] Since service-sector job growth has been concentrated in industries with relatively low efficiency, the potential for those industries to streamline their processes using IT or other means suggests further constraints on service job growth, other things being equal.[18] Nevertheless, merely installing IT-based systems does not guarantee job reductions. For example, as an executive of a major diversified service firm observed, the use of IT in a lean company does not necessarily result in less staff in front-of-the-house activities: the check-in line may be shorter and the service faster and more accurate, but the number of clerks may stay the same.

Nonetheless, fears of job loss in the work force as a whole can strongly affect the ability of an organization to adopt new tools and systems in a timely and cost-effective manner. Moreover, these fears may arise even when management adopts IT for reasons other than staff reduction. This issue should be addressed directly and dealt with to the greatest extent possible through the adoption of such actions as expansion of internal retraining programs, shifts of affected personnel to other activities within the organization, sweetening of early-retirement packages, and when necessary, provision of substantial outplacement services. These measures can help foster a positive attitude about change.

Applications of IT also affect career prospects more generally, including professional development, pay and promotion opportunities, the ability to stay in a given geographic area, and reporting relationships and requirements. This broad complex of changes in the content of jobs will affect job satisfaction and the quality of working life. Both the levels and the extent of supervision may change with new applications of IT. As organizations become flatter and more decentralized, the line between staff and line functions will continue to blur. One executive at a major communications company described the changing role of managers:

> The whole character of the relationship between a manager and employees changes. Teams are empowered, which means that the role of the manager switches from being a director of activities to a facilitator, a coach, and a thought leader.

Line managers may not only decrease in numbers, as suggested by flatter organizations, but are also likely to need new substantive and managerial skills.

Even when job loss is not perceived as a potential result of the introduction of IT, employees may resist change because they do not understand what is being imposed on them. Smooth transitions depend on employee acceptance, and a major factor in obtaining that acceptance is the extent of employee participation in planning. Moreover, early and genuine employee involvement in system planning also enables the resulting system to incorporate and complement employees' domain knowledge and process skills. For these reasons, employees and their representatives should be involved as early as possible in technology-related decision-making and implementation processes.

IT applications alter the knowledge and skill requirements of personnel. They are likely to increase the intellectual demands on knowledge workers—the workers who are responsible for interpreting, analyzing, and taking action on the basis of information received throughout the company. For example, access to previously unavailable data enabled by the use of IT (e.g., hour-by-hour sales in a retail establishment), and the potential of such data to lead to competitive advantage, create a requirement for knowledge workers to develop appropriate analytical skills, both to interpret relevant data and to disregard irrelevant data. In addition, the cooperative work that IT enables among dispersed workers means that these workers must now know how to cooperate and share information with each other in order to use groupware (collaboration technology) and shared information resources to the best advantage.

Substantially redesigned activities (e.g., complete redesign of insurance claims-processing procedures) generally require much more extensive education and training programs. For example, the product management and engineering vice president of a major communications company noted,

> We're expecting people to be able to be more than just technically able. We're expecting them to have the capacity to make decisions. That's what we're trying to do. Our objective is to move decision making lower so we're asking people to be able to acquire skills to do that, and, of course, working in team kinds of arrangements people, by necessity, have to have much, much stronger interpersonal skills.

On the one hand, as indicated by Larry Bacon of the Travelers Companies, the resulting jobs may be more professional than the original ones. On the other hand, some applications of IT may require less cognitive effort on the part of employees (as in the case of IT-based systems that can provide real-time guidance or advice to users, or even IT-based cash registers and bar-coding that eliminate the need for cashiers to do arithmetic).[19]

Combined changes in organization, job content, tools, and infrastructure will make it necessary for managers to develop new skills and new hiring strategies; they may also change demand for retraining.[20] The new skills go far beyond those traditionally associated with "retraining" or IT, such as the skills needed to use spreadsheets or word processors. In many cases, specific training related to new IT applications may need to be supplemented with broader education in a variety of areas—e.g., supervising a different kind of work force, integrating a variety of separate activities into team processes, making better use of enhanced communications capabilities, leading technological change, and so on.

Questions about who will train whom, how, when, and where, need to be answered before any hardware or software changes are instituted.[21] Further, given the anticipated rate of technological change in the decades to come, (re)training can be expected to be a continuing rather than a one-time or infrequent need. Depending on how it is implemented, IT affects learning curves for both individuals and organizations overall.

Individuals at all levels of the organization may be affected as the use of IT permeates a company's activities. Many may have increased responsibilities, in part because using IT may make it possible for each individual to do more. Employees may feel more empowered or have a greater sense of ownership of work, although not necessarily as a result of intentional organizational redesign. For example, high-level managers can use IT to exercise a greater degree of control over their work, even when assistants would be available to perform such work. Such ownership may lead to the reduction or elimination of intermediate rungs in the corporate hierarchy (a job-loss issue), but as importantly it may also lead to a more finely tuned match between the ultimate work product and the understanding and insights of senior management. At the same time, greater ownership may tempt managers to appropriate the benefits of using IT more for themselves than for their enterprises; specifically, some managers may try to decrease their personal risks of error by uneconomically increasing the amount of data they seek before making decisions.[22] Such changes in organization and management are often not anticipated initially by companies embarking on new applications of IT but emerge as the use of IT diffuses through the company. Companies that do not pay deliberate managment attention to organizational issues often find that previously existing roles and relationships reassert themselves in ways that put a ceiling on how much benefit can be achieved with the new technology and/or subvert and undermine the changes that the new technology has enabled, thereby pushing the organization back in the direction of the status quo.

IT-enabled decentralization is often associated with changes in job content and hierarchies.[23] Specifically, IT can be used to combine multiple tasks within jobs and to support cross-functional teams. Customer service affords an example: telephone and computer systems provide tools for a single individual to receive and handle a variety of inquiries. Cross-functional jobs and teams imply more comprehensive knowledge and the ability to manage flexible and loosely coupled staff resources. For example, one communications company vice president described the movement toward cross-functional jobs as a trend toward "caseworkers"[24] for applications in customer service, provisioning, and network configuration activities, suggesting that database and expert-system technology made such jobs possible. This approach to reengineering has reduced time requirements by a factor of 10 and costs by a factor of 3 to 4.

Similarly, IT can be used to support the flattening of hierarchies, as fewer people and fewer jobs are needed to relay and concentrate information when electronic databases and communications provide some of those functions. Middle managers, as well as technical and administrative staff in service activities, thus face special challenges in their work and careers. As currently deployed, IT systems handle particularly well activities that require complex collections of repetitive and routine tasks, including such things as data collection, information transfer, reproduction, monitoring, scheduling, and the like. For example, Roger Ferkenhoff described a recent restructuring of Sears' vertical business groups (automotive, home appliances, and so on) where the elimination of a layer of management was made possible by company-wide access to computing and communications systems. Both elimination or simplification of some jobs and enhancement of others are possible.

Finally, IT-based systems may also be a necessary part of a work environment that is on the cutting edge of expanding business frontiers. The leaders of an industry seek the best talent available, and such people are most often attracted by the challenge of working on state-of-the-art business problems. Craig Goldman of Chase Manhattan, for example, pointed to the value of investing in good desktop technology to reduce attrition of technical staff. To the extent that exploitation of IT is a necessary component of a successful approach to such problems, firms that hope to lead an industry cannot afford to scrimp on the technology needed to stay at the cutting edge.

CONCLUSIONS

Intense domestic and international competition, a lackluster economy, and other business pressures are leading companies to look beyond incremental change. They are redefining their purposes, goals, and images, redesigning work processes in fundamental ways, making major changes in both management structures and work locations, and reconstituting their employee work forces. Such changes will continue throughout the coming decade, and many analysts feel this circumstance will become the norm for the foreseeable future.[25]

Although it is not possible, in a general sense, to say that a "right way for firms to use IT" has emerged, IT can be used by firms to develop a vast new array of alternatives for organizing activities. Some of that opportunity for choice can be seen in the different approaches (in terms of technologies and processes overall) that companies in a given industry have taken to carry out the same fundamental activity. However, IT can also be used with homogenizing results. For example, producers of a wide range of products may be interconnected by the same EDI system, a system that imposes a common process for order-related activities. The trend toward interconnectivity and the possibility of a national information infrastructure suggest that, to at least some extent, technical standards will increase commonalities for IT-related tasks across organizations.

The chief conclusion to be drawn from the committee's activity-level inquiry is that the use of IT has so greatly increased the opportunities for designing service activities to meet a variety of performance goals that new perspectives are required for organizational learning, understanding, and assessment. Neither researchers nor decision makers have a base of empirical evidence or well-established precedents on which to rely in understanding how IT can be used most effectively to support work flows within and across enterprises. Further, as discussed in other chapters, the actual outcomes of such efforts are influenced by a number of factors in addition to IT (such as competition, employee skill base, and especially managerial capability in organizational and activity design). **IT alone does not create impacts; its effects reflect a host of decisions made and actions taken—wisely or not—by a range of stakeholders including senior managers, technical professionals, and users.**

Because the rapid pace of IT change does not appear to be slowing, new possibilities for designing activities, restructuring them within firms, and linking them across firms will continue to emerge. And because continuous change is to be expected, today's right answer is perhaps tomorrow's wrong solution. Moreover, as suggested by Merrill Lynch's Howard Sorgen, what is a right answer today is not always clear.

> What we are going to suffer through, I believe, for the next 3 years in the application of information technology is a significant number of false starts, as technology organizations attempt to deploy workstation-based solutions for large-scale problems. Since many of these organizations lack the management experience and technical maturity to make the proper choices in hardware and software, some of their experiments will fail—due not only to their own lack of appreciation of the requirements of a robust "production-ready" operation, but also because the support tools available for many years for the mainframe environment are simply not mature enough to support high-volume, transaction-processing applications on a workstation-based technical platform.

At the same time, smarter decisions can be made today about how to use investments introduced some time ago. This observation was made by Larry Bacon of the Travelers Companies:

> One of the things we've seen has been enormous cost reduction over the last 2 or 3 years in our industry, and a great deal of that has been that people have reached down and really gone and taken advantage of the things they automated years ago. So if they automated something and they could eliminate 200 positions, maybe they reduced 150 initially. Now they go back and they not only get the other 50 they should have, but they say, "Now that we're doing business this way, I can do this and I can do that, and I can do these things better, and maybe I can close these 6 offices because now I can do it with this number of offices." They have made much bolder strokes. But that's a recognition of where they are today rather than a premeditated, "We're going to automate and do this."

The volatility in the application of IT and the restructuring of activities entails an organizational need for flexibility, an ability to change quickly, and the capacity to experiment regularly—with the expectation of some successes and some failures. The cost of continued experimentation—and the likelihood of both successful and unsuccessful trials—should be considered explicitly in firms' strategic planning for technological change. Moreover, within organizations "training" will, in consequence, become an everyday issue. However, it has been observed that within firms the pace of implementation of new technologies has slowed; technology push is being weighed against organizational needs, available resources, and capabilities for assimilation. This more cautious approach to the use of innovative IT may result in better planning, evaluation, and implementation.

How to value or assess the performance of service activities is an issue that calls for more data and analytical models than are currently available. Repetitive activities are much easier to measure than others, and service performance metrics in the past have usually been based on what is easy to measure.[26] Since it is difficult to measure the more complex and nonroutine things that organizations do, it is inherently problematic to determine whether the acquisition of new IT has made their performance better. This conclusion underscores the need for new activity-level metrics.

The availability of such metrics would have important policy consequences. The capacity of both service enterprises and service activities within manufacturing and other enterprises to create value added for customers and to increase their own real productivity is important to the levels of wealth created by the nation. With 77 percent of all U.S. employment in service industries and another (approximately) 10 to 12 percent in service activities within goods-producing companies, increasing the productivity of service activities—whether within a company or in a separate service company—seriously affects the nation's capacity to increase real wages over time.

One of the more important conclusions that emerges from the study of the impact of IT on service performance at the activity level is the profound effect it will have on employees. Use of IT is an important factor in helping to increase the value added, and hence the wage potentials, of service jobs at all levels from the high-paying professional and managerial levels to the low-paying entry level. Because service jobs provide the entry- and early developmental-level jobs for the country—and many of these depend on extensive use of IT to create high value added—effective deployment and implementation of IT in services are critical to developing the output potentials of recent entrants into the nation's work force. Moreover, as companies redesign their processes and structures, their needs for particular skills and numbers of employees in their work forces will undergo major shifts. These changes call for preparations and responses by individuals, employers, and government at all levels.

The IT-enabled ability to relink activities in a myriad of configurations will profoundly influence the structure of U.S. industry, the organization of companies, and the nature and location of future jobs. How firms and industries restructure themselves will have major policy implications for job design, changes in occupational mix, and education and training. The outcome of such restructurings will have profound effects on productivity in all industries, the competitiveness of U.S. companies and industries in international markets, the number and nature of employment opportunities, and the effectiveness of huge and ongoing investments in IT.

NOTES AND REFERENCES

[1] It should be noted that process innovation is not a new construct. However, unlike product innovation, process innovation has not been widely recognized until relatively recently as a potential source of significant organizational performance improvements. For further discussion of this point, see, for example, Tornatzky, L., T. Solomon, T.K. Bikson, and others, 1982, "Contributions of Social Science to Innovation and Productivity," *American Psychologist* 37(7):737-746; Tornatzky, L., W. Hetzner, J.D. Eveland, and others, 1983, *The Process of Technological Innovation: Reviewing the Literature*, National Science Foundation, Washington, D.C.; and Tornatzky, L., and M. Fleischer, 1990, *The Processes of Technological Innovation*, Lexington Books, Lexington, Mass.

[2] Kiesler, Sara, and Lee Sproull. 1992. "Group Decision Making and Communications Technology," *Organizational Behavior & Human Decision Processes* 52(1):96-123.

[3] Recent changes in services at the department and process levels of organizations have spawned new families of measures, but the committee believes that most of these efforts are still narrowly defined (see *The Master Measurement Model of Employee Performance.* n.d. The Society of Incentive Travel Executives Foundation, New York). An activity-level analysis can help broaden the viewpoint and open the way to making revolutionary changes.

[4] When the use of new technologies and approaches leads to new combinations of previously separate activities, for instance, traditional measures of performance are problematic at best—and perhaps outright misleading or useless.

[5] The committee also examined the work of several prominent European scholars on the impact of information technology on work in service industries. However, since these individuals tend to study non-U.S. institutions, and institutional and national differences between the United States and Europe (e.g., the German apprenticeship system, government funding of industry) are often profound, it is very hard to compare macroeconomic-level issues such as productivity. In addition, the work of these people focuses on levels of analysis that are finer-grained than even the activity level, with no particular ties to economic performance. Thus, such work was considered relatively peripheral to the issues the committee was addressing.

[6] A good treatment of the use in measurement of data indicating customer satisfaction can be found in Zeithaml, Valarie A., A. Parasuraman, and Leonard L. Berry, 1990, *Delivering Quality Service: Balancing Customer Perceptions and Expectations*, Free Press, New York.

[7] Bureau of Labor Statistics employment projections are developed using a detailed input-output model and a variety of economic and demographic data. In addition, analysts determine factors that have previously exerted a strong influence on the behavior of important projection results, and then make assumptions, based on past experience and professional judgment about future trends in specific industries and occupations, about their influence in the future. This exercise includes evaluation of particular technologies in specific jobs or industries. The entire process is repeated every 2 years.

[8] Service occupations include cleaning and building service occupations, food preparation and service occupations, health service occupations, personal service occupations (such as barbers and child care workers), private household workers, and protective service occupations.

[9] This is not to deny the existence of activities that are relatively industry-specific, such as patient care activities in the health care industry. Billing, an activity that is relatively generic across many industries, is handled in a unique way within the telecommunications industry due to industry-unique regulatory requirements.

[10] See Boynton, A.C., B. Victor, and B.J. Pine II. 1993. "New Competitive Strategies: Challenges to Organizations and Information Technology," *IBM Systems Journal* 32(1):40-64.

[11] The close intermingling of properties of new technologies with properties of technology-dependent tasks is not a new outcome; indeed, such reciprocal effects have long been described by sociotechnical systems theory. Still, that theory has typically been applied to help explain relationships between new manufacturing tools and tasks involving the production of goods; IT bears a similar relationship to information-intensive service activities in both manufacturing and service firms.

[12] Computer Science and Telecommunications Board, National Research Council. 1991. *Keeping the U.S. Computer Industry Competitive: Systems Integration*, National Academy Press, Washington, D.C.

[13] The increase in convenience can be contrasted with the notion of "quality service" defined as a high level of service. Thus in some instances IT and other tools are helping to provide more personalized service, while in other instances, IT is helping customers be served more quickly by diminishing interactions with service-provider personnel.

[14] Camp, Robert C. 1989. *Benchmarking: The Search for Industry Best Practices That Lead to Superior Performance*, Quality Press, Milwaukee, Wisconsin.

[15] Strom, Stephanie. 1992. "Computerized Record-Keeping for Retailers," *New York Times*, May 20, p. D-6.

[16] See, for example, Carey, Susan. 1992. "Airlines Seek to Cut Back-Office Costs by Establishing Off-Shore Operations," *Wall Street Journal*, November 30, p. B-6D.

[17] See Prokesch, Steven. 1993. "Service Jobs Fall as Business Gains," *New York Times*, April 18, p. 1.

[18] Baumol, William J., Sue Anne Batey Blackman, and Edward N. Wolff. 1989. *Productivity and American Leadership: The Long View*, MIT Press, Cambridge, Mass.

[19] A good discussion of this issue can be found in Bulkeley, William, 1992, "Computer Use by Illiterates Grows at Work," *Wall Street Journal*, June 9, p. B1.

[20] However, when an activity remains substantially unchanged (e.g., typing reports on a word processor rather than a typewriter), specific task training may be all that is necessary.

[21] Note that some needs for new skills can be met by the use of IT, both through IT-based training systems (satellite classes, computer-aided instruction systems, and so on) and through the incorporation of knowledge and reference information into production systems (help functions, knowledge-based systems, and so on).

[22] Doorley, T., A. Gregg, and C. Gagnon. 1988. "Professional Service Firms and Information Technology: Ongoing Search for Sustained Competitive Advantage," *Managing Innovation*, National Academy Press, Washington, D.C.

[23] For more discussion of this point, see Zuboff, Shoshana, 1988, *In the Age of the Smart Machine: The Future of Work and Power*, Basic Books, New York.

[24] This term is attributed to business analyst Michael Hammer, who has written and consulted widely on reengineering.

[25] Davenport, Thomas H., 1993, *Process Innovation: Reengineering Work Through Information Technology*, Harvard Business School Press, Cambridge, Mass.; Davenport, Thomas H., and James E. Short, 1990, "The New Industrial Engineering: Information Technology and the Business Process Redesign," *Sloan Management Review*, Summer, pp. 11-17; and Hammer, Michael, 1990, "Reengineering Work: Don't Automate, Obliterate," *Harvard Business Review*, July-August, pp. 104-112.

[26] In addition to the reference provided in Note 3, see also Thor, Carl, 1986, "Using Nominal Group Technique to Establish a White-Collar Productivity Measurement System," *Productivity Brief*, No. 51, American Productivity Center, Houston, Texas; and Thor, Carl, 1991, "Performance Measurement in a Research Organization," *National Productivity Review*, Autumn, pp. 499-507.

5
Improving Decision Making About Information Technology

Analyses at the macroeconomic, industry, firm, and activity levels have attempted to assess the impact of using IT at those levels. At the enterprise level a number of studies and articles have indicated (1) shortcomings in how some companies have managed IT, particularly when they first began investing in IT, and (2) a lack of correlation between the amount a company invests in IT and its return on assets, returns to shareholders, or profits per employee.

To understand more thoroughly why companies have had such variable experience with their investments in IT, the committee asked experienced executives a series of structured questions (see Appendix D). The questions were intended to probe for any important problems executives had encountered in implementing IT systems, how they had attacked those problems, and what issues remained. While often admitting previous—and current—management problems, many executives indicated they had made significant improvements in their management practices and were currently modifying their processes to achieve further effectiveness. This chapter summarizes some of the interesting problems and solutions encountered.

Paul Strassmann, a former executive of the Xerox Corporation and director of defense information at the U.S. Department of Defense, analyzed the inconsistent relationship between investment in IT and service firm performance between 1977 and 1987 (Figure 5.1). He concluded, "A computer is only worth what it can fetch at an auction. IT has value only if surrounded by appropriate policy, strategy, methods for measuring results,

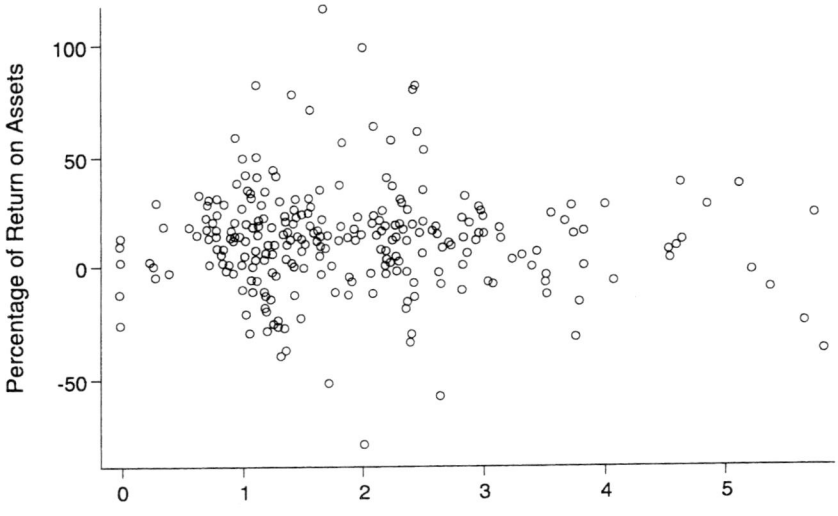
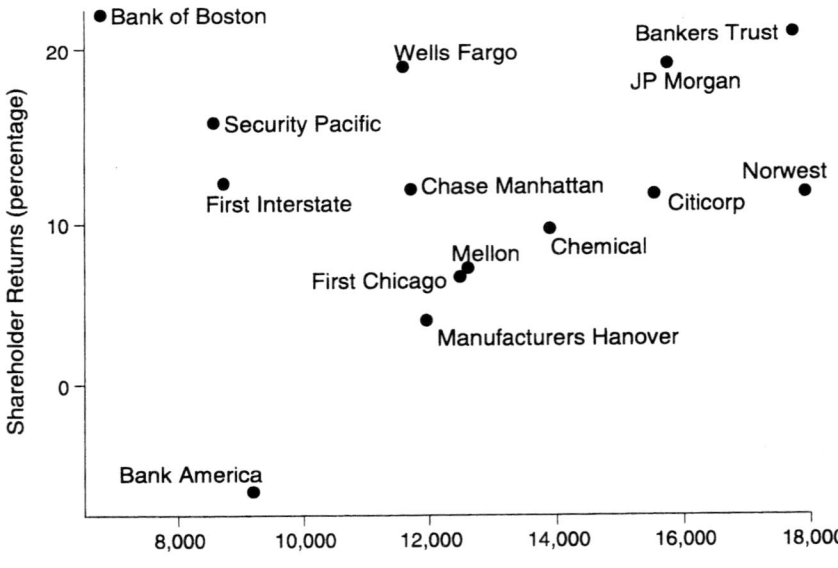

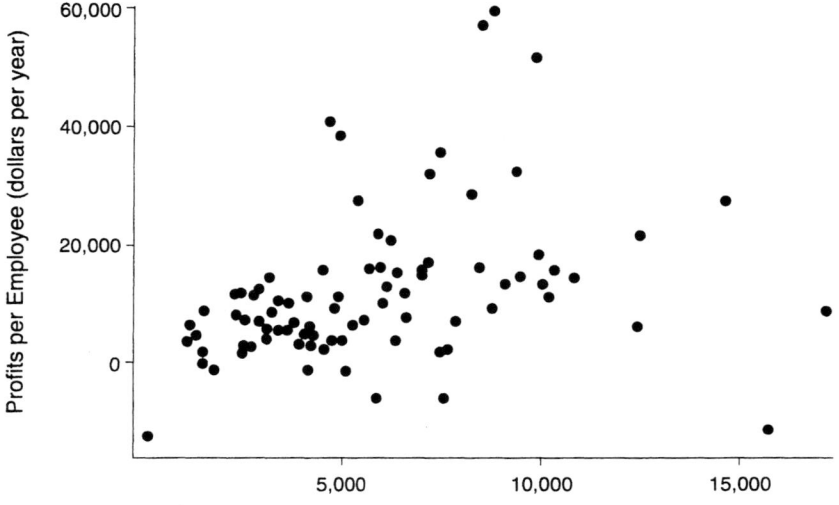

FIGURE 5.1 Investment in information technology and service performance: an inconsistent relationship. SOURCE: Reproduced with permission from Strassmann, Paul. 1990. *The Business Value of Computers,* Information Economics Press, New Canaan, Conn., p. xviii. Copyright 1990 by Information Economics Press.

project controls, talented and committed people, sound organizational relationships, and well-designed information systems. . . . The productivity of management is the decisive element in whether a computer helps or hurts."[1]

The committee concurs in this assessment. Box 5.1 provides a further illustration from software applications development. As Figure 5.1 suggests, standard measures of output make it appear that some companies' investments in IT have paid off well, whereas those of other companies with comparable opportunities have not. More often than not, good management has made the difference. Generally problems with obtaining a payoff from investment in IT, when they exist, lie not in the capacity of the technology but in the planning and implementation of systems. Good management can overcome many technological deficiencies, while poor management can prevent returns from otherwise productive technologies. The latter has often happened, for example, when corporate managers have left decisions to technical experts who were not knowledgeable about the strategic factors, operating variables, or organizational dynamics involved in implementation. A variety of studies (listed in Appendix A) have set forth many of the common shortcomings in the management of IT.

> **BOX 5.1 The Impact of CASE Tools on Productivity**
>
> Experience drawn from software engineering highlights the importance of management. Computer-aided software engineering (CASE) tools such as programming environments and debuggers were originally sold and marketed as tools that could increase the productivity of programmers by an order of magnitude. However, a variety of studies indicate that the use of CASE tools makes far less difference to programmer productivity than does the choice of the particular individuals to do the programming job; when CASE tools are not used, programmers are unproductive, but the use of CASE tools is not a guarantee that programmers will be productive. It turns out that when a programming project is competently managed, the impact of CASE tools is more easily observed.
>
> SOURCE: Bill Curtis, Software Engineering Institute, Carnegie Mellon University, Pittsburgh, Pa.

COMMON PROBLEM AREAS IN THE MANAGEMENT OF INFORMATION TECHNOLOGY

The following section addresses some of the identified problem areas in the management of IT and summarizes observations about them made during the committee's interviews.

Lack of Competition

One claim is that service companies have been protected by regulations and geography from domestic and foreign competition more than their manufacturing counterparts.[2] Hence they have not been forced to compete and respond to changes as quickly. However, this explanation is incomplete. Interviews verified that these two factors might have slowed potential changes in regulated airlines, health care, banking, and communications companies. Yet no professional service, retail, wholesale, entertainment, or international banking company mentioned these factors as relevant. Still, there is no question that more recent instances of restructuring in service industries have coincided with increased deregulation, cross-border trade, foreign direct trade, and depressed domestic markets.

These factors may help to explain previous slow responses to change in some types of companies but as a full explanation seem inconsistent with the facts that (1) U.S. service companies have consistently been among the first to adopt new technologies, (2) other countries (particularly in Europe, and Japan) have been even more sheltered in key service industries like communications, transportation, distribution, and finance, and (3) U.S. service companies' performance in most areas has compared very favorably with that of the companies of other industrial countries. (See Chapter 1.)

Inadequate Planning and Follow-up

Inadequate planning and follow-up have undoubtedly been significant problems in implementing IT projects for many service-sector firms. Although at the time of the committee's interviews many respondents indicated that their procedures for planning deployments of IT were comparable to those used for investments in other technology, they often candidly admitted that they had experienced earlier problems. Early investments were often pursued to acquire short-term savings in labor—by merely automating existing practices—rather than to generate longer-term gains or strategic potentials. Investments in duplicative or incompatible programs sometimes occurred.

In many instances, the costs associated with development and ongoing support required for major new information systems were underestimated. This was especially true for the maintenance, the updating of software, and the retraining costs associated with such systems. As was noted in Chapters 3 and 4, introduction of IT frequently leads to a variety of job changes that may have far-reaching implications across an entire company. Often, the nature and scale of these implications have not been fully explored as part of planning for IT. As a result, job changes were made less smoothly, and changes in performance evaluation and reward systems unnecessarily lagged deployment of IT systems.

Some respondents cited problems of underestimating incremental usage created by new systems that quickly exceeded acceptable utilization ratios in data centers—later leading to unexpected costs for further central processing power. Unanticipated costs for support and additional computing power increased both total investments and the bureaucracies to operate data centers—and thus lowered long-term returns. As Roger Ballou, president, Travel Related Services Group (USA), American Express, noted,

> One place an awful lot of people get into trouble is by not looking at the fully loaded costs of technology investment. If you analyze the costs of just bringing up the system and its ability to offset existing paper reporting, it can look very effective. But when you look at the full ramifications in terms of CPU [central processing unit] utilization on an ongoing basis, staffing support to provide help-desk functions for it, and so on, it can change both the cost and seeming returns on the investment. We recently built an on-line reporting system using existing software. We did have to pay a few hundred thousand dollars for disk drives and things like that. With programming, the total investment was probably several million. However, the ongoing operating costs of this system are probably running at $300,000 to $500,000 a month. If you are not careful, you also keep using available CPU time incrementally, and all at once you have to buy a large new chunk of CPU capacity for the next project.

Resistance and Inefficiencies in Work Practices

As noted in Chapter 3, the mere fact of access to desktop computing does not necessarily improve the effectiveness with which knowledge workers (i.e., the individuals in an organization who are responsible for interpreting and analyzing raw data and information and converting them to useful knowledge) can pursue their jobs. In many cases, knowledge workers have used IT to do more busy work without necessarily enhancing output—spreadsheets can be recalculated, presentations fine-tuned, or manuscripts revised more frequently with little noticeable benefit. In a related realm, respondents often questioned whether they had achieved sought-after communications benefits from more powerful desktop tools. Many said they had not yet found effective ways to stimulate or measure better communications through electronic mail or other computer communications systems.

A serious challenge—underestimated by several of the companies interviewed—comes from the long time that it takes to change traditional work practices and corporate cultures. When personnel are uncomfortable with a new work environment and lack clear direction, they often attempt to maintain their old procedures in parallel. Such employees often feel that their basic skills and organizational worth are being undermined. Knowledge workers, in particular, often seek new grounds to justify their presence and search out other things to do as work is removed from their queue.

J. Raymond Caron, president of CIGNA Systems, illustrated these concerns when he noted,

> When we began to automate some of our agents' activities, we thought we would have less work coming into our central offices for the underwriters to do and there would be a shift in the workload. That didn't happen, primarily because we underestimated the amount of work required to change traditional underwriting practice. And without a design change in the overall process, we didn't really achieve our goals. We now also have hundreds of financial types who are wizards at spreadsheet work. You have to ask the question, "How many times do you have to display this kind of data and who cares?"

Corporate policies that consciously promote continuity in employment and job security may work against achieving institutional changes, although they do help address some of the employee concerns discussed in Chapter 4. As Daniel Schutzer, vice president, Citibank, said,

> As a nation we have had a population boom and a need for full employment. We have had a reluctance until recently to lay people off, in part because we didn't have global competition until then. Now we're seeing a terrific downsizing as a result of the technology introductions of the past decade or two. This is a permanent restructuring. We'll never see those jobs come back again.

Excessive Project Scope

For many years, IT vendors and popular journals overemphasized the importance of large-scale "system solutions." Managers too often responded by seeking to install mega-projects with high visibility. Such projects generally have multiple objectives that must be reconciled and integrated across several divisions. Mega-projects tend to become very complex. And they often take inordinate amounts of time, investment risk, and political compromises to bring into being. As a result, even companies with well-established track records for innovative uses of IT have experienced difficulties with large-scale IT projects—as the examples of Federal Express (successful with Cosmos II, unsuccessful with Zap-mail) and American Airlines (successful with SABRE, unsuccessful with CONFIRM) testify. Citibank's Schutzer underscored these difficulties:

> When something becomes a big magnet project, everybody becomes focused on it. They throw in everything but the kitchen sink that they think about but might or might not really need. The business people don't necessarily know how easy or hard something is to do, and they are encouraged to be more elaborate by programmers or by technical project engineers. Before you know it, you're designing for many more functions than you can possibly deliver or need. The technical guys in an effort to promote the project have usually given unrealistic schedules, which the business people may believe because they don't know enough about the technology, or delve deeply enough into the details. Then one of three things happens: (1) Everything just gets so complicated it blows up, and you get major business reverses. (2) People just get tired and kill it quietly. Or (3) you announce a premature success and switch the thing over too soon without adequate testing. In any one of these scenarios, the result is a disaster and the hero whose ego is on the line usually dies.

Respondents explained why such mega-projects had been major sources of corporate IT investment inefficiency. First, because of their complexity, such projects cost more in time and investment terms. Second, by the time they were implemented, competitors might also have come out with similar systems, often at lower costs because of cheaper technologies developed during the innovator's prolonged development time. Third, because of delays, large programs also ran a much higher risk of not being matched to corporate or customer needs by the time they were implemented. When queried, most respondents said they now broke large-scale programs into a series of smaller projects and implemented these incrementally. (For details, see section below, "Compressing Project Scope and Payback Time.")

Technology-driven Investments in IT

Respondents reported that in earlier years, many purchases of IT were technology- or vendor-driven, rather than being determined by business needs or opportunities. At that time, many service firms had relatively little experience with advanced technologies and often lacked the expertise to articulate precisely their needs for IT or to challenge IT solutions proposed by vendors. Because of rapid advances in equipment, vendors usually could promise much greater technical capacity and flexibility at lower cost. Not wanting to lose competitiveness, top managers in service enterprises might agree to equipment purchases based on optimistic projections by lower-level technology champions and vendors. Frequently, important support systems—like software, optical scanning, labeling, or materials-handling systems—were inadequate, making it difficult to use the computers' full capabilities.

For example, many retail firms experienced major problems in using electronic scanning systems as a source of data for marketing, profitability analyses, customer micromarketing, and other service features at the customer interface. Existing software was too expensive to implement on mainframe computers; scanning equipment was not sufficiently accurate; bar-coding labeling was not as comprehensive or readable as retail applications required. Only as needed subsystems became available—especially vendor-generated labeling and decentralized microcomputing power—was full implementation possible.

Substantial improvements in IT, falling costs of IT, increasing customization of IT to meet user needs, diffusion of IT expertise throughout the ranks of senior management, and a much broader base of experience with IT have increased user sophistication substantially in recent years.

Difficulties in Software Development

Given the widespread availability of IT hardware and "shrink-wrapped" software, the only significant technological advantage that most innovators can keep as proprietary is software developed in-house. As critical as software is, however, software engineering is often very difficult to discipline. For a variety of reasons, software developers are often reluctant to take advantage of structured computer-assisted software engineering tools or macro programs (like METHOD 1,2) that would help to ensure the accuracy, completeness, and speed of their work. Meaningful metrics for tracking the output of software development have been particularly difficult to devise. Commonly used measures such as lines of code completed per day generally do not reflect either the complexity of a problem or the quality of the code, while function point systems are difficult to implement. As an example of the problem, Jon d'Alessio, then staff vice president and chief information officer, McKesson Corporation, stated,

> We don't have any formal measures of our own internal systems development productivity. We don't do function points or lines, or anything like that. There has been a great reluctance to do it by our systems staff. We have had major debates on what to measure, how to measure it. Basically, in the past we have had a culture of very creative people who were artists in building systems. We're trying to move it toward an engineering, disciplined approach. But artists don't like to be measured, and I'm not sure the engineers do either.

Difficulties in software development and engineering are not unique to the business community; software engineering remains a major challenge at the research frontiers of computer science.[3] The biggest problem today in software development is the inability to produce software on a large scale. Software development managers have treated software too much like an art form whose process of creation cannot be improved through the application of sound design and engineering principles. However, developments in the 1980s suggest that understanding of how to build large software systems efficiently and well is improving, and companies are beginning to achieve significant returns on investments devoted to software development. To some extent, the knowledge being developed has been codified.[4]

Some companies like AT&T, Arthur Andersen, and Marriott have systematized particular aspects of software development. But respondents to the committee's interviews said that new techniques and metrics for ensuring quality and productivity in software development are still required. The need for better standards and diffusion of software management capabilities will intensify as user systems become larger and more interactive. These may be the crucial bottlenecks to future IT progress.

CRITICAL ISSUES IN THE MANAGEMENT OF INFORMATION TECHNOLOGY

Other issues critical to the management of IT were identified in the committee's interviews and in its own deliberations. Many of the basic themes are not new, but the emphasis needed within each has changed. The most pervasive themes for improving the use of IT relate to (1) developing genuine information and IT strategies focused on achieving competitive advantage, (2) implementing cross-functional reengineering and restructuring of processes and organizations, (3) actively involving users and customers throughout the processes of design and implementation of IT projects, (4) developing customer-driven measures of quality, (5) compressing the scope and payback time of projects, (6) improving postproject audits, (7) carefully benchmarking processes and performance against those of outside sources, and (8) installing performance-evaluation and reward systems that are customer driven and that develop intellectual capital.

Information and IT Strategy Seeking Competitive Advantage

Most interviewed executives acknowledged the importance of having an IT strategy. However, the committee found that a majority of the firms contacted described their IT strategies as primarily components or extensions of divisional strategies. For the most part, programs were evaluated and prioritized as a part of divisional planning processes and subsequent procedures for allocating capital. Information technologies were regarded by a majority of the interviewed companies primarily as enablers for other desired divisional or corporate goals (e.g., cost reduction, new-product development, quality improvement). These companies' "IT strategies" were more long-range plans for investment in and installation of IT than explicit plans for integrating IT as part of a competitive positioning strategy. Some companies also had a separate corporate platform integration strategy with its own priorities. Further, some companies reported having a special information systems committee at the corporate level to review and coordinate individual strategic programs. Time horizons for IT plans varied considerably, but 80 percent of respondents operated on either a 3- or 5-year time horizon—updated annually through capital budgets and specific operational plans keyed in at 6-month to 1-year intervals. (See Question Box 1 in Appendix D.)

CIGNA Systems provides an interesting summary example of such practices. J. Raymond Caron noted,

> We have eleven businesses within CIGNA, and we have a strategy for each. Division by division is the way we put the plans together. In essence each division first puts down its wants and needs. Then the divisions prune this list by setting priorities in terms of capital availability and payoff. They draw a line in terms of what they agree to do and what they take off the table. In addition there is a corporate "platform integration" strategy. This is a kind of umbrella for all twelve systems in terms of data centers, computer platforms, communications, and applications. This largely has to do with CIGNA-Link, which is our PC LAN communications interconnection facility for all our businesses worldwide. Decisions about those are made at the corporate level, and we set overall guidance and direction at that level. As each division puts its strategies, plans, and budgets together, it is incumbent upon them to use those directions. The central infrastructure is budgeted and evaluated separately as a corporate investment, with a charge-back system based upon the amount of use that each area makes of a service.

A long-term plan for investing in IT and installing IT is an important beginning point, but a more strategic view (as has also been generated by CIGNA) is desirable. Many interviewed companies said that they had hired at top levels professionally trained IT managers familiar with the business. But with only a few exceptions, neither top managers nor the new IT managers described genuine information strategies that (1) would lead to distinctiveness or competitive preeminence for their companies or (2) provided specific quantitative targets to ensure that the set objectives were met. The committee believes that any information or IT plan is most likely to be successful when it is part of a well-integrated strategic plan that contains such elements. As applications of IT move from an emphasis on traditional cost-cutting toward more strategic concerns, a well-defined strategic process for integrating IT and customer needs becomes particularly important. Edward Hanway, president of CIGNA Worldwide, described his company's approach:

> We are using a team-oriented approach and a lot of new software technologies that allow a "try it, test it, fix it" type of development effort—as opposed to our historic approach, which was a long, involved, planning and document preparation process. We've been adamant in motivating these multifunctional teams, pushing them to realize that the challenge is not simply to save money. Efficiency is important, but the big issue is how successful we are with a customer or in the market.

Another critical component of any comprehensive information and IT strategy is engagement in that strategy by all levels of the organization. The mere involvement of chief executive officers, chief operating officers, and chief financial officers in developing the company's information strategy is not sufficient; true understanding and commitment are essential. To exploit the potential of IT in facilitating strategic change requires consistent long-term support across all divisions. Only top management can provide the patience, consistency, and reward structures that make it possible to execute forward-looking strategies despite urgent operating pressures. These are complex tasks requiring top-level finance, human resource, and operating champions to lead needed changes. For many companies, ensuring such leadership may require making major changes in the selection and promotion criteria used for top managers themselves.

Cross-Functional Reengineering and Reorganization

Successful installation of IT increasingly requires that both information technologists and user groups look beyond their old functional boundaries. Both applications-specific expertise and familiarity with the latest IT are critical. Ensuring continuous integration between technologists and users throughout planning and implementation both improves results and shortens design cycles. In the words of Edward Hanway,

> By closely integrating the people who do the IS [information systems] work into the management structure of the business units, we have gotten terrific results in a much quicker time frame than we ever would have hoped for previously. Attitudinally, there has been a major change. Now, there is none of that age-old "we versus they," or "throw the requirements over the wall and expect us to deliver" mentality. . . . The productivity of IS people has increased dramatically as a result.

Changing interfunctional processes usually requires readjusting organizational structures across those functions. Major restructuring, in turn, involves significant risk and takes time to accomplish smoothly. As a result, large organizations often implement such changes incrementally. To reduce risks they frequently run a series of smaller trials or experiments with potential new organizational modes, develop coaches for these modes, create systematic ways to learn from their experiments, and then attempt to diffuse this learning throughout the firm. All this takes time and continuous management attention.

To exploit IT effectively in such cases, the committee thought it helpful for managers to develop an explicit transition plan involving certain key steps. Critical among these is how to "reskill" the organization for its new roles—particularly for the flexible, multiskilled, team-oriented structures that seem to be emerging. Neither public education nor company training programs have been particularly attentive in the past to meeting the needs for new skills. Many companies lack experience with new organizational and operating modes and may need to seek the necessary expertise outside their own boundaries. As part of the process of change, companies often need new methods for evaluating the contributions of individuals and teams. Important among these are measures and incentives for their line managers to develop people (and systems) as "knowledge-based assets" (a topic discussed below in the section "Customer- and Knowledge-driven Performance Evaluation and Reward Systems").

Many respondents commented that the first performance gains from IT's use were often obtained by merely automating existing activities. But over 70 percent of respondents said that in today's environment, careful process analysis and reengineering are key to improving benefits from the use of IT. In its classic form, reengineering involves a series of rather well-understood steps:

1. Analyze the total process to determine whether it should be done at all, that is, whether its value added exceeds its costs;

2. Analyze each major step within the process to determine its value added versus its cost and whether it can be eliminated, simplified, or consolidated with another step;

3. At each major step, analyze each component activity, eliminating, consolidating, or simplifying those that remain;

4. Map the remaining component activities into a new system and analyze to see where further steps may be eliminated, consolidated, or simplified;

5. Install new organizational structures and systems specifically designed to implement the remaining activities as efficiently and effectively as possible; and

6. Follow up to ensure that the new process is operating as intended.

When ineffective processes are not reengineered, the application of IT to those processes simply results in performing ineffective processes more rapidly. Respondents often noted that important contributions to productivity and effectiveness through the use of IT frequently came less from the computerization of existing activities than from the transformation of a process itself.[5] Successful automation is often targeted first toward those steps that are most onerous, complex, boring, or time consuming. By defining and analyzing the steps and outputs of these processes down to their smallest repeatable microelements, IT-based systems can be introduced that operate at lowest cost, yet still maximize flexibility, control quality, and capture essential information for future use. When these steps were carefully undertaken with user and customer participation, startling results were often reported. Roger Ballou of American Express described that company's process and gains as follows:

> If you don't reengineer the work flow to take advantage of the technology, you're just doing the same inappropriate things quicker. People have a tendency not to think about what the technology will let them do once it's in; they just do what they're doing today. In a simple example, our business travel operations historically had something like 31 manual checks done to ensure accuracy, lowest fare, and things like that. In two stages we automated about 75 percent of those quality assurance checks. To do this right we had to reengineer the whole work flow of the reservation process and ticketing functions in our offices.
>
> If we had just put the automation in, because of the 25 percent of checks that still have to be done manually, we probably would not have generated any substantial savings. But by designing a statistically valid sampling technique that could ensure accuracy levels above 98 percent on this manual 25 percent, we have been able to generate tremendous savings. We have a department of process engineering that provides the technical expertise for these tasks, but they do it in and with the offices affected. We call the process "brown paper reviews," because when they go into the offices they use big sheets of brown paper to lay out the process engineering work flows of all steps, working with counselors and with office personnel to get ownership of the solution.

A cross-functional and strategic orientation to process development is critical. Without it functional groups are likely to introduce IT on an internal ad hoc basis without considering performance gains that might be obtained by looking outside their traditional organizational boundaries. Such an approach often has led to major suboptimizations. Because most organizations tend to grow initially around specialized functional expertise, over time a number of steps may be built into business processes merely to accommodate functional decision making and the power politics associated with functional structures. Appropriate reengineering can break down these structures and substitute cross-functional processes and team decision making, offering new opportunities and payoffs. Increasingly, improved communications and capabilities for data exchange enhance and enable these opportunities.

At CIGNA Corporation, Melvin Ollestad, senior vice president, Claims, Employee Benefits Division, described how his corporation's cross-functional reengineering is specifically matched to customer needs:

> The company has a Systems Development Methodology (SDM) for cross-functional design. In our division, first of all we now try to decide how we want to run the business, what is the best way to serve customers. We try to understand exactly what that means and to reengineer how we want to deliver each specific service. Then we put in place the technology to support us in doing that. We had become functionalized within the offices so that we had one group of people opening the mail, a second doing basic inputs to record a claim, a third group to do data entry, another group for the adjudication process, other specialists on various kinds of claims for reference purposes, and still another group that generally answered questions, phone calls, and so on.
>
> The idea of putting together teams of people and dedicating them with appropriate IT support to customers appeared to be a good way to get a needed transformation. It has had the benefit of aligning us much better and more deeply with our customers. The customers like it a lot. The employees feel better about having control, being able to make decisions, and being heard. We also find that we need fewer management supervisory people, and the ones we do have are in a facilitating mode, which is more rewarding to them as people get used to the process.

Interviewed companies repeatedly reported that, when cross-functional reengineering is focused on specific problems, total processing times could drop from days or weeks to a few hours or minutes. Box 5.2 presents an example from the literature. From the customer's viewpoint, cross-functional structures also often prove to be much more effective with respect to quality, improving both efficiency and responsiveness to customers' needs.

J. Raymond Caron of CIGNA Systems described that company's approach to cross-functional reengineering and the benefits received from that approach:

> **BOX 5.2 Reduction of Application Processing Time at the IBM Credit Corporation**
>
> The IBM Credit Corporation provides financing for potential customers of IBM computers, software, and services. Prior to reengineering of operations, a typical credit request took approximately 6 days from submission to approval. Several people handled each request: order takers, credit checkers, pricers, and the like. However, managers discovered that the actual processing time for the typical credit request was 90 minutes: for most of the 6 days, the credit request sat on someone's desk. The company reengineered its operations, replacing specialists in the different departments with a single generalist—a "deal structurer"—who processed an entire credit request from beginning to end. For difficult applications that might require more expertise for proper processing, the deal structurer calls on a small pool of specialists. IBM Credit Corporation cut its average turnaround time from 6 days to 4 hours; in addition, it now processes 100 times as many deals as before with a slightly smaller work force.
>
> SOURCE: Hammer, Michael, and James Champy. 1993. *Reengineering the Corporation: A Manifesto for Business Revolution*, Harper Collins, New York, May.

We now have two kinds of reengineering. We have functional reengineering and what we have termed *strategic reengineering*. In a functional reengineering setting, we work with a claims department, an underwriting department, or a marketing department, looking at the processes within the function. The more powerful and difficult approach is strategic reengineering. Strategic reengineering looks at the way a business is performed from the customer's viewpoint, and slices it across our very strong functions. This approach clears things up very quickly in terms of what adds value, what does not add value, what gets in the way of meeting customer needs, and what the cost is of providing products and services. We try wherever possible to include in the effort customers, distributors, and all of the organizations within the business that are involved with the value chain, as well as suppliers. This type of reengineering takes a lot of effort to do because of our strong historical functional organization bias. But we find it yields the most results.

At BankAmerica, Martin Stein, vice chairman, noted,

One of the effects of IT is that we now have really two types of organizations. We have our traditional hierarchical, vertical organization, where we tend to centralize things like back-office functions. But IT has also created a real operating organization which goes the other way, and that's based on cross-functional teams. Our COIN [Customer On-line Information Network] system has worked because people formed a cross-functional design team to match this process where you couldn't tell users from technology people. The projects that succeed on a large scale appear to have those characteristics; the ones that fail don't. We're at the point now where if we don't see that type of informal cross-functional work team organization, we won't do the project.

Carefully implemented, cross-functional process mapping and reengineering—along with use of self-directed teams—can result in the elimination of numerous steps and often two or three organizational layers involved in managing interfunctional processes. For companies interviewed by the committee, such approaches frequently resulted in real-time (computer-based) interactions and much-enhanced (personnel-based) responses to customers. For example, self-directed "800 number" teams supported by new IT systems often consolidated various order-processing, customer-inquiry, customer-response, field-dispatching, and trouble-shooting activities that had built up huge functional bureaucracies in the past. Such interfunctional applications were among the highest "quick-payoff" applications of IT reported in interviews.

Traditional hierarchical management structures are difficult to reconcile with the needs of cross-functional teams. Successfully reengineered business processes often result in very flat, network, team, cluster, inverted, or other new organizational modes.[6] Indeed, the full realization of benefits from using IT generally requires not just extensive investments in hardware but a complete overhaul of the firm's traditional organizations, systems, practices, and culture. Very few respondents said that they had an explicitly stated goal of flattening an enterprise's organizational structure by using IT. Such goals, announced publicly, might generate considerable resistance to change. However, the potential payoff is high enough to warrant conscious consideration—and planning—for organizational restructuring in any proposed process change. In fact, a majority (60 percent to 80 percent) of companies interviewed by the committee found that the use of IT had had an impact on their organizational structure (e.g., changing spans of control, facilitating organizational flattening, or encouraging use of self-directed teams). But very few had made a full transition to supporting their new organizational structures with both new customer-oriented measures of performance and new reward systems. Many said that they were experimenting with such changes now. Companies reported both increased centralization (usually in data centers or databases) and increased decentralization (usually in operations) resulting from their use of IT. (See Question Box 5 in Appendix D.)

Continuous User and Customer Involvement

Direct and intimate user involvement in the specification, design, and implementation of IT systems was a strong contributing condition for success in the vast majority (over 85 percent) of the companies interviewed by the committee. (See Question Box 6 in Appendix D.) This is not surprising, since the applications-specific knowledge needed for effective implementation is far more likely to reside in the minds of users (whose job it is to understand the application) than in the minds of information technologists (whose job it is to understand the technology).

Many of the companies interviewed by the committee found that external customers also have a valuable role to play during the planning and installation of IT-based systems. Unfortunately, relatively few companies directly involved such customers beyond early specification stages—i.e., in system design or implementation. Because customer needs ultimately define the nature and success of many applications, direct input and feedback from external customers can be very helpful in creating effective IT systems. As IT applications become more strategic, involving external customers may become even more important. Modern software and improved development practices can facilitate the kind of highly interactive prototyping that greatly increases both the quantity and quality of user input. The most effective user and customer involvement occurs when:

- *Users and customers participate interactively.* Since user and customer needs are often difficult to conceptualize and articulate, close user interaction with information technologists, or still better, interaction with possible prototypes, can help uncover hidden but real needs. Focus groups and experimental facilities for testing consumers' responses are important ways to obtain input, but observing users interacting with a prototype can add important new insights. A vice president of a major airline described that company's approach:

> We have consumer inputs for our system designs from the airports where we have implemented test systems. In addition, we have user inputs from the people who are actually working at the counter. For them, we use a prototyping technique where we actually are coding and developing right along with the users. As we put in a feature, they will recommend changes, redesign it, implement it, continually modify it, until we have reached something we all feel is satisfactory.

- *Users and customers are involved continuously.* Because many factors critically affecting usability are decided not in original specifications, but in design and implementation stages, many companies have found it very helpful to involve users and customers throughout implementation. As BankAmerica's Martin Stein stated:

If we can't get user commitment, no matter how important the system is, we won't do it. We try to do reengineering with each process change. But it is not a complete reengineering before installing the technology. It's almost an existential process. We reengineer it as we go along. One of the things we discovered is that if we are really smart, we get the benefits we say, but often it turns out that we don't get them from the places we thought we would. If you have a situation where there is a clear general idea of what the payoffs are and there are compelling economics, as you go along you get more perfect knowledge of where the gains are and can guide the process in those directions. Each reengineering iteration seems to refine it. We use interfunctional teams to let us design within these dynamics.

- *Groupware technology facilitates collaboration.* Collaboration among technologists, users, and customers located in geographically separated sites can be cumbersome and can make rapid changes and iterations difficult. Moreover, maintaining multiple versions of a large development system can become a logistics nightmare. Technology that provides computer support for cooperative work, called "groupware," can reduce the impact of physical dispersion, as well as provide for managing a system with multiple developers or multiple users. At Chase Manhattan, Craig Goldman, senior vice president and chief information officer, reported,

Using Lotus Notes my developers, working with customers, can develop applications in hours and days that once took months and years. These are very user-friendly applications, with a high degree of rapid prototyping. Now our customers can actually see the development taking place before their eyes. What this has done is to make them believers that things can be done. They have wound up spending more time than they ever would have in the past working with the developers, interfacing with them, and actually developing the technology. We have come up with better input and better ideas from the key people using the technology, and also better products coming out the back end because there was greater involvement on the part of customers. In some of our areas, this involvement extends to surveys that go right out to our external customers.

Customer-driven Measures of Quality

One of the more important trends in managing IT is the attempt to develop better metrics to measure and manage quality from the customer's viewpoint. As in manufacturing, companies' financial measures of revenues or returns may provide poor gauges of the quality of output, especially in the short run. Several respondent companies had developed elaborate formal nonfinancial measures of service quality. The most straightforward of these involved internal engineering metrics. Since service quality is often produced in the same moment that the service is consumed, many respondents had installed on-line (real-time) IT systems to ensure the delivery of crucial elements of quality that could not be achieved otherwise.

Thus when financial service representatives pull up the file on a new product, they are constrained by numerous rules, limits, and procedures—built into the software—to ensure that all relevant data are checked and that no impermissible commitments are made. The customer is served faster and more accurately, yet the costs of internal processing and errors are reduced. Fast-food operations' electronic systems ensure that inventories do not go stale, staffing levels are maintained, cooking temperatures and cycles are correct, customer bills are properly itemized and added, and so on. Such systems allow relatively untrained people to perform tasks accurately that they previously could have performed only imperfectly, if at all. For more sophisticated professional activities, such as design or maintenance operations, architectural management, legal work, accounting audits, bioassays, real-estate evaluations, and investment banking, on-line IT systems have been implemented to ensure a thoroughness, consistency, and quality never before possible.

However, despite their utility, engineering metrics and IT systems that monitor the performance of internal operations can ensure only that internal operations are proceeding as designed, not that those internal operations are providing the customer with real value. Moreover, what the company regards as higher-quality output (more customized service, or a faster response) may not in fact be perceived by customers as more desirable, especially if they must pay more for it. Companies have often found upon checking that customers cared far more about reliability in delivery or pleasant personalities in contact people than about fast response times. They can discover this only by interviewing customers.

As a result, sophisticated companies are beginning to pay substantial attention to measures of quality that are customer-based. A surprising number (43 percent) of the companies interviewed by the committee had instituted such measures.[7] Although companies try to collect as much data as possible through automated means, a complete evaluation procedure should also normally include some random visits, customer sampling, and personal observations as assessment tools. These are especially important in understanding certain significant dimensions of point-of-contact service performance—like cheerfulness, creativeness, responsiveness, professionalism, or other key characteristics of personal service.

Service companies in particular have taken a leadership role in developing customer-oriented measures of quality. Quality in services often requires extensive interaction at the point of customer contact, is of prime importance to the customer, and has a high potential impact on future sales. As in manufacturing, there tends to be a strong positive correlation between service quality and lower cost. The elimination of errors in producing a service decreases the costs of coordination and rework, customer service costs, and customer complaints (to say nothing of the unmeasured and possibly greater costs of losses of goodwill at the customer level). Two examples suggest the kinds of approaches companies take to improve levels of customer service while decreasing costs:

- McKesson has defined 42 "customer satisfactors" that it surveys externally and measures internally on a routine basis. A seven-page questionnaire goes to over 1000 customers every year, and updates are made quarterly on a smaller set of factors considered to be the most important. McKesson is now trying to link these "satisfactors" to its compensation-incentive systems. At the strategic level, McKesson also emphasizes five themes for competitiveness: customer-supplier satisfaction, people development, market positioning, relative net delivered cost, and innovation. For all of these factors, McKesson uses internal and external metrics to track its own and competitors' positions as perceived by customers.

- MCI, in addition to using on-line measures of technical quality, does in-depth customer surveys about twice a year and uses the results of other customer questionnaires administered at a lower level of detail (10 questions) monthly. In addition it makes extensive use of focus groups and other techniques to check its general image. Every customer with more than approximately $30,000 a month in billings is surveyed in detail once a year, either informally or through in-depth interviews. The in-depth interviews are done by an outside company. MCI does its own statistical analysis of the surveys that come in from the samples for residential customers. It also uses focus groups to get a more personalized feel for how those customers are responding to particular services. MCI uses formal measures of loss rates, geographically, by customer service center. In its business communications division, MCI measures these quality factors by branch office at 132 branches. It also measures loss rates by customer segment and does an extensive employee satisfaction survey every 18 months, considering that to be an important factor in customer service.

Respondents reported on a number of other experiments aimed at measuring service quality at the customer level. Nevertheless, interviews indicated little direct use of customer-driven metrics in measuring the performance of specific departments. There was an even greater gap in converting such measures into performance incentives for contact groups. And at the time of the interviews, no companies had converted either the results of customer surveys of quality or data on customers' observations into useful financial measures of service performance. These are important areas for future management attention.

Compressing Project Scope and Payback Time

Increasingly, companies face the dichotomy that while they seek to increase paybacks from IT through more strategic (usually more complex and longer-range) programs, the life cycle of each generation of technology is becoming shorter. To manage this anomaly, many interviewed companies said that they now proceed incrementally on large IT projects.

These companies said that they consciously seek to break such projects down into smaller, more discrete segments—each of which can (1) be justified individually and (2) be integrated incrementally into an agreed-upon system architecture. The broad goals of the overall project and its general costs and benefits are analyzed. Then the output and input characteristics of each major module (and its needed interface standards) are established. These are used to discipline all subsidiary project designs. Then the program is broken down into definable smaller projects, each with finite timing and payoffs. As early projects are successfully implemented, they help to reduce the real and perceived risk on the total project. Early paybacks lower the present value of the total investment. Initial feedback from early projects can be used to guide those that come later in the sequence. Overall project management is simplified and more focused. And there is less political resistance to large-scale projects as early successes ease concerns.

To implement changes in large systems incrementally, companies indicated that they often developed and tested individual modules on a small scale or in a single operating division. As these projects proved their viability, they might then be integrated for testing with other successful projects on a local scale or be rolled out as discrete projects across various divisions. As a result of such practices, companies could achieve faster paybacks (by not having to wait for the entire program to be completed), and risks were reduced.

Despite the rapid rate of improvement and turnover that abbreviates the life cycle of much IT equipment, only a minority (30 percent) of the interviewed companies said that they had a special "hurdle rate" for IT investments vis-à-vis other investments. (See Question Box 1 in Appendix D.) Instead, they adjusted for the relatively quick obsolescence of IT equipment by introducing faster depreciation rates into their calculations.

As a prioritizing device, some companies sought 6- to 9-month payoffs on IT projects. Others noted that among successfully implemented projects, the time to actual payoffs rarely exceeded 3 years. For example, Chase Manhattan's Craig Goldman said, "In the data center arena, you have to pay project investments back in the year you make the investment. We are planning on reducing our absolute costs over the next 3 years, every year while we enjoy a 25 percent volume growth; there's a program to support it." At CIGNA Corporation, James Stewart, executive vice president and chief financial officer, stated: "Increasingly we are shortening the planning time frame. We are focused on shorter-term paybacks rather than building galactic systems. The planning time frame has shortened from the traditional galactic 2 to 3 years down to 6 months."

Planning for payback within shorter periods helps manage technological risks. Fast and effective implementation can also have strong strategic significance. As McKesson's Jon d'Alessio said,

> On the application side, you get the possibility of a competitive edge for a while. But the lead time for your corporation is not very long; you clearly don't get a sustainable edge because competitors can respond so quickly. How efficiently you implement, how effectively you do it, and how quickly and well you translate concepts into better customer service—those are the things that differentiate companies.

Many companies interviewed by the committee had further improved control by (1) demanding that divisional systems follow corporate-wide interface and software standards for compatibility and interoperability, (2) employing corporate-level allocation and follow-up processes for interdivisional strategic and infrastructure projects, and (3) using more systematic preproject analyses and postproject audits than in earlier years.

Postproject Audits

The committee found that virtually all interviewed companies reported using formal evaluation procedures for IT projects (which lent themselves to such analyses) before investments were made. (See Question Box 2 in Appendix D.) But postproject evaluations were less universally pursued. A majority (64 to 68 percent) did attempt audits on certain types of projects, notably cost-reduction and new-product programs. Audits for other types of projects were less frequent. (See Question Box 3 in Appendix D.) Postproject audits were often said to be erratic or spotty. This was of some concern to both the committee and to many respondents, despite the fact that a large majority of respondent companies that had undertaken overall assessments claimed acceptable to high payoffs on their IT investments. Some examples illustrate various viewpoints:

• At the Travelers Companies, Larry Bacon, senior vice president, commented,

> Do we do postinvestment audits consistently across the board? No, it's very spotty. Our decentralized style dictates that the divisions run their own businesses. Some divisions do audits very rigorously; others don't. On each project, however, we try to make sure that we do capture the intended benefits.

- At SuperValu, H.S. Smith, vice president, said,

We do cost-benefit analyses prior to the execution of each project. In the past we haven't really been very religious about auditing after the fact. We have audited our capital appropriations, but we don't capitalize software, so we have not audited the results of that.

- At Citibank, Daniel Schutzer said,

I think we are probably equally guilty with everyone else as far as keeping records and checking how well we succeeded on projects and whether we really did achieve expected benefits. We constantly check the milestones for the development itself: whether we delivered in 2 years for the $5 million proposed or whether we slipped and overran. But we don't really systematically ask: Is the project increasing revenue the way we thought? Is it reducing costs or personnel? Sometimes, if there is an immediate reduction of personnel, that measurement may be taken. But for some of the other kinds of incidental benefits—revenue increases, expense savings—it's not clear to me that we do a good job of following up.

Many had installed more rigorous procedures in the last few years. They thought that installing such procedures would undoubtedly force operating and information systems managers to concentrate more on specifying and achieving planned gains, and that this presumably would improve future measured performance gains from using IT. However, in the committee's interviews very few companies mentioned going to the next high-payoff step of systematically analyzing postproject audits to ascertain and catalog those success or failure patterns that could assist in selecting and managing future IT programs. There was little evidence that formal post hoc evaluations were directly used to guide future capital or program budgeting allocations. Further, such appraisals were seldom used to evaluate line managers' performance or to set metrics for incentive plans. All these seem worthy considerations in improving future program management.

Benchmarking Against Specialized Outside Providers

Benchmarking examines how one's own performance of an activity compares to that of others performing the same activity. Benchmarking studies generally provide better information about business processes than about specific costs. Definitions of data and what is included in various cost categories vary widely among companies. These definitional problems are compounded by all of the usual problems about measuring service output. Consequently, comparisons of best-practice processes generally are more productive. Companies can make significant gains (1) by evaluating and modifying "best practices" observed externally and (2) by deploying their own best practices more widely internally. In addition to improving many processes directly, comparisons with outsiders can also send signals to groups within the company being benchmarked that their performance can be checked against that of outside service groups and that they must keep up with competitive practices.

The committee found that benchmarking had generally been undertaken only relatively recently. Most interviewed companies benchmarked primarily against other competing peer firms. Only a few (less than 30 percent) mentioned benchmarking against internal "best-in-class" activities in their own firms or in noncompeting external firms. Fewer still benchmarked against specialized external service providers—like ADP Services, EDS, or ServiceMaster—which have widespread reputations for efficiency. Although outsourcing of data centers has become a $7 billion to $10 billion industry in the United States and Japan,[8] few interviewed companies mentioned outsourcing as a direct result of their benchmarking studies. More often they updated, consolidated, or modified their internal processes themselves. A major exception was MCI. Richard Liebhaber noted:

> Where I get my view of 5- or 10-year technology is by visiting vendors. People ask me how many development engineers I have working for MCI. I say I have 19,000—but they don't work for me—they work for 74 vendors. I view all those vendor engineering people as working for me. So, we go out into their laboratories, find out what they are doing, and influence what they are doing.

A particularly useful type of benchmarking can result when groups of companies voluntarily pool their own information and agree jointly to sponsor a consulting firm to undertake a detailed study of comparative practices. Data on relative performance are then fed back to individual firms. Each firm's own data are specified for its internal use, but the identity of the remaining participants is disguised by normalizing size (or other distinguishing features) and identifying competing companies only as A, B, or C. For the companies interviewed, such practices offered useful relative calibrations, although not specific financial standards for service performance. For example,

- CIGNA Corporation used outside consultants to compare unit costs of its back office and data centers versus competitors' unit costs for such services (in terms of tape drives, databases, CPUs, and so on). This engineering cost-driven study did not address returns on investment or make specific comparisons with specialized outsiders such as EDS.
- BankAmerica compared its IT performance against that of other competitive institutions in terms of certain key measurements of effectiveness on an anonymous basis. It also used noncompeting peer groups (such as the member companies of the Research Board) for similar comparisons, but it had not specifically evaluated its overall investments in IT with respect to paybacks.

The following quotes summarize how some other successful companies approached benchmarking:

- At Chase Manhattan, Craig Goldman said,

We have done some very specific studies both internally and with the help of external sources to peg us vis-à-vis competition in a number of key areas. In one, we hired Nolan Norton. They took our data from five or six major facilities and compared them to a cross-section of other companies. There was a second study done by Price-Waterhouse that said on an individual basis, each of those data centers were efficient—and significantly more cost-effective than if we outsourced them. Overall we found we are close to being as efficient as we could get from an outsourcing contract today. By doing further consolidations, we will be more efficient. In addition, we hired Booz Allen to look at our major competitors and to give us some comparative data both on efficiency levels and relative performance trends. We have also made major strides in migrating to common platforms and systems, looked around the network, and picked up the modules from each sector that made the most sense.

- NationsBank's Patrick Campbell, senior vice president, Technology Planning, described that company's approach:

In Dallas, we have a very strong IT user community. For example we have J.C. Penney's, Frito-Lay, American Airlines, Southwest Airlines, and so on. We have begun dialogues with representatives of these firms in "user communities" or "user groups." By exchanging information with noncompetitors, we can take pages out of their book just about every day and not have to reinvent the wheel. This benchmarking group is very selective about who can join. One of the rules is that the prospects need to be Dallas-based so we have close proximity. Basically, participants must be at the corporate office level and hold the position of senior technology planner on the company team. None of the companies can compete directly with one another.

We also benchmark our internal operations against established outsourcing suppliers on a continuing basis. We do "best-in-class" analyses of their processes as well. We try to position ourselves between the outside vendor community, like AT&T or IBM, and our customers. One of the benchmarks to which we compare ourselves is the ability to provide IT services to our internal and external users at a competitive price. In other words, if AT&T can perform a service for 12 cents a minute, our gauge is to be *less* than 12 cents per minute. If we can do that, we are basically in a sound business position; we are not a net overhead cost the way many organizations are.

Benchmarking has received widespread attention only in recent years. Even so, the most common type of benchmarking appears to be a comparison of a firm's performance in a given activity to that of other peer companies. Comparisons to specialized service providers, to smaller firms, and to firms not in the same industry are much rarer. Since activities are relatively generic (as noted in Chapter 4), it should not matter to the benchmarking company whether the best-practice provider of a given activity is a peer company or an external specialized service provider. Including specialized external service providers in the comparison group can be especially useful, because such companies make their living by concentrating on an activity and providing it more efficiently or effectively than others.

Customer- and Knowledge-driven Performance Evaluation and Reward Systems

A company's prosperity in the long run is intimately linked to the way in which its reward structures are aligned with its corporate goals. The committee discussed in depth the question of whether in corporations of the future, the management of intellect (or intellectual processes) and the capital embodied in knowledge-based assets will be the primary bases on which they compete. Even today, knowledge-based service activities such as research, design, product or process development, buying, trading, marketing, advertising, systems integration, software development, and logistics management contribute most of the value added in manufacturing enterprises. Whole service industries like consulting, accounting, financial services, the law, health care, entertainment, and many aspects of the communications field also depend on the value added by intellectual processes.

The most valuable assets of firms in these industries typically lie in their technological and professional know-how, their flexible response and innovation structures, and their knowledge about customers and markets. These assets reside in the minds of individual staff members, in software programs, in information and management systems, and in the databases of the companies. Indeed the management of intellectual capital may well be a major factor in determining who survives and who does not in the coming years. To quote Walter B. Wriston from *The Twilight of Sovereignty*, "Information, in the words of Leon Martel, is 'rapidly replacing energy as society's main transforming resource.'"[9]

Some studies have suggested that the management-evaluation and incentive infrastructures of companies have not yet been adjusted to take full advantage of the opportunities that the use of IT offers.[10] The committee's interviews support these contentions as they pertain to performance evaluation and reward structures. If a firm's competitive edge rests on its knowledge-based assets and its superior customer service, reward systems need to be able to measure such assets, to recognize individuals and teams whose work contributes to superior customer service, and to reward these people accordingly (Box 5.3 gives an example).

> **BOX 5.3 A Knowledge-based Reward System**
>
> In 1992, Salomon Brothers was planning to install an employee compensation system based on the knowledge that people bring to their work. A new employee with no knowledge about the financial business receives a certain level of base pay. Employees are organized into teams that specialize in various products such as corporate bonds. To earn a raise, the employee must complete an assignment on a certain set of skills; as the employee masters a wider and wider variety of skills through progressively more difficult assignments, his or her compensation will increase.
>
> Salomon Brothers expects that employees trained under this new arrangement will complete transactions more quickly. But it expects its biggest payoffs from how decisions about new products and evaluations of new businesses are made.
>
> SOURCE: Gabor, Andrea. 1992. "After the Pay Revolution, Job Titles Won't Matter," *New York Times*, May 17, Business Section, p. 5.

However, few respondents reported direct connections between (1) their customer-based measures of performance and quality and the incentives offered to those handling contacts with end customers (although many said they were currently experimenting with such arrangements) or (2) improvements in knowledge-based assets and rewards given to managers. It is ironic that financial markets often reflect the value of intellectual assets (through a company's "Q value," i.e., its market value versus the replacement value of its physical assets) but that the company's own books and performance-evaluation systems rarely do. The value of such assets does not appear in published financial data or in the "asset" accounts used for internal controls. The omission of such factors in performance evaluation and reward systems could pose major long-term problems for service companies competing in a customer-driven, information-intensive era.

SUMMARY AND CONCLUSIONS

Although a large percentage of interviewed companies felt they had received adequate to high payoffs from using IT, there were a number of areas in which the committee thought managers could seek greater performance advantages. Principal among these were (1) developing and obtaining top management commitment to genuine information and IT strategies focused on gaining strategic advantage, (2) more extensive cross-functional reengineering and reorganization of processes affected by IT, (3) expanded user and customer involvement in all aspects of the design and implementation of IT projects, (4) improved customer-driven measures of quality installed and in use, (5) an increased focus on shorter-term payoffs for IT investments within a long-term strategic framework, (6) better-developed postproject audits, (7) more external benchmarking and increased consideration of "best-practice" processes from outside specialist service groups, and (8) expanded use of customer- and knowledge-driven performance measurement and reward systems throughout the firm. Even the committee's sample of sophisticated respondent companies often needed improvement in these areas. Most of the problems respondents reported in achieving payoffs from investment in IT—when such problems existed—came not from overinvesting in IT, but from management inadequacies in planning and implementing IT systems. Both Chapters 3 and 5 have highlighted some of the more interesting ways experienced managers have found to improve their success in using IT's potentials. Nevertheless, there is room for further improvement.

NOTES AND REFERENCES

[1] Strassmann, P. 1990. *The Business Value of Computers*, Information Economics Press, New Canaan, Conn.

[2] Roach, S. 1989. "Pitfalls of a New Assembly Line: Can Services Learn from Manufacturing?," Morgan Stanley, New York. Also, Roach, Stephen S. 1991. "Services Under Siege: The Restructuring Imperative," *Harvard Business Review*, September-October, pp. 82-91.

[3] Computer Science and Telecommunications Board, National Research Council. 1992. *Computing the Future*, National Academy Press, Washington, D.C. Also, Computer Science and Technology Board, National Research Council. 1989. *Scaling Up: A Research Agenda for Software Engineering*, National Academy Press, Washington, D.C.

[4] Humphrey, Watts S. 1989. *Managing the Software Development Process*, Addison-Wesley, Reading, Mass.

[5] In these cases, IT itself is not irrelevant. IT often provides a key element in the new process.

[6] A discussion of these organizational modes can be found in Quinn, James Brian, 1992, *Intelligent Enterprise*, Free Press, New York, Chapters 4 and 5.

[7] Other studies indicate that many service institutions lack such formal feedback techniques for measuring the quality of services. For example, one study found that 70 to 90 percent of all banks were in this category. See Giesler, E., and A. Rubenstein. 1988. "Measurement of Efficiency and Effectiveness in the Selection, Usage, and Evaluation of Information Technology in the Services Industries," Joint Meeting of Institute for Illinois and Industry Information Council, August 31.

[8] The National Academy of Engineering is currently studying some important aspects of outsourcing that will be discussed in a forthcoming National Academy of Engineering report, *Preparing a Global Economy: A New Mission for U.S. Technology*.

[9] Wriston, Walter B. 1992. *The Twilight of Sovereignty*, Scribners, New York.

[10] McKensie, R., and R. Walton. 1988. "Implementation of Information Technology: Human Resource Issues," MIT, Sloan School of Management, Management in the 1990s Program, Cambridge, Mass.

6
Information Technology in Services: Implications for Public Policy

Information technology (IT) has contributed to the growing economic importance of services, and that contribution is expected to increase substantially. This report has documented, for example, the dramatic growth in electronic transactions, yet the fact that most business transactions still involve direct cash or paper checks suggests that what has been seen to date is only the beginning of a long-term transition in the conduct of services. Continued advances in computing and communications technologies, development of new features and applications, and increases in their affordability and ease of use will drive the further integration of IT into services.[1] Pacing that integration will be growth in the understanding of how best to select, introduce, support, and manage IT. Inasmuch as people learn from early successes and failures, future applications are expected to be more successful on average than those of the past. Experimentation will continue; there will still be failures as well as successes in the use of IT in services.

The spread of IT to date owes much to market forces—there has been no explicit national policy aimed at promoting the use of IT in services. As discussed in Chapter 2, conditions in different industries have motivated different types and rates of IT application; as discussed in Chapter 3, specific applications arise from conditions, options, and approaches perceived by individual management teams. The accumulated experience with IT in services now raises questions about potential market inefficiencies and implications for social welfare, concerns that may argue for public policy intervention. How rapidly and smoothly can adjustments be made to take place? How can the benefits and costs be widely and fairly distributed? How can positive impacts be facilitated and negative impacts ameliorated? How can policymakers better track and anticipate relevant trends? This chapter first discusses some important policy issues and then introduces some specific policy options related primarily to (1) employment shifts associated with the use of IT, (2) investment in IT, and (3) research relating to the application of IT and the changing structure of the economy that the committee believes should be seriously considered. The emphasis is on identifying areas of need rather than detailed specification of recommended actions. Implications for management action are discussed in Chapter 5.

IMPLICATIONS FOR MACROECONOMIC AND FISCAL POLICY

As this report is being written, the slow economic recovery is motivating public policy interest in economic growth. One important contributor to economic growth is investment, and one vehicle often suggested for stimulating investment is tax incentives.[2] However, this study indicates that there is no evidence that significant lack of investment in IT has slowed growth in productivity, while there is evidence that a number of (sometimes measurable) benefits have accrued in several industries. Moreover, continuing improvements in IT's functionality and affordability suggest that IT will be used to help lower entry barriers in some markets as well as open possibilities for new kinds of business.[3] **Any investment stimulus enacted by government should not discriminate against investment in IT (software and support as well as hardware). The market should decide how to allocate investment dollars among alternative uses of capital.**

The findings of this study also suggest that the benefits of investment in IT within the U.S. will not all be captured domestically. IT is being used to facilitate the globalization of business, enabling enterprises to manage effectively over a wider geographical area and to shift some activities and associated employment overseas. Greater availability of capital overseas and the worldwide integration of markets and capital resources through IT are other factors promoting globalization. Thus, in the absence of mechanisms to reward local spending, there is no guarantee that policies designed to encourage investment or demand will necessarily increase jobs within the United States. Because of its collateral effects, investment overseas is not necessarily a macroeconomic problem, but it may create problems for local communities in which job losses may occur. Local job creation may require incentives for local investment.

One type of IT-related investment with many local benefits is investment in the domestic telecommunications and information infrastructure.[4]

The proliferation of IT to date has relied in part on a strong national telecommunications network (specifically, a complex of local and national networks). Large enterprises have built their own, private networking capabilities to contain costs, secure advanced capabilities, and gain competitive advantages, but smaller enterprises, in particular, depend on the public infrastructure that is provided by telecommunications service companies.[5]

A second arena likely to benefit from a powerful telecommunications and information infrastructure is the private home. Widespread access to networked IT in private homes is likely to lead to the creation of large home-based markets for new products (e.g., devices or services based on or enabled by multimedia technology). Consistent with the pass-through-of-benefits phenomenon discussed in Chapter 3, these new markets will in all likelihood generate public or private financial gains that far exceed those realized by the first companies entering these new markets.

The increasing integration of computing and communications, the assimilation of IT as part of the infrastructure of an enterprise, and the growing dependence of enterprises on IT all indicate that advanced information infrastructure will be important to achieving the benefits of IT in service activities. Information infrastructure can also assist in the delivery of training, as recommended above; there is growing interest at all levels in the use of electronic networks to deliver educational services.

To date, market forces have generally worked well in providing access to IT benefits. But in some geographical areas, selectively stimulating the growth of information infrastructure—particularly for small business, educational institutions, medical care systems, and the home—could enhance interactions among all these units, promote expansion in both the number and types of jobs in the service sector, and possibly lead to the creation of entirely new service industries. **Given the potentially broad impacts, information infrastructure—including investment in relevant research and development—deserves special consideration in public policy.[6] However, wherever possible, the United States should allow the market to optimize the allocation of resources.** The country has an opportunity to expand on the relative advantage it currently has in many areas of telecommunications. A number of countries (e.g., newly industrializing and central European nations) have obviously weak infrastructures; but virtually all countries have targeted information infrastructure for improvement as a vehicle for economic development and growth.[7]

BACKGROUND ON EMPLOYMENT ISSUES RAISED BY INFORMATION TECHNOLOGY IN SERVICES

It is impossible to isolate the effects of IT on employment from the many other factors that affect it. In general, the application of new technology may initially give rise to job displacement and job change because by definition new technology changes the way output is produced as well as the output itself. Historically, the evidence indicates that the displacement effects have been temporary: over the long term, new technology and production processes tend to promote productivity, competitiveness, and economic growth, all of which contribute to job growth over time.[8] MIT's Robert Solow and others have estimated that 70 to 90 percent of economic growth has depended on the application of new technologies and technological innovations. Thus, although job opportunities diminished in agriculture and more recently in manufacturing due to automation and other factors, the number of people employed overall grew, particularly in service industries. Lower prices and the introduction of new products contributed to growth in employment, particularly in services; service-occupation employment, for example, experienced substantial growth between 1980 and 1990.[9] It is precisely this history that troubles some analysts: Will the combined strengthening and slimming of services now trigger (or accompany) new economic growth somewhere, or does the diffusion of IT and other technologies from agriculture through manufacturing to services imply that there is nowhere left for sufficient growth in jobs to occur? In addressing this question, several issues must be considered.

As discussed in the macroeconomic analysis of Chapter 1, IT applications in services particularly affect white-collar jobs. Bureau of Labor Statistics forecasts, executives interviewed by the committee, committee members, and a number of studies all anticipate slower growth in some white-collar occupations in the near future, resulting (in part) from increased use of information technologies. The first to be affected have been lower-level, administrative and clerical occupations; more recently, the number of paraprofessional and technician occupations has been contracting in some industries. IT is also enabling the ongoing reductions in middle-management positions, and it is expected to diminish growth in sales positions as sales-related applications proliferate.[10] For example, the increased use of IT is likely to have contributed to the higher displacement rates evident in retail trade and "other services," compared to manufacturing, during the 1980s.[11]

Although the executives interviewed for this study were asked primarily about strategic and technical issues related to the introduction of new IT systems, many indicated that reductions had occurred in the size of their company's work force. For example, Larry Bacon of the Travelers Companies described the elimination of 200 positions following the introduction of automation systems (Chapter 4); at McKesson, the use of PCs by customers has resulted in large cuts in the number of order takers, salespeople, buyers, and functional managers (Chapter 3); Ford reduced its accounts payable staff by 75 percent through implementing IT systems (Chapter 4). Certainly in the short term, and in particular job categories, firms, or industries, introduction of new IT can have significant effects on employment that may not be fully offset by growth elsewhere.

Some of the observed displacement may reflect subtle and indirect shifts of labor effort, including the shifts to efforts on the part of customers mentioned in Chapters 3 and 4. Such shifts reflect not only managers' decisions about how to reorganize work within an organization, but also changing levels of expertise and changing preferences within the general population.[12] Increased use of IT-based systems may also have fostered the recent growth in part-time and temporary employment, some of which may be among people who would prefer full-time employment (and are therefore underemployed).

At least some observed and anticipated displacement reflects slow modernization of relatively low-technology industries. Service job growth in the past decades was concentrated in industries that have lagged in their (overall) use of computing and communications (e.g., health care, legal services, and retail).[13] The comparative inefficiency of these industries casts doubt on the notion that they will continue to support significant job growth.

Complicating the problem of assessing changes in employment levels is the fact that IT is used to facilitate the relocation of jobs at all levels, both within the country and between countries. Even if the absolute amount of work or jobs remains constant, people do not tend to move with jobs, and so job movement can have the effect of (local) job displacement.[14] Companies with heavy data-entry requirements (e.g., airlines, insurance companies, and some database service providers) have used foreign clerical workers for several years to reduce costs.[15] More recently there has been growth in the use of foreign professionals for software development, especially for lower-level coding but increasingly for higher-level work.[16] While evidence of these trends is largely anecdotal, that evidence suggests growth in the use of lower-wage foreign labor in service activities over the past 5 years.

Thus, while the absolute fraction and number of white-collar jobs transferred to foreign citizens is still small, the trend raises questions about both the number and quality or distribution of job opportunities that will remain available to U.S. citizens over time. Entry-level jobs are the first to go offshore, but higher-level jobs are also moving. On the other hand, jobs are created in the United States by foreign-owned (as well as U.S.-owned) enterprises. All of these trends are facilitated by improvements in communications technologies, and all are part of a pattern that has led some economists to posit an emerging global division of labor and economic activity.[17]

It is difficult to forecast where new jobs will be created, which leads some analysts to predict a rise in unemployment or a job shortage. However, overall, job growth is reasonable to predict. The past decade alone witnessed growth in opportunities in such areas as health care, environmental services, and, particularly relevant, IT-related services (software development, network-based services, training in the use of IT, systems integration, remote IT facilities management, and so on). Although job creation has been concentrated in small, entrepreneurial firms (across all industries), these firms and their employment patterns are relatively difficult to track.[18]

The most obvious trends suggest principally that job growth (and job levels) among traditional large employers will be depressed in the near term. However, the implications for overall employment levels are not clear. Although large firms continue to be large and important employers, the percentage of the working population that larger firms employ has been falling[19] and the identity of the largest firms has changed over time. Simultaneously, new companies and the new jobs associated with them have been growing. The enabling effects of using IT in these new enterprises have not been measured.

An added problem lies in labeling: the conventional division of the economy into agriculture (plus mining and forestry), manufacturing, and services suggests that we have run out of sectors. But the service sector is so heterogeneous that only a more fine-grained identification of subsectors or new sectors is likely to illuminate underlying changes in employment patterns. It is possible that new kinds of businesses will emerge from both the manufacturing and service sectors that would give rise to yet another kind of sector. However, it is unlikely that such developments will be recognized quickly, given the difficulty of detecting them in economic data.

Whether or not there is a temporary rise in unemployment, the content of jobs is changing. IT-based systems have been associated with a shift toward intellectual activities, manipulation of information about things or people (as opposed to manipulation of physical materials), and increased attention to the information content or corollaries of products (e.g., airline reservations and frequent flyer services as well as air transport, customization of insurance policies, and so on). With computer systems focused on the mechanics of collecting, storing, processing, and retrieving information, people have more time to do what computers do not do as well—people-to-people interaction, creating new ideas, and so on—making use of information delivered by technology. In addition, as the technology delivers more and more data, people will be called on to use and work with it, in some cases to be more analytical. These are the changes in most jobs that lie behind observations about the rise of the "knowledge worker." Ironically, the rise of the knowledge worker is associated with renewed attention to process engineering: the essence of reengineering is the gathering of information and the conduct of analysis to help improve "production" processes (food preparation and delivery, transport of people and cargo, and so on).

The average complexity of service jobs appears to have risen; by varying definitions, there are more knowledge workers, and higher levels of education are required for entry-level jobs. Flatter organizations and the popularity of team organizations, both enabled by the use of IT, imply that the work force of the future will need better communication and coordination skills. These changes in jobs are evident in many industries; they are occurring more rapidly and extensively in some industries (e.g., financial services) than in others (e.g., retailing). Other changes in skill requirements are predicted by management analysts—the need for a broader set of skills and more problem-solving ability to meet a wider set of responsibilities—but it is not clear how broadly these changes are taking hold in practice.

THE NEED FOR POLICY INTERVENTION TO EASE EMPLOYMENT TRANSITIONS

Although this report has concentrated on impacts in companies and industries that use IT, its positive benefits at these levels may be accompanied by negative side effects, most notably impacts on the labor force. Employment impacts may be direct or indirect, depending on how, where, and when IT is used. As discussed in Chapters 3 and 4, IT is used as a tool by managers to systematize or reorganize production processes and enterprises, effect transitions from old to new lines of business, and shift activities within and between enterprises, locations, and time periods. Layers are being eliminated from the job structures of enterprises, implying broader job definitions, while the mix of activities within firms is often becoming more focused, implying a narrower band of functions for personnel in such enterprises. All of these changes are occurring in the context of limited economic growth and structural changes in service industries, as discussed in Chapter 2, plus domestic and international competitive pressures that motivate businesses to seek greater efficiency.[20]

The trends listed above raise the specter of *job displacement* (the elimination of specific jobs or the reduction in growth for such jobs compared to what would have been under the original conditions) and *job change* (changes in the nature and mix of tasks that make up jobs). These changes are likely to continue, because computer-based technologies and their applications are often reconfigured over time and because people learn over time how to use these technologies better.

It is beyond the scope of this report to quantify potential displacements associated with IT in services or their duration. Broad trends and the difficulty of interpreting them are outlined above. **Based on those trends, the committee concludes that some displacement, including significant loss of current types of jobs, is inevitable, although new and different jobs are likely to be created. As with past technology-induced displacements, public policy intervention may be necessary to ameliorate impacts on communities and individuals.**

The changes in service activities addressed in this report are part of a larger pattern of changes in employment opportunities that has been characterized in *Workforce 2000*[21] and other studies; the inferences from this report are in harmony with other, more broadly based analyses that create an expectation for a more volatile job market. This study reinforces and amplifies concerns about the transitions in employment that are likely to take place over the next 5 to 10 years.

A central concern for public policy is how to ease worker dislocation, reducing negative social impacts (such as unemployment, underemployment, and reduction in household income) and facilitating the economic transition. The current economic system is characterized by short-term notification of displacement, loss of health insurance and pension plans with job loss, limited outplacement assistance, and limited unemployment insurance and employment service programs. Absent change (such as movement toward portable, universal health insurance), the conditions described in this report suggest that a growing number of people may be faced with loss of insurance benefits as well as loss of income. Such programs as advance notice, retraining, employment search assistance, portability of benefits, and temporary income support during job search have been suggested as appropriate by various parties. These measures imply interdependent but separate roles for employers, government, and individuals. This committee did not take a specific position on the relative merits of these proposals.

As has been noted by others, measures (such as training, retraining, and other types of adjustment assistance) will probably be needed;[22] the challenge is to develop innovative and effective approaches. Also important will be encouragement of job creation through economic growth, including the investment in new, entrepreneurial businesses and information infrastructure (see "Implications for Macroeconomic and Fiscal Policy" above). Calibrating policy measures will require closer monitoring and analysis of trends (see "The Need for Additional Research to Guide Policy Making" below), to permit timely if not proactive responses.

Reinforcing conclusions developed by other studies, the committee believes that there is a clear need for increased training of many types. Both retraining for existing members of the labor force (in anticipation of new jobs and a new mix of jobs) and education and training to make prospective entrants to the labor force more versatile (in anticipation of ongoing change in jobs and careers and periodic retraining) will be needed. Especially important, given changes observed in service activities (see Chapter 4), will be the development of skills relating to the handling and use of information, including a solid foundation of basic skills ranging from reading, writing, and mathematics to problem-solving skills. Developing such skills for individuals already in the labor force implies a departure from the job-specific, task-oriented training typical of employer-based programs. In particular, it implies a need for relatively frequent or ongoing training.[23]

This study underscores the need for training at all levels within organizations. In particular, job trends associated with the use of IT raise added concern about training for the people at the bottom of the labor force, the people with the least skills who would be suited for some of the jobs most likely to be displaced or changed through the use of IT. Inequalities in the earnings distribution have widened recently, reflecting greater growth at lower wage levels and reductions in middle-level opportunities due in part to shifts in the mix of jobs by occupation and industry.[24] Inasmuch as information-related and problem-solving skills remain restricted to a small subset of the population, further shifts toward "knowledge work" will make it more difficult for people with limited or weak skills to obtain good jobs.[25] This study thus adds to concerns raised by others about the quality of basic (K-12) education (and also vocational education); the majority of the labor force consists of people who have at most a high school diploma. Looking at the other end of the employment spectrum, it should also be recognized that training will be needed for professional and managerial personnel to facilitate their own use of IT, prepare them to manage IT better, and convey new approaches to the organization of work.

Questions arise as to the degrees of responsibility held by individuals, employers, and government for training and retraining. Many of the changes discussed in this report are beyond the ability of individual members of the labor force to influence. A fundamental question is how to assist the employee in making transitions, with help from the employer as well as support from government (at all levels). As suggested above, portability of benefits illustrates one mechanism for facilitating transitions. Since willingness as well as ability to pay for these measures will affect what is done, incentives may be needed for individuals and employers.

THE NEED FOR ADDITIONAL RESEARCH TO GUIDE POLICY MAKING

A recurring theme in this report has been that limited data yield limited understanding. Problems in collecting and aggregating data are significant reasons why available macroeconomic data neither prove nor disprove claims about the level of impact investment in IT has had on performance in services.

The conventional distinctions between manufacturing and services, which underlie the collection, analysis, and presentation of publicly available data, undermine useful analysis. Available data do not help to track the changes and blurring of industry structures and identities resulting from shifts in who does which activities, where, and when (e.g., the roles of both hospitals and insurance companies in providing managed care, the retailer-like roles of transportation service providers, and so on). And the data that are available obscure the fact that production of goods and services involves many comparable activities. For example, data regarding employment from major companies that produce goods may be tallied only within manufacturing, thus obscuring large volumes of service activity (such as research, marketing, and training) also produced within those companies.[26]

Because each industry has different performance indicators, developing a comprehensive body of measurements is a huge task that is far from being accomplished.[27] Even with perfect measures of output, it may still not be possible to separate out the effects of various factors, including the use of IT, that affect output and other dimensions of performance. In addition to technology, those factors include changes in the skills of management, the education and training of the work force, economies of scale and scope, technology change in general, government regulations, collective bargaining, and so on. **Detailed microeconomic studies building on the kinds of issues revealed by the committee's interviews, macroeconomic studies, and organizational studies are necessary to better measure and understand the contributions of multiple factors and how they interact.**

Given the apparent significance of small firms to growth in the economy and in employment, valuable insights could be gained from more research specifically focused on how smaller enterprises use IT and with what effects. Insights available through the literature and through interviews tend to be limited to the experiences of large firms—researchers tend to find it easier to identify and work with larger firms, and that tendency may bias understanding.[28]

Although the committee did not have the resources to investigate smaller-company practices systematically, members cited examples of individual smaller companies that had developed extremely fast response capabilities, strong cross-functional team-oriented cultures, team management and reward systems, and very productive desktop IT systems for enhancing communications. These enterprises already exhibit many of the characteristics larger companies seek through more disaggregated organization and activity-based competitive structures. Smaller enterprises also differ in other significant ways. They can often rely on direct person-to-person communications and more informal information systems. Because of the increasing importance of small enterprises in creating jobs, introducing IT innovations, and utilizing IT in new ways, special study of small enterprises' use of IT would seem a worthy goal for future research.

Finally, more systematic attempts to compare experiences with IT internationally may be useful, in part to benefit from different perspectives on elements of performance, concepts and measurements, and trade-offs in the use of IT and in part to capitalize on the extensive tradition in other countries (especially in Europe) of studying social and organizational impacts of technology. **Since use of IT will be a critical factor in international competition, it would be prudent to systematically compare and monitor progress and impacts in other countries.**

Improving Federal Macroeconomic Data Gathering and Analysis

There is a need for improved statistics about existing activities and for statistics that capture the development of new services. Policymakers, in particular, need better data to monitor and plan for changes in the economy. Better statistics could provide a clearer picture of the economy, illuminating shifts in investment, employment, products, productivity, and other dimensions relevant to government and industry. In particular, there is a need for an expansion in scope, i.e., data about more industries. As was noted, detailed data are available for only a fraction of the service-oriented economy. Fundamental to these is a need for a more refined classification of activities, firms, and industries that would guide the collection and analysis of data. For example, it would be useful to have more specific data on selected skill classifications and occupations within each industry class. It would also be useful to separate out significant service business components within firms that predominantly produce goods. The complications and costs of obtaining more detailed data are well recognized.

Broader and improved capture of changes in quality and measurement of other factors that contribute value for customers could also help to put statistics on productivity into perspective. Existing measures focus primarily on industries whose outputs are captured by gross national product data. The service-sector interviews undertaken by the committee plus both anecdotal and more formal evidence suggest that many of the performance gains in services—particularly those associated with intangible improvements in quality or those realized as cost savings, greater convenience, or increased flexibility or variety—may not be captured by the industry producing the benefit.[29] At a gross level, these shifts may be reflected in the financial performance of a company. But where competition within an industry is heavy and financial gains are passed through to customers or suppliers as savings, there may not be an obvious correlation between benefits to customers and the firm's or industry's financial performance.[30] Progress in developing and using hedonic price indexes suggests that there are some opportunities to develop better measurements of output quality and customer benefits, although delivering against those opportunities may take time and be difficult to realize.

The need for better economic statistics has been recognized for some time; it is made more urgent by the cumulative impact of cutbacks in federal statistical programs during the 1980s. A number of recommendations for improving statistics on productivity and services were made in an earlier National Research Council report (Box 6.1). **Although progress has been made in implementing several of the Rees Panel's recommendations, more work is needed, and the committee therefore endorses those**

BOX 6.1 Rees Panel Recommendations for
Better Statistics

Recommendation 3: "The Panel recommends that the Bureau of Labor Statistics and the Bureau of Economic Analysis explore methods for estimating the implications of error reduction in component measures for the **reduction of overall error in productivity measures** beyond that corrected by routine revisions." (p. 7)

Recommendation 4: "The Panel recommends that the Bureau of Economic Analysis (BEA) and the Bureau of Labor Statistics (BLS) seek to improve their existing price indexes and to develop auxiliary measures of price change. These new auxiliary measures should **take into account more adequately the types of quality change that are not now measured.** . . .

Among the adjustments that could be incorporated in the new measures are **adjustments . . . for changes in value to users resulting from the introduction of improved products; estimates of the value to users of improvements in performance that are achieved without increases in real costs; and estimates of the present value of future savings in operating efficiency made possible by design changes and improvements. . . .** " (p. 8)

Recommendation 6: ". . . the Panel does agree that for the study of many important social problems—for example, improvement of the health status of the population—**definitions of output and input that go well beyond those currently used to measure productivity are required. . . .** " (p. 10)

Recommendation 14: "The Panel endorses . . . calling for the Census Bureau to collect, as an integral part of each economic census, **data on the purchases of intermediate services** as well as materials by establishments." (p. 13)

Recommendation 17: "The Panel recommends that government agencies **support research aimed at improving knowledge about the sources of productivity change.** These agencies should be especially attentive to research that focuses on measuring **technical and organizational change and new product and service innovation. . . .**" (p. 15)

NOTE: Emphasis added.

SOURCE: National Research Council, Panel to Review Productivity Statistics. 1979. *Measurement and Interpretation of Productivity,* National Academy of Sciences, Washington, D.C.

recommendations. Specific proposals were also captured in the recent Presidential Economic Statistics Initiative (the Boskin Initiative). That initiative called for a 5-year, $230 million effort, a significant portion of which was aimed at improving service industry statistics.[31] Such an initiative, if funded, would help to ameliorate some of the problems of concern to the committee; momentum in this area must not become a casualty of the transition. It is hoped that the Clinton administration will enhance and build on these recommendations with its own program. Note also that the need for better statistical data is largely independent of issues related specifically to IT and productivity.

The committee urges the federal administration to promote a significant upgrading of statistical programs. At a time when more and more enterprises are recognizing the value of information to the performance and expansion of their businesses, it behooves the government to collect and make use of better information about the changing economy.

Improving Data and Accounting Principles Related to Investments in Information Technology

Available data provide information on investments in computing and communications hardware, which is treated for tax and national statistics purposes as a capital investment. However, IT hardware represents only a fraction of the investment needed to make IT effective. Committee members (based on their experiences in developing, installing, operating, and maintaining systems) and other analysts have noted that hardware may constitute only about one-third of the total investment in a system (and that proportion has been declining). Other components of IT system cost include, in particular, the cost to develop, purchase, or maintain software plus associated training, support, integration, upgrading, and other services. All of these costs are expenses under current accounting principles and practices and are not captured in a firm's capital accounts. Increases in the outsourcing of elements of information technology—from telecommunications to databases to software development to data center operations—tend to further raise the percentage of IT costs that are expensed rather than capitalized. A consequence of particular concern is that the value of software in generating income is not obvious to management, investors, or policymakers—even when a specialized software system, such as a computerized reservation system, is critical to strategic advantage. Software has become a major asset to corporations that is not reflected in their balance sheets.[32]

Improving the valuation of software will be difficult. There are different and sometimes conflicting interests among analysts, investors and owners, managers of organizations using software, managers of organizations producing software, and tax authorities, among others. These different perspectives have come out recently in the development of legislation that would affect the tax accounting treatment of software, as one of several "intangible assets";[33] similar issues arise concerning the treatment of research and development spending. Discomfort with capitalizing software over a long period of time arises from difficulties in predicting with reasonable precision the value and life of a software system; there is concern that any piece of software may have a relatively brief useful life, and it may be replaced or upgraded through an ongoing process of "maintenance" that blurs the identity of the software in question. **The committee recommends that the Financial Accounting Standards Board (FASB) and the Congress look at ways to improve the usefulness and monitoring of accounting data on investments in both purchased and internally developed IT systems (especially software and databases) to better support fiduciary management and performance measurement.**[34]

Increasing Awareness of and Investments in Research Related to Information Technology in Services and Service Quality Measurements

Committee interviews with executives suggest that corporate R&D on the use of IT to develop new service products and processes is underappreciated, underestimated, and probably underfunded.[35] Committee deliberations and interviews with executives of large companies plus published materials reveal a pattern of experimentation that takes place in service industries, in which companies develop and try out new applications, software, and systems.[36] Such projects or programs are not necessarily classified or analyzed as research by the companies that undertake (and pay for) them, but they contribute to a larger pattern of trial, error, and success that drives new applications of IT in services and shapes the competitive landscape within industries.

The committee concluded from its assessment that more emphasis needs to be placed on research and development relating to services, including the applications of IT in services. This greater emphasis is needed across the board—in firms, institutions, and government. Such emphasis should include both process and product innovation.

It is not possible to estimate how much relevant R&D takes place in or for services, but there is anecdotal evidence that support from both corporate budgets and federal programs for academic research for these efforts is limited. This situation reflects a larger problem of limited support for R&D explicitly focused on process or organizational issues. Academic analysts, including committee members, have observed that it is difficult to get funding for such research. Enterprises should not be discouraged by accounting conventions from experimenting with these technologies, given their proven contributions to competitiveness; rather, financial incentives for such experimentation should be considered. Although R&D within an industry is typically funded by the industry directly, broader, longer-term, or academic research often presumes federal government support. This form of broad stimulus would fall within the realm of macroeconomic and fiscal policy, discussed above.

Another vehicle for motivating more innovation among service industries may be an increased effort to apply the Baldrige Award to services. According to literature describing the award, up to two awards annually can be given in the three categories of manufacturing, services, and small business. However, of the awards presented through 1992, ten went to manufacturing companies, four to small businesses, and only three to service firms; many consider the criteria for the award to be aimed largely at manufacturing.[37] Although the Baldrige Award program has generated some controversy, it has increased attention to critical elements of performance, especially quality. It has helped spread quality-oriented attitudes, terminology, and measurements. The perceived availability of a special award in services could facilitate experiments and more widespread measurement of quality at the level of enterprises or firms.

OTHER POLICY ISSUES IDENTIFIED BY THIS STUDY

The increasing use of IT in services raises other concerns that should motivate examination of existing public policies or consideration of new policy. Those concerns relate to such issues as privacy, remote work, competition policy, and intellectual property. Although detailed exploration of such issues was beyond the scope of this report, the committee believed it important to identify them, to increase awareness and to signal that further analysis would be useful to determine where private actions may be insufficient to meet public interests.

One area where further policy action is already under debate is that of protection of an individual's rights to limit access to personal data, building on the base provided by the Privacy Act of 1974 (which was directed to the public sector). Policy measures in this area will affect choices service and other organizations can make in selecting and implementing information technology. For example, as discussed in Chapter 3, electronic databases are being used by more and more organizations to store personal data to support customer service operations, marketing, credit approvals, and other service activities. The proliferation of applications, equipment, networks, and network interconnections means that growing numbers of people have potential access to kinds of data (such as health, income, and credit records) heretofore physically less accessible.[38] These circumstances imply a greater risk of unauthorized access to or use of personal data. In addition to these potentials for abuse, there are questions about the collection and review of data by employers about their employees, a capability facilitated by the use of IT, some of it in the context of electronic monitoring of employee behavior. This practice has already raised concern among some employees, unions, and privacy advocates as well as policymakers.

Privacy is not the only consideration. The ability of service providers to assemble information regarding so many different aspects of an individual's life so as to provide better service also provides the capability to deny service. For example, caller-identification telephone technology enables a called telephone to display the number of the calling telephone. Such technologies can be used to call up a customer profile based on telephone numbers associated with previous orders, and it can also be used to ignore or give lower priority to service requests that come, for example, from low-income regions of a city. Insurance companies can use detailed information about an individual to generate a customized insurance policy for that individual, but they can also use that information as the basis for denying insurance policies (e.g., for health care) to individuals deemed "high-risk" (e.g., those who test HIV-positive).

Another impact of the use of IT with social ramifications is the facilitation of remote work.[39] **This effect can result in the shifting of work to other countries.**[40] **It can also have more positive effects locally, in the context of "telecommuting" and the movement of work to where people are rather than the converse.** Telecommuting—whether via satellite offices, home offices, or other field locations—will change the social structure of organizations, the geography of industries (domestically and internationally), the demand for office space, and so on. Presumably, these practices will grow because they are perceived to have performance benefits and because falling costs for IT will make them increasingly affordable and easy to implement. There may also be environmental, safety, and energy conservation benefits inasmuch as work-related travel is diminished. The potential for more home-based work could affect a wide range of people, including individuals who have difficulty getting to or functioning in conventional work environments; such individuals would include the disabled, people with dependent care responsibilities, and those without access to adequate transportation.[41]

Shifts in activities among industries engendered by the use of IT raise questions about laws and regulations aimed at constraining the competitive behavior (e.g., pricing, collaborative ventures, mergers and acquisitions, and so on) of firms. Developments within the service sector point to increased competition across industries (and sectors), making it harder to target programs to specific industries. Increases in outsourcing and in electronic linkages to trading partners raise questions about the boundary between cooperation and collusion. For example, recent government attention to the use of computerized reservation systems as a possible mechanism for collusion on pricing illustrates some of the disagreement about how information technology can and should affect competitive conduct.[42] Since electronic communication among businesses and across industries is expected to expand, and since IT is expected to enable continued reorganization of businesses, it may be that the goals of competition policies (such as antitrust policy) may be better served by a focus on specific kinds of transactions rather than on institutions. This is an issue that warrants further exploration by Congress and appropriate executive branch agencies.[43]

Another area of business (and individual) behavior where current policy might need reexamination is intellectual property rights. Protection of intellectual property will be a factor affecting the rate, nature, and ownership of investments in information infrastructure, including information- and network-based service businesses. Software has already given rise to both uncertainty and assumptions regarding the existence or lack of intellectual property protection.[44] Particularly relevant to services are the implications of increased electronic networking for the protection of intellectual property associated with materials made available electronically over networks. The debate has just begun in this area.

Finally, IT could be better used to enhance the policy-making process itself. IT can be used to facilitate both the collection of highly refined data by government and the use of that data for faster and better decision making and therefore potentially better and more responsive services to citizens. Such government activities as approval of eligibility for entitlement and assistance programs could be made more responsive and accurate, drawing on experiences elsewhere; indeed, ongoing federal agency efforts to modernize their systems show that the potential is recognized. Improving government effectiveness by better use of IT is an area of high potential payoff already recognized by the Clinton administration.[45] It deserves special in-depth study.[46]

NOTES AND REFERENCES

[1]IT will be present not only on its own, but also in the form of embedded components in a wide variety of equipment and products that may themselves be linked to more conventional or obvious IT.

[2]An option contemplated by the new administration is tax credits for incremental investments in equipment. See Greenhouse, Steven. 1992. "Economists Back Clinton on Investment Tax Credits," *New York Times*, November 16, pp. D1-D2. Also, see Landau, R. 1988. "U.S. Economic Growth," *Scientific American* 258(June):44-52.

[3]Birch, David L. 1989. "Statement by David L. Birch Before the U.S. House of Representatives Small Business Committee," transcript of testimony, September.

[4]It must be recognized that information infrastructure in any one locale is increasingly likely to be linked to such infrastructure elsewhere, through regional, national, and international connections.

[5] It should be noted that most private networking by large enterprises involves the use of "public" network facilities. Through leasing of circuits and ports and through software, real or "virtual" allocations of facilities are made. Virtual private networks, enabled by software to preempt access to certain facilities, are expected to become more available to smaller users over time. Nevertheless, conventional public infrastructure is expected to continue to provide a lifeline for smaller users who need occasional access to trading partners and service providers.

[6] Public policy attention to information infrastructure has already expanded considerably during the Clinton administration, and both the 102d and 103d Congresses have introduced related legislation. In addition, both the legislative and executive branches have taken steps to develop and implement a national research and education network program (the NREN component of the High Performance Computing and Communications program), which is expected to contribute to and interconnect with a broader national information infrastructure. The HPCC program is premised in part on a recognition that technology development and infrastructure are interrelated. A new fifth component is called Information Infrastructure Technology and Applications.

[7] National Telecommunications and Information Administration. 1991. *The NTIA Infrastructure Report: Telecommunications in the Age of Information*, NTIA Special Publication 91-26, U.S. Department of Commerce, Washington, D.C., October.

[8] Cyert, Richard M., and David C. Mowery (eds.). 1987. *Technology and Employment: Innovation and Growth in the U.S. Economy*, National Academy Press, Washington, D.C.

[9] Rosenthal, Neal. 1992. "Evaluating the 1990 Projections of Occupational Employment." *Monthly Labor Review* 115(8):32-48.

[10] Note that one form of sales that is fundamentally a creation of IT capability and capacity, telemarketing, appears to be growing. Meanwhile, the technology behind telemarketing (switches, storage units, call distributors, and so on) is becoming more sophisticated.

[11] Podgursky, Michael. 1992. "The Industrial Structure of Job Displacement, 1979-89." *Monthly Labor Review* 115(9):17-25.

[12] The epitome of this phenomenon is the transformation of employment for telephone operators. It is by now a cliche that, absent automation, two-thirds (or more) of the population might have to work as telephone operators to sustain contemporary calling volume. But rather than simply eliminate operator tasks, many were shifted to telephone company customers—telephone users are operators, based on old definitions of operator jobs. Two developments made this shift possible. One was, indeed, computerization of the telephone system, especially the installation of computer-controlled switches, computer-based databases for customer and billing information, and so on. The other was the slow but inexorable training of hundreds of millions of people to memorize huge strings of digits for input to the telephone system through a crude terminal, the touch-tone telephone. This training, or more specifically, the knowledge in the population of telephone customers regarding how to make direct-dial calls, is a vital complement to the technology in the displacement of operators.

[13] Baumol, William, Sue Anne Batey Blackman, and Edward N. Wolff. 1989. *Productivity and American Leadership: The Long View*, MIT Press, Cambridge, Mass.

[14] An exception may apply for highly skilled occupations and individuals. There was reportedly job growth, especially in IT-related occupations, among high-skilled immigrants during the late 1970s and early 1980s.

[15] Carey, Susan. 1992. "Airlines Seek to Cut Back-Office Costs by Establishing Offshore Operations," *Wall Street Journal*, November 30, p. B6D.

[16] Computer Science and Telecommunications Board, National Research Council. 1993. *Computing Professionals: Changing Needs for the 1990s*, National Academy Press, Washington, D.C.

[17] Wolff, Edward N. 1991. "Productivity Growth, Capital Intensity, and Skill Levels in the U.S. Insurance Industry, 1948-86," *The Geneva Papers on Risk and Insurance* 16(59, April):173-190.

[18] Although the diffusion of IT into smaller enterprises could slow job growth within small firms, the launching of new businesses should continue to create new jobs both directly and indirectly. See Birch, David L. 1989. "Statement by David L. Birch Before the U.S. House of Representatives Small Business Committee," transcript of testimony, September.

[19] Note that the Fortune 500 share of total nonfarm employment has been decreasing from a peak of around 20 percent during the late 1960s and early 1970s. That share is now about 10 to 11 percent. See "Where the Jobs Aren't," *Wall Street Journal*, August 10, 1992, table drawing on Kemper Financial Services data.

[20] The most recent employment conditions reflect a recession and slow recovery. The concern in this discussion is with secular or long-term trends as opposed to the inevitable short-term shifts associated with the business cycle.

[21] Johnston, William B., and Arnold E. Packer. 1987. *Workforce 2000—Work and Workers for the 21st Century*, Hudson Institute, Indianapolis, Ind., June.

[22] See Cyert and Mowery, 1987, *Technology and Employment*.

[23] For further discussion of this point, see Zuboff, Shoshana, 1988, *In the Age of the Smart Machine: The Future of Work and Power*, Basic Books, New York.

[24] For a discussion of how many factors contribute to the growth in earnings inequality, see Grubb, W. Norton, and Robert H. Wilson, 1992, "Trends in Wage and Salary Inequality, 1967-1988," *Monthly Labor Review* 115(6):23-37. Note that some of the trends associated with IT could entail shrinkage in current low-wage jobs; this is already evident in forecasts for slower growth in clerical jobs, for example. Questions arise about the types of jobs that may be available for the people who would have taken such jobs.

[25] Kutcher, Ronald E. 1988. "Growth of Services Employment in the United States," pp. 47-75 in *Technology in Services: Policies for Growth, Trade, and Employment*, Bruce R. Guile and James Brian Quinn (eds.), National Academy Press, Washington, D.C.

[26] What is tallied where depends on whether the services represent final, as opposed to intermediate (component), output. Resources for final output are tallied directly; resources associated with intermediate output are reflected in final goods and services. This practice supports the objective of measuring trends in final goods and services, but it obscures intermediate-production trends of interest for understanding qualitative changes in the structure of the economy.

[27] An exhaustive body of data may neither be practical nor justify the expense. Also, note that even if that body of measurements existed, one could not simply add industry-specific measures together to generate an aggregate economy-wide measure. But more detail than is currently available is needed to understand how activities, enterprises, industry, and the economy are changing.

[28] Indeed, the relative growth in employment among smaller firms and, historically, smaller firms' limited success with IT may be another factor explaining why measured service performance has been weak.

[29] Available data do not (and may never) capture adequately the contributions to standards of living that IT may support. As measured, growth in productivity contributes to increases in the standard of living, but it is only one element. The creation of whole new industries and the increased flexibility and variety of products and services available are other elements.

[30] For example, computerized reservation systems for airlines and automated teller systems for banks provide greater customer convenience, but, although they could not provide competitive service without these tools, even airlines and banks with leading CRS and ATM systems have had financial difficulties over the past few years.

[31] If funded, the Boskin Initiative would have emphasized Bureau of Economic Analysis (BEA) programs (macroeconomic data on investment and output) and Bureau of Labor Statistics (BLS) programs (employment and productivity measurement), as well as Bureau of the Census programs that contribute to BEA and BLS statistics. Planned Census Bureau improve-

ments, for example, are aimed at better measuring the output of industries that provide multiple services, better measuring the purchases of services by manufacturing firms, and better estimation of the emergence of new services.

[32] The committee conducted many discussions on the shift from physical to intellectual capital. Many factors obscure the value of software in the eyes of executives, investors, and policymakers more accustomed to and familiar with physical capital: software's intangibility and inscrutability to the layperson, its character as intellectual capital, and the seeming lack of durability of software, which is associated with its ease of duplication and potential to be quickly outmoded or bested by rival products. The situation has been compounded by traditional perspectives in the accounting community, which are oriented toward the cost and proceeds of physical property, plant, and equipment and which reflect concern about the potential for misleading financial reporting as a product of estimating the value of intangibles or making changes in financial metrics. All of these concerns are valid, but all militate against a recognition of the shift from physical and money capital to intellectual capital.

[33] In the case of software acquired through business acquisitions, that legislation provides for writing off the cost over 14 to 16 years. The software industry has objected that that long period will raise costs and adversely affect international competitiveness, since the useful life of software is only a few years at best.

[34] According to FASB literature, "The mission of the Financial Accounting Standards Board is to establish and improve standards of financial accounting and reporting for the guidance and education of the public, including issuers, auditors, and users of financial information.... The FASB develops broad accounting concepts as well as standards for financial reporting. It also provides guidance on implementation of standards...." FASB has come under some criticism lately, due in part to its support for a proliferation of accounting standards, but it remains the logical entity to study this issue.

[35] Inasmuch as service innovation is associated with entrepreneurial firms while research funding tends to be concentrated in larger firms and universities, there may be a systemic constraint on service research funding.

[36] For example, Kmart developed and tested a new system to track traffic in stores and relate traffic patterns to purchase patterns. See Schwadel, Francine. 1991. "Kmart Testing Radar to Track Shopper Traffic," *Wall Street Journal,* September 24, pp. B1 and B5. On a larger scale, Federal Express's pioneering attempt to introduce a fax network service and AT&T Bell Laboratories' early attempts to introduce cellular telephony represented experiments in the application of IT.

[37] Although no service awards were made in 1991, awards went to the Ritz-Carlton Hotel Company and AT&T Universal Card Services in 1992 and to Federal Express in 1990.

[38] The public uproar over the Equifax-Lotus proposal to distribute customer profile data and controversy over the accuracy of and access to credit-agency records are but two indicators of growing public concern about data, although in general the public may not fully understand how much data about individuals is being collected and becoming available.

[39] CSTB has launched a new study of technology for telecommuting.

[40] Although some shifting from domestic to offshore employment may take place, that phenomenon may convey positive benefits in the form of improvements in foreign standards of living and diminution of immigration pressures. However, such benefits would be realized over a much longer term than the employment shifts that produce them.

[41] The Comprehensive National Energy Policy Act of 1992 (P.L. 102-486) directed the Department of Energy to conduct an analysis of telecommuting and its social and environmental impacts, impacts that would be fostered by IT.

[42] Tolchin, Martin. 1992. "U.S. Sues 8 Airlines Over Fares," *New York Times,* December 22, p. D1.

[43] Those agencies would include the Office of Management and Budget, the Department of Justice, and the Federal Trade Commission.

IMPLICATIONS FOR PUBLIC POLICY

[44] Computer Science and Telecommunications Board, National Research Council. 1990. *Intellectual Property Issues in Software,* National Academy Press, Washington, D.C.

[45] Making government more efficient and more responsive, in part through the use of information technology, is one of the priorities of the technology program introduced by the federal administration in February 1993. See Clinton, William J., President, and Vice President Albert Gore, Jr. 1993. "Technology for America's Economic Growth, a New Direction to Build Economic Strength," February 22. IT use in government was given special consideration in Vice President Albert Gore's *National Performance Review—From Red Tape to Results,* distributed electronically over the Internet on September 7, 1993.

[46] The potential for using IT to enhance government is not new to the federal government or lower levels of government. However, the stream of reports issued by the General Accounting Office and even by the Computer Science and Telecommunications Board attests to the significant opportunity for improvements in the acquisition, use, and management of IT in government.

Appendixes

Appendix A
Selected Research on Economic and Strategic Impacts of Information Technology

TABLE A.1 Selected Research on Economic and Strategic Impacts of Information Technology

Reference	Type of Research	Unit of Analysis	Performance Construct and Measure(s)
Alpar and Kim (1990)	Econometric Time series Cross-sectional (1979 to 1986)	Firm/small business unit (759 banks)	Productivity (multifactor)
Applegate et al. (1988)	Theory, description	Managers	Productivity Flexibility Creativity
Attewell and Rule (1984)	Review of management information systems literature	Individual Management Organization	Number and quality of jobs, management decision making, organizational dealings with clients and customers
Baily and Chakrabarti (1988)	Economic analysis and simulation	Company	White-collar productivity
Baily and Gordon (1988)	Methodology review	Aggregate economy vs. industry	Average labor productivity and multifactor productivity
Banker and Kauffman (1988)	Econometric Cross-sectional	Firm/small business unit (508 branch banks)	Competitive advantage (marginal bank branch deposit share as contribution to reducing costs)
Bender (1986)	Correlational Cross-sectional (1983)	Firm (132 life insurance companies)	Operating cost efficiency
Benjamin et al. (1984)	Case studies and surveys; prescriptive	24 companies	Strategic opportunities
Bikson and Eveland (1986)	Literature review, retrospective application of sociotechnical systems	Organization (diverse range)	"Successful" implementation (user, management satisfaction)
Blumenthal (1987)	Theory review	International National	Productivity and impacts on industry and employment

APPENDIX A

Input Measure(s)	Key Findings (Brynjolfsson and Bimber Hypothesis Code)[a]
Total information system expenses; labor; capital; time deposits	10% increase in IT associated with a 1.9% decrease in total costs. IT contributed to reduction in demand deposit amount and an increase in time deposits. IT is capital using and labor saving.
IT	Discusses present and future impacts of computers on managers. Emphasizes increased flexibility, new structures. (IE)
Computing	Significant disagreement and/or conflicting studies in every major dimension examined. (IE)
Electronics innovation	Proposes 3 potential explanations for the IT paradox in white-collar context: mismeasurement, distributional rather than productive effects, information value problem: Price decreases in technology lead to more technology purchased rather than decreased cost; also suggests may be just transitional time lag. (IC)
Output per hour, multifactor	Uncovers large measurement errors but finds that they explain at most 0.5% of the 1.5% slowdown in aggregate productivity. Key contributing errors are undervaluing of variety, service quality, and convenience. Adjustments applied to the banking industry produce much stronger productivity growth than do government analysis/statistics of productivity growth. (IA)
Presence of ATM at a branch. Connection to regional shared ATM network	Use of ATMs enables branch to protect rather than grow market share. Bank customers evidenced willingness to pay for regional access to shared electronic banking networks.
Total IT expenses	Higher IT spending associated with higher unit cost efficiency.
IT	IT can help firms establish new markets and redistribute profits in existing markets. (IE)
Process of introduction of new technology	What is needed is an integrated view, in which decisions about tools, uses, and users are seen as essential properties of a strategy that is iterative and emergent, learning from its own successes and failures over time and committed to change as a continuous fact of life. (IIE)
Programmable automation	Confronts dilemma in the popular view: increased use of programmable automation leads to increased competitiveness and other benefits to industry while threatening job loss and other negative consequences to workers. (IIB)

TABLE A.1 Continued

Reference	Type of Research	Unit of Analysis	Performance Construct and Measure(s)
Bresnahan (1986)	Econometric methodology	Financial sector	Spillover to customers downstream
Cecil and Hall (1988)	Prescriptive, descriptive	Company	Performance
Cron and Sobol (1983)	Correlational Cross-sectional	Firm (138 surgical wholesalers)	Profitability (return on assets; profits/sales; return on net worth). Competitive advantage (5-year sales growth)
Curley and Pyburn (1982)	Case studies of 13 organizations, survey of additional 33	46 manufacturing and service industries	Improved productivity (managerial, clerical, professional)
Dertouzos (1989)	Descriptive, prescriptive, models	Economy	Productivity
Feldman and March (1981)	Review of literature, theory	Organizations (wide range)	Use of information
Franke (1987)	Econometric (1958 to 1983)	Financial sector (insurance and banking)	Productivity (average labor). Capital (ROI)
Fudenberg and Tirole (1985)	Economic model development	Firm	Net cash flow
Giesler and Rubenstein (1988)	Descriptive, survey of 20 banks and interviews	Bank	Competitive performance
Graham (1976)		Firm	Performance
Harris and Katz (1991)	Correlational Time series (1983 to 1986)	Firm (40 life insurance companies)	Operating cost efficiency (operating expenses/ premium income)
Hirshleifer (1971)	Economic models	Private vs. social	
Kraut et al. (1989)	Case with lagged, time-series design (methodology emphasis)	Company (one public utility)	Productivity, quality of work, attitudes toward computers

Input Measure(s)	Key Findings (Brynjolfsson and Bimber Hypothesis Code)[a]
Technological innovation	Benefits to the public that were derived from computerization of financial services were five times the expenditures on computers. (IA)
IT	Fundamental changes in strategy and organization are required to produce significant benefits. (IE)
Number of software applications	Firms with extensive automation are either very strong or very weak financial performers.
Office automation	Meaningful improvements in productivity require active management of an ongoing learning process that brings about changes in the way people think about the work they do. (IB)
Computer field, technology, and theory	Questions value of increased work quality; develops method for measuring computer productivity and defines a value of information. (IIC)
Acquisition of information	Offers a critique of the decision-theoretic model of information acquisition and use in organizations; provides alternative explanations for the common observation that information often seems to be acquired excessively. (ID)
Total IT capital stock	Declines in productivity of capital vs. labor productivity associated with specific technological innovations. (ID)
Early or late adoption	Develops game-theoretic model of rent-dissipation in the timing of introduction of new technologies. (IC)
IT	Three-quarters lacked any formal evaluation procedure; only 3 viewed IT in terms of strategic goals and long-term growth. (IID)
	Better managerial decision making would apparently contribute positively to performance, yet questions if IT materially contributes to the quality of decision making. (IIC)
IT expense ratio IT cost efficiency ratio	Top-performing firms had higher growth in IT expense ratios and lower growth in operating expense than did weak performers.
	Private value of information may have no relationship to the social value, principally because of rent dissipation; shows that information may have negative social value if it destroys opportunities for insurance and risk-sharing. (IC)
Automation of record system	Extends a simple impact model (1) by expanding what one considers the technology to be, (2) by identifying individual and organizational contingencies that moderate impact, and (3) by recognizing bidirectional nature of technological change. (IIF)

TABLE A.1 Continued

Reference	Type of Research	Unit of Analysis	Performance Construct and Measure(s)
Loveman (1988)	Econometric Time series Cross-sectional (1978 to 1984)	Firm/small business unit (60 manufacturing small business units)	Productivity (average labor)
Malone et al. (1987)	Conceptual framework and prescription	Firm and market structures	Costs of coordination
Mark (1982)	Methodology review	Service industry	Labor productivity
Nelson (1981)	Critique and economic model development		
Noyelle (1990)	Correlation	U.S. and French retailing industry	Productivity measure and employment
OECD (1988)	Descriptive, socio-economic analysis	Individual to international	Employment, productivity growth
Osterman (1986)	Econometric time series (1972 to 1987)	Industry (40 service and manufacturing industries)	Productivity (clerical employment volume/output; managerial employment volume/output)
Parsons et al. (1990)	Model	Firm (2 large banks)	Multifactor productivity
Pentland (1989)	Survey (1988)	Individual (1100 Internal Revenue Service agents), Department	Productivity (labor hours/audit), Output quality (client reports)
Porter and Millar (1985)	Some case examples, prescriptive		Competitive advantage
Roach (1991)	Trend comparisons (1950 to 1989)	Service sector	Productivity (employment volume/output)
Sassone and Schwartz (1986)	Method to quantify benefits	Departments (4) of large corporations (587 individuals)	Dollars saved by restructuring work activities

APPENDIX A   223

Input Measure(s)	Key Findings (Brynjolfsson and Bimber Hypothesis Code)[a]
Total IT capital stock	Increases in shares of IT capital have insignificant effects on productivity. (IA)
Electronic communications, electronic brokerage, and electronic integration	IT reduces the costs of coordination and thus leads to more coordination-intensive organizational forms, such as markets. (IE)
Labor	Describes the problems in measuring service productivity and attempts of the Bureau of Labor Statistics to correct them. (IA)
	Emphasizes evolutionary models over traditional economic theory of productivity. (ID)
Conventional productivity	Severe measurement problems in services.
New technologies	Possible reasons for failure at aggregate levels: (1) economy, (2) lags in translating potential gains in productivity into actual gains because of problems of organizational and institutional adaptation, (3) disequilibrating effects of technical change in relation to international trade. (IIE)
Aggregated number of mainframes; number of central processing units	Each 10% increase in computing stock associated with 1.8% decrease in clerical employment and 1.2% decrease in managerial employment. Found lagged effect; displacement partially reversed after initial impact.
IT and operating data	IT coefficient in translog production function small and often negative.
Laptop computer use	No discernible improvement in productivity. Major discrepancy between users' perceptions of improved productivity and actual results.
IT	IT affects competition in 3 ways: (1) it alters industry/value-chain structure, (2) it supports cost and differentiation strategies, and (3) it spawns entirely new businesses. (IE)
Total IT capital stock	Large-scale increases in ratio of IT capital stock to other shares of capital, coupled with stagnant productivity, suggest no payoff from IT investments. (IID)
Office automation	Reports on poor status of cost-justification procedures, difficulty of measuring the dollar value of investments in new technology. (IIA)

TABLE A.1 Continued

Reference	Type of Research	Unit of Analysis	Performance Construct and Measure(s)
Strassmann (1990)	Correlation	Company (38 service companies)	Percent return to shareholders
Thurow (1987)	Theory—challenges economic assumptions Prescriptive	Service-sector businesses	Productivity growth
Venkatraman and Zaheer (1990)	Quasi-experiment Time series (1985 to 1987)	Individual (78 insurance agents)	Productivity (number of policies in force, number of new policies) Effectiveness (total premiums and commissions)
Weitzendorf and Wigand (1991)	Model case study	Company (2)	Performance

[a]Code gives elements of Brynjolfsson and Bimber hypotheses outlined below:

I. Economic Hypotheses

   A. *Measurement error:* Outputs (and inputs) of information-using industries are not being properly measured.
   B. *Lags:* Time lags in the payoffs from information technology make analysis of current costs versus current benefits misleading.
   C. *Redistribution:* Information technology is especially likely to be used in redistributive activities among firms, making it privately beneficial without adding to total output.
   D. *Mismanagement:* The lack of explicit measures of the value of information make it particularly vulnerable to misallocation and overconsumption by managers.
   E. *Business transformation:* Measures of gross output do not well capture the benefits that motivate expenditures on information technology and information workers.

Input Measure(s)	Key Findings	(Brynjolfsson and Bimber Hypothesis Code)[a]
Various IT ratios, weighted differently	No correlations between various IT ratios and performance measures.	
Movement to bonus system, value-added maximization, delayed management fast track	Our institutions, styles, and beliefs have not adapted to realities of new technologies, leading to too many managers and too much information gathering. (ID)	
Electronic integration with insurance carriers	No improvement in operating efficiency. No improvement in effectiveness.	
IT	Interactive model of information use.	

II. Behavioral Hypotheses

  A. *Quantity of work:* For the production of a fixed level of output by a firm, the introduction of information technology increases rather than decreases the volume of work required.
  B. *Nature of productivity:* Information technology increases the efficiency of individuals, work groups, or departments in the performance of certain tasks without contributing to the overall productivity of the firm.
  C. *Quality:* Improvements in work quality from the use of information technology are not affecting productivity.
  D. *Purchase decision:* The decision to purchase information technology is not made on the basis of maximization of quantifiable productivity.
  E. *Organizational factors:* Firms are failing to undertake the necessary organizational adaptations to realize the potential productivity gains inherent in the information technology that they have purchased.
  F. *Technology:* Other problems are so strongly depressing service-sector and white-collar productivity that any small gains from new technology are not noticeable.

SOURCES: Derived from the literature reviews in papers by Brynjolfsson, Erik, and Bruce Bimber, 1991, "Information Technology and the 'Productivity Paradox,'" Working Paper, Brookings Institution, Washington, D.C., Feb. 7; Brynjolfsson, Erik, 1991, "The Productivity Paradox of Information Technology: Review and Assessment," Center for Coordination Science Technical Report #130, December; and Wilson, Diane D., 1992, "Assessing the Impact of Information Technology on Organizational Performance," Sloan School of Management, Massachusetts Institute of Technology, (revised), May 1.

REFERENCES

Alpar, Paul, and Moshe Kim. 1990. "A Microeconomic Approach to the Measurement of Information Technology Value," *Journal of Management Information Systems* 2:55-69.

Applegate, Lynda M., James I. Cash, Jr., and D. Quinn Mills. 1988. "Information Technology and Tommorow's Manager," *Harvard Business Review*, November-December, pp. 128-136.

Attewell, P., and J. Rule. 1984. "Computing and Organizations: What We Know and What We Don't Know," *Communications of the ACM* 27:1184-1192.

Baily, Martin, and Alok Chakrabarti. 1988. *Innovation and the Productivity Crisis*. Chapter 5, "Electronics and White-Collar Productivity," Brookings Institution, Washington, D.C.

Baily, Martin Neill, and Robert J. Gordon. 1988. "The Productivity Slowdown: Measurement Issues and the Explosion of Computer Power," pp. 347-431 in *Brookings Papers on Economic Activity*, William C. Brainard and George L. Perry (eds.), Brookings Institution, Washington, D.C.

Banker, R.D., and R.J. Kauffman. 1988. "Strategic Contributions of Information Technology: An Empirical Study of ATM Networks," in *Proceedings of the Ninth International Conference on Information Systems*, Minneapolis, Minn., December.

Bender, D.H. 1986. "Financial Impact of Information Processing," *Journal of Management Information Systems* 3.

Benjamin, Robert I., John F. Rockart, Michael S. Scott Morton, and John Wyman. 1984. "Information Technology: A Strategic Opportunity," *Sloan Management Review*, Spring, pp. 3-10.

Bikson, Tora K., and J.D. Eveland. 1986. *New Office Technology: Planning for the People*. Work in America Institute Studies in Productivity, #40, Pergamon Press, New York.

Blumenthal, Marjory S. 1987. "Economic Impacts of Automation," *Oxford Surveys in Information Technology* 4.

Bresnahan, Timothy F. 1986. "Measuring the Spillovers from Technical Advance: Mainframe Computers in Financial Services," *American Economic Review* 76(34, September).

Cecil, John L., and Eugene A. Hall. 1988. "When IT Really Matters to Business Strategy," *McKinsey Quarterly*, Autumn, p. 2.

Cron, W.L., and M.G. Sobol. 1983. "The Relationship Between Computerization and Performance: A Strategy for Maximizing the Economic Benefits of Computerization," *Information and Management* 6:171-181.

Curley, Kathleen Foley, and Philip J. Pyburn. 1982 "'Intellectual' Technologies: The Key to Improving White-Collar Productivity," *Sloan Management Review*, Fall, pp. 31-39.

Dertouzos, Michael L. 1989. "Computers and Productivity," LCS 25th Anniversary Volume, Massachusetts Institute of Technology, MIT Press, Cambridge, Mass.

Feldman, Martha S., and James G. March. 1981. "Information in Organizations as Signal and Symbol," *Administrative Science Quarterly* 26:171-186.

Franke, Richard H. 1987. "Technological Revolution and Productivity Decline: Computer Introduction in the Financial Industry," *Technological Forecasting and Social Change* 31:143-154.

Fudenberg, Drew, and Jean Tirole. 1985. "Preemption and Rent Equalization in the Adoption of New Technology," *Review of Economic Studies* 52:383-401.

Giesler, Eliezer, and Albert H. Rubenstein. 1988. "How Do Banks Evaluate Their Information Technology?" *Bank Administration*, November.

Graham, John. 1976. *Making Computers Pay*, John Wiley & Sons, New York.

Harris, Sidney E., and Joseph L. Katz. 1991. "Organizational Performance and Information Technology Investment Intensity in the Insurance Industry," *Organization Science* 2:263-296.

Hirshleifer, Jack. 1971. "The Private and Social Value of Information and the Reward to Inventive Activity," *American Economic Review*, pp. 561-574.
Kraut, Robert, Susan Dumais, and Susan Koch. 1989. "Computerization, Productivity, and Quality of Work Life," *Communications of the ACM* 32(February).
Loveman, Gary. 1988. "An Assessment of the Productivity Impact of Information Technologies," MIT Management in the 1990's Program, 88-054, July.
Malone, Thomas W., Joanne Yates, and Robert I. Benjamin. 1987. "Electronic Markets and Electronic Hierarchies," *Communications of the ACM* 30(6, June).
Mark, Jerome A. 1982. "Measuring Productivity in the Service Sector," *Monthly Labor Review*, June.
Nelson, Richard R. 1981. "Research on Productivity Growth and Productivity Differences: Dead Ends and New Departures," *Journal of Economic Literature* 29:1029-1064.
Noyelle, T., ed. 1990. *Skills, Wages, and Productivity in the Service Sector*, Westview Press, Boulder, Colo.
Organisation for Economic Cooperation and Development (OECD). 1988. *New Technologies in the 1990's: A Socio-economic Strategy*, OECD, Washington, D.C.
Osterman, Paul. 1986. "The Impact of Computers on the Employment of Clerks and Managers," *Industrial and Labor Relations Review* 39:175-186.
Parsons, D.J., C.C. Gotlieb, and M. Denny. 1990. *Productivity and Computers in Canadian Banking*. University of Toronto, Department of Economics, Working Paper #9012, June.
Pentland, Brian. 1989. "Use and Productivity in Personal Computing," *Proceedings of the Tenth International Conference on Information Systems*, Boston, Mass., December.
Porter, Michael E., and Victor E. Millar. 1985. "How Information Gives You Competitive Advantage," *Harvard Business Review*, July-August, pp. 149-160.
Roach, Stephen S. 1991. "Services Under Siege—The Restructuring Imperative," *Harvard Business Review*, September-October, pp. 82-91.
Sassone, Peter G., and A. Perry Schwartz. 1986. "Cost-Justifying OA," *Datamation*, February 15.
Strassmann, P. 1990. *The Business Value of Computers*, Information Economics Press, New Canaan, Conn.
Thurow, L. 1987. "Economic Paradigms and Slow American Productivity Growth," *Eastern Economic Journal* 13:333-343.
Venkatraman, N., and Akbar Zaheer. 1990. "Electronic Integration and Strategic Advantage: A Quasi-Experimental Study in the Insurance Industry," *Information Systems Research* 1:377-393.
Weitzendorf, T., and R. Wigand. 1991. *Tasks and Decisions: A Suggested Model to Demonstrate Benefits of Information Technology*, Working Paper, Institut für Informationswissenschaft, Graz, Austria.

Appendix B
Methods for Deriving Bureau of Economic Analysis Measures of Output

As part of the National Income and Product Accounts (NIPA) series, the Bureau of Economic Analysis (BEA) of the Department of Commerce publishes annual measures of gross product originating (GPO) by industry in current and constant dollars to supplement the measures of gross national product (GNP) for the U.S. economy as a whole. These data are useful for understanding the diversity of movement in output among the various component industries of the economy. However, for a variety of reasons, principally data limitations, these measures do not have the same degree of accuracy as the overall measures of GNP.

When requested, the Bureau of Labor Statistics (BLS), the federal government agency that develops the government's measures of productivity, does make available the productivity measures that could be derived by relating these data on output to the corresponding data on labor input. Because of the limitations in the data, however, the BLS does not publish these measures as part of its regular set of productivity indexes.

In the framework of the national accounts, the relevant measure of output for purposes of gauging productivity is the constant-dollar GPO. To derive this measure the BEA uses three principal methods.[1] One is termed *double deflation*, another *extrapolation*, and the third *direct deflation*. The method chosen for each service industry usually depends on the availability of adequate data.

In the double-deflation method, constant-dollar GPO is derived as the difference between current-dollar gross or final output divided by an appropriate output price index, and the current-dollar intermediate input (materials and purchased services) divided by an appropriate input price index. In the extrapolation method, constant-dollar GPO is derived by extrapolating the base-year current-dollar GPO from some related series such as constant-dollar gross (not net) output, employment, or the number of hours worked. In the direct-deflation method, constant-dollar GPO is derived by dividing each year's current-dollar GPO by either a gross output price index or an hourly earnings index.

Generally, the double-deflation method is used whenever possible, since it is most consistent with the definition of GPO, namely, final output minus intermediate input. For the other methods to be appropriate approximations, certain assumptions are made. In the extrapolation method, the assumption is that the change in constant-dollar gross output is the same as the change in constant-dollar input. In the direct-deflation method, the assumption is that the changes in the output price deflators and the input price deflators are the same.

In recent years there have been substantial improvements in the NIPA data, and the number of industries for which double deflation is used has increased. Table B.1 shows the methods currently used to derive the constant-dollar GPO for the various service industries. As can be seen, double deflation is used for a substantial number of service industries.

However, the quality of the double-deflation estimates varies considerably. Table B.2 lists the various measures of output prices and other data and the sources of data used to derive the constant-dollar gross output portion of GPO as measured by the double-deflation method. These data come from both government and private sources, and the definitions in many cases differ considerably from those underlying the current-dollar estimates.

Although double-deflated gross output is generally calculated by dividing the current-dollar output by an output price index, as shown in Table B.2, in some cases, part of the constant-dollar gross output is deflated and part of it is based on direct extrapolation of base-year quantitative output measures. This is the case in local and interurban passenger transportation, where gross output for taxicabs is based on revenues deflated by the consumer price index for taxi fares; but gross output for intercity buses is based on base-year current-dollar revenues adjusted by changes in total passenger-miles; gross output for other local transit services is based on base-year revenues adjusted by changes in the number of passenger trips; and gross output for school buses is based on base-year revenues adjusted by changes in employment. Thus, measures for local and interurban passenger transportation by definition cannot take into account changes in productivity that may have taken place, and in some cases, the output price indexes used to deflate output are not price indexes but cost indexes. As such, deflated output measures cannot take into account changes in productivity.

In developing measures of constant-dollar input to subtract from measures of constant-dollar gross output, changes in the composition of the

TABLE B.1 Methods for Estimating Constant-Dollar GPO for Various Service Industries

Industry	Method
Transportation	
Railroads	Double deflation
Local passenger transit	Double deflation
Trucking and warehousing	Double deflation
Water transportation	Double deflation
Air transportation	Double deflation
Pipelines	Double deflation
Transportation services	Extrapolation
Communications	
Telephone and telegraph	Double deflation
Radio and television broadcasting	Double deflation
Electric, gas, and sanitary services	Double deflation
Retail trade	Double deflation
Wholesale trade	Double deflation
Finance, insurance, and real estate	
Banking	Extrapolation
Credit agencies	Extrapolation
Security and commodity brokers	Double deflation
Insurance carriers	Double deflation
Business and personal services	
Hotels and other lodging places	Double deflation
Personal services	Double deflation
Business services	Extrapolation
Auto repair services and garages	Double deflation
Miscellaneous repair services	Double deflation
Motion pictures	Direct deflation
Amusements and recreation	Double deflation
Health services	Double deflation
Legal services	Double deflation
Educational services	Double deflation
Social services	Direct deflation
Miscellaneous professional services	Direct deflation
Private household services	Direct deflation
Government	
General government	Extrapolation
Government enterprises	Extrapolation

SOURCE: U.S. Department of Commerce, Bureau of Economic Analysis. 1991. *Survey of Current Business,* January.

TABLE B.2 Sources of Data for Output Price or Other Measures Used in Deriving Double Deflation GPO Measures for Various Service Industries

Industry	Price or Other Measure[a]
Transportation	
Railroads	IPD from revenue ton-miles and passenger-miles from AMTRAK data
Local passenger transit	
Taxicabs	CPI for taxi fares
Intercity buses	Passenger-miles from ABA
School buses	Employment from BLS
Local transit	Passenger trips from APTA
Trucking and warehousing	Ton-miles from DOT
Water transportation	Index of ton-miles for deep sea from BEA, ton-miles for other water transportation from DOD, and ton-miles of marine cargo from DOD
Air transportation	Separate revenue passenger-miles for domestic and international travel and freight ton-miles by DOT
Pipelines	Ton-miles from AOP
Communications	
Telephone and telegraph	PPIs for local telephone and toll telephone services and direct advertising
Radio and television broadcasting	Index based on cost per 1000-member audience
Electric, gas, and sanitary services	
Electric utilities	Kilowatt-hours from EEI
Gas utilities	BTUs of gas for resale and BTUs of gas utility sales from AGA
Sanitary services	CPI for water and sewage maintenance
Retail trade	
Eating and drinking places	CPIs
Other	Base-year margin times sales deflated by CPIs
Wholesale trade	
Merchant wholesalers	1982 gross margin rate-weighted sales deflated by PPIs
Manufacturers' sales offices	For equipment rental, IPD from BEA capital stock data; for rest, PPIs
Agents and brokers	PPIs
Finance, insurance, and real estate	
Security brokers and services	
Commissions	Number of public securities orders from SEC and NYSE
Mutual funds	IPD for securities commissions
Underwriting	New securities registrations from SEC
Trading gains	IPD for GNP
Commodity brokers	IPD for GNP
Insurance brokers and agencies	Insurance carrier deflators weighted by commissions from A.M. Best Co.
Real estate services	IPD for PCE
Business and Personal Services	
Hotels, rooming houses	Laventhol & Horwath room-rate index
Laundries and dry cleaners	CPIs from BLS
Shoe repair shops	CPIs from BLS

Continues

TABLE B.2 Continued

Industry	Price or Other Measure[a]
Photographic studios	CPIs from BLS
Beauty shops	CPIs from BLS
Barber shops	CPIs from BLS
Funeral services	CPIs from BLS
Automotive rental	CPIs from BLS
Automotive repair services	CPIs from BLS
Electric repair shops	CPIs from BLS
Watch and jewelry repair	CPIs from BLS
Furniture repair	CPIs from BLS
Miscellaneous repair shops	Average earnings from BLS
Amusement and recreational services	
Dance studios and schools	CPIs from BLS
Theatrical producers and entertainers	CPIs from BLS
Bowling alleys and pool halls	CPIs from BLS
Commercial sports	CPIs from BLS
Health services	
Physicians and dentists	CPIs from BLS
Nursing and personal care facilities	HCFA input price index
Hospitals	Composite deflator of hospital room CPI and HCFA input prices
Medical and dental laboratories	CPIs from BLS
Outpatient care facilities	CPIs from BLS
Health and allied services, not otherwise classified	CPIs from BLS
Legal services	CPIs from BLS
Education services	
Private schools and libraries	PCE deflators
Private education housing and meals	PCE deflators

[a] Abbreviations:

ABA	American Bus Association	EEI	Edison Electric Institute
AGA	American Gas Association	FCC	Federal Communications Commission
AOP	Association of Oil Pipelines	GNP	Gross national product
APTA	American Public Transit Association	HCFA	Health Care Financing Administration
BEA	Bureau of Economic Analysis	IPD	Implicit price deflator
BLS	Bureau of Labor Statistics	M-E	McCann-Erickson Co.
BTU	British thermal unit	NYSE	New York Stock Exchange
CPI	Consumer price index	PCE	Personal consumption expenditures
DOD	U.S. Department of Defense	PPI	Producer price index
DOT	U.S. Department of Transportation	SEC	Securities Exchange Commission

SOURCE: U.S. Department of Commerce, Bureau of Economic Analysis.

TABLE B.3 Sources of Data for GPO Series Based on Extrapolation and Direct Deflation

Industry	Method	Source of Data
Transportation services	Extrapolation	BEA employment
Banking	Extrapolation	BEA employment
Credit agencies	Extrapolation	BEA employment
Real estate	Direct deflation	Trade source rent index for office buildings
Holding companies	Extrapolation	BEA employment
Business services	Extrapolation	BLS employment weighted by Census Bureau receipts
Motion pictures	Direct deflation	BLS prices and earnings
Social services	Direct deflation	BEA average wages and salaries
Miscellaneous professional	Direct deflation	BEA average wages and salaries
Private households	Direct deflation	BLS prices
Government		
General	Extrapolation	BEA hours worked weighted by measures of experience
Government enterprises	Extrapolation	BEA and Census Bureau employment and BLS output indexes

SOURCE: U.S. Department of Commerce, Bureau of Economic Analysis. 1991. *Survey of Current Business,* January.

material and other input have to be taken into account in deriving the appropriate input price indexes. To do this an input-output table, which measures in some detail the purchases from one industry by another, is used. The last fully developed input-output table is for 1977. To update this information for the current measures, changes in the composition were estimated by assuming that both constant-dollar gross output and input have changed at the same rate since 1977.

Table B.3 provides information on the sources of data used to develop GPO measures in those industries for which the double-deflation method is not used. In many of these cases, and particularly for financial institutions, extrapolation was used, and the base-year revenues were adjusted by changes in employment or wages and salaries. In such cases, measures of output do not reflect changes in productivity that have taken place.

NOTE

[1] For a detailed description of the estimating methods used for the measures of constant-dollar GPO, see De Leeuw, Frank, Michael Mohr, and Robert P. Parker, 1991, "Gross Product by Industry, 1977-88: A Progress Report on Improving the Estimates," *Survey of Current Business,* January, pp. 23-37.

Appendix C
Procedures for Deriving Bureau of Labor Statistics Measures of Productivity for Service Industries

The Bureau of Labor Statistics (BLS) measures of productivity are in the form of indexes of output per unit of labor input derived from dividing an index of output for an industry by the corresponding index of labor input.

INDUSTRY-LEVEL MEASUREMENT OF OUTPUT

Table C.1 describes the procedures used by the BLS to derive the indexes of output for each of the service industries for which it publishes productivity measures. A summary of those methods follows. Table C.1 also provides Standard Industrial Classification code information to clarify industry definitions as they are used by the BLS.

Transportation

The BLS publishes indexes of productivity for five transportation industries: railroads, intercity buses, intercity trucking, air transportation, and petroleum pipelines. These measures cover 35 percent of transportation employment.

NOTE: This appendix updates and expands on previous work presented in Mark, Jerome A., 1986, "Measuring Productivity in Services Industries," pp. 139-159 in *Technology in Services: Policies for Growth, Trade, and Employment*, Bruce R. Guile and James Brian Quinn (eds.), National Academy Press, Washington, D.C.

TABLE C.1 Methods Used by the Bureau of Labor Statistics to Derive Indexes of Output for the Service Industries

Industry	SIC[a]	Procedure
Railroads	4011 pt.	Freight ton-miles and passenger-miles weighted with labor expenses. Freight ton-miles adjusted by unit-revenue-weighted commodity ratios.
Bus carriers, Class 1	411, 413, 414 pt.	Intercity and local indexes combined with employment weights. Four components of each index—passenger-miles, passengers, charter passengers, and deflated freight revenue—combined with revenue weights.
Intercity trucking	4213	Indexes for general freight, specialized carriers, and household-goods carriers combined with employment weights. Freight ton-miles for components of each index combined with employment weights.
Air transportation	4512,22	Freight ton-miles and passenger-miles separately weighted for domestic and international services.
Petroleum pipelines	4612,3	Unweighted barrel-miles.
Telephone communications	481	Separately deflated revenues from local, wide-area toll service (WATS), measured toll (MTS) and miscellaneous services.
Electric utilities	491,493 pt.	Kilowatt-hours for 7 classes of A & B service and 4 classes of Rural Electrification Administration service combined with revenue weights.
Gas utilities	492,493 pt.	Therms sold for residential, commercial, industrial, and other classes of service combined with revenue weights.
Gas and electric utilities	491,2,3	Output indexes for electric and gas utilities combined with employee-hour weights.
Scrap and waste materials	5093	Scrap index based on tons by types of scrap combined with unit-labor-requirement weights. This index combined with wastepaper index using employment weights.
Hardware stores	5251	Deflated merchandise line sales combined with employment weights.
Department stores	5311	Merchandise line sales for 16 departments separately deflated with consumer price indexes. Deflated department sales then combined with employment weights. This index of output then combined with deflated mail-order sales using employment weights.
Variety stores	5331	Deflated sales for 29 merchandise lines combined with gross margin weights.

Continues

TABLE C.1 Continued

Industry	SIC[a]	Procedure
Grocery stores	5411	From 1958 to 1972 for general grocery stores, deflated merchandise line sales for meat, produce, dry grocery, dairy, frozen food, and other departments combined with labor-cost weights; from 1972, gross margin weights used. For specialty stores, merchandise line sales separately deflated and aggregated. The two indexes then combined with all person-hour weights.
Retail bakeries	546	Deflated merchandise line sales combined with gross margin weights.
Retail food stores	54	Indexes for grocery stores and retail bakeries combined with index for other food stores using hours of all persons for weights. Index for other food stores derived by combining indexes for meat, fish markets, fruit stores, markets, dairy stores, and confectioneries with employee weights. Detailed indexes based on deflated merchandise line sales combined with gross margins.
New- and used-car dealers	5511	Combined count of new- and used-car sales and deflated parts and service sales with employment weights.
Auto and home supply stores	553	Deflated merchandise line sales combined with gross margin weights.
Gasoline service stations	5541	Sales deflated by price index from consumer price indexes (CPIs) weighted by merchandise line sales.
Men's and boys' clothing stores	5611	Sales deflated by price index from CPIs weighted by merchandise line sales.
Women's clothing stores	5621	Sales deflated by price index from CPIs weighted by merchandise line sales.
Family clothing stores	5651	Sales deflated by price index from CPIs weighted by merchandise line sales.
Shoe stores	5661	Sales deflated by price index from CPIs weighted by merchandise line sales.
Furniture and home furnishings stores	571	Merchandise line sales for individual SIC 4-digit industries deflated with matching CPIs combined with gross margin weights. Indexes then combined with all person-hour weights.
Household appliance stores	572	Merchandise line sales for individual 4-digit industries deflated with matching CPIs combined with gross margin weights. Indexes then combined with all person-hour weights.

TABLE C.1 Continued

Industry	SIC[a]	Procedure
Radio and television stores	573	Merchandise line sales for individual 4-digit industries deflated with matching CPIs combined with gross margin weights. Indexes then combined with all person-hour weights.
Eating and drinking places	58	For each type of outlet (restaurants, cafeterias, and so on), CPI-deflated merchandise line sales combined with gross margin weights. Outlet indexes in turn combined with employment weights.
Drug and proprietary stores	5912	Prescription sales, meals and snacks, and general merchandise sales deflated by matching CPIs. Deflated sales then combined with employee-hour weights.
Retail liquor stores	5921	Deflated merchandise line sales combined with gross margin weights.
Commercial banking	602	Indexes for three major banking activities (deposits, loans, and fiduciary) combined with employment weights. Measure for deposits includes demand deposits (based on number of checks and electronic transactions) and estimated number of transactions in time and savings accounts. Measure for loans based on number of various types of loans combined with employment weight. Measure for fiduciary activities based primarily on number of trust accounts.
Hotels and motels	7011	Separate indexes for hotels, motels, and tourist courts combined with employment weights. For each index, receipts for various activities (e.g., room rentals, food sales, beverage sales, etc.) are deflated with matching CPIs.
Laundry and dry cleaning services	721	Deflated revenues from 8 types of laundry and dry cleaning services combined with employment weights.
Beauty and barber shops	7231,41	Beauty shop index based on deflated revenues for 14 types of services and barber shop index based on deflated revenues for 13 services combined with all person-hour weights.
Automotive repair shops	753	Receipts from 12 industry activities deflated by matching CPIs and combined with employment weights.

[a]Standard Industrial Classification system code.

SOURCE: Bureau of Labor Statistics, unpublished data.

Conceptually, the measures for the transportation industries are easier to develop than those for other service industries because transportation industry output—the movement of goods or passengers over distances—is more easily quantified. Units of output in transportation have two dimensions, quantities and distance, that reflect how much has been transported how far. As such, ton-miles, passenger-miles, barrel-miles, and so forth are the primary indicators of output for these series of indexes.

For the most part, historically, these data have been available from the regulatory agency of the particular transportation industry, such as the Interstate Commerce Commission (ICC) or the Civil Aeronautics Board. In many cases, however, there are data gaps that place certain limitations on the measures. For example, it is sometimes impossible to adjust the measures of output adequately for changes in the average length of haul. The labor requirements associated with the movement of freight and passengers are usually greater for short hauls than for long hauls. Therefore, a shift from a long haul to a series of short-haul trips or vice-versa could be interpreted as a change in productivity, although only the mix of trips has changed.

For the two major freight-carrying industries, railroads and trucking, undifferentiated data on ton-miles are reported for various classes of freight operations. In trucking, the ton-mile data are reported separately for general freight, specialized carriers, and carriers of household goods. But the measures of output should reflect the kinds of commodities handled and the average distance they are moved, since they represent separate types of services. The preferred way to develop such measures would be to combine the tonnage and average haul of each commodity with its respective requirements for labor input and then aggregate the results for all commodities transported. Unfortunately, this cannot be done with currently available data.

However, for the railroad industry, information on tonnage for separate commodities is available from the ICC for about 170 commodity lines, ranging from agricultural and mining products to motor vehicles and scientific instruments. Several years ago similar information was available for the trucking industry, but its collection has been discontinued. The BLS uses these data to adjust the overall measure of freight ton-miles for changes in the composition of goods carried.

Although this adjustment for commodities hauled represents an improvement over undifferentiated ton-mile figures, refinements cannot be developed to the extent desirable. The adjustments to the index for the commodity hauled are made in terms of unit revenue weights. The underlying assumption, therefore, is that differences in labor requirements among commodities are similar to differences in unit revenues. Since labor costs constitute more than half of each industry's total operating costs, this assumption may not

APPENDIX C 239

be unreasonable; however, the proportions could conceivably differ by commodity. In deriving the index of total industry output for each of the transportation industries, the freight ton-mile measure (adjusted or not) is combined with the revenue passenger-mile measure.

The deregulation of many transportation industries has resulted in the elimination of some of the operating statistics previously published and used to develop the indexes of output. As a result, some of the measures for the transportation industry have had to be extended on the basis of more limited information. The BLS has been cooperating with other government agencies to ensure that adequate statistics remain available for transportation industries.

Communications

The BLS index of productivity for telephone communications covers about 70 percent of the employment of the communications sector. The index of output is derived as a weighted aggregate of revenues adjusted for changes in price for four different categories of telephone service: local calls, measured toll service (MTS), wide-area toll service (WATS), and all other services, including private-line service. The data on revenue are collected and published by the Federal Communications Commission. Deflators are derived from price indexes compiled and published by the BLS under its Producer Price Index program.

The measure of deflated revenue includes revenues from private-line services. It also accounts for TV, radio, and computer transmission by telephone industry facilities as well as directory services.

Despite the detail that is included in the measure of output, improvements could be made if information were available on the intensity of use of telephone equipment by customers. The number of calls made can vary without revenue also varying proportionately because of flat charges such as WATS-line or local-call charges. To the extent that the number of such calls varies over time, the index overstates or understates changes in output.

Electric, Gas, and Sanitary Services

Services rendered by public utilities range from the provision of light, heat, and water to the disposal of solid and liquid wastes. In this area the BLS currently publishes indexes of productivity for electric utilities, gas utilities, and a combination of the two.

The measure for electric utility output covers all privately owned utilities, which account for roughly 80 percent of the total output generated in the United States. Output is defined in terms of kilowatt-hours generated and distributed. The measure of the output of gas utilities is defined in terms of therms (one therm equals 100,000 British thermal units) delivered to customers by all privately owned companies (which account for 95 percent of total gas output).

Since the labor requirements per kilowatt-hour or per therm are higher for residential than for commercial and industrial customers and are higher for small establishments than for larger ones, BLS differentiates among both kilowatt-hours and therms by type of customer.

Retail Trade

Although the BLS has been publishing measures of productivity for retail trade industries since 1975, the number of such industries has increased markedly in recent years. At present, indexes are available for 11 important industries—retail food stores, franchised new-car dealers, gasoline service stations, apparel and accessory stores, furniture and appliance stores, eating and drinking places, drug and proprietary stores, and liquor stores. Apparel and accessory stores are further broken out into men's and boys' clothing stores, women's ready-to-wear stores, family clothing stores, and shoe stores. Also, furniture and appliance stores are disaggregated into furniture and furnishings stores, and appliance stores. Work is currently under way on measures for hardware stores, auto and home supply stores, and department stores.

For most retail trade industries, data on gross sales in current dollars, deflated by appropriate price indexes, are used to estimate real output. This method can yield good measures of real output if adequate consumer price indexes can be developed that reflect the price movements of the various commodities sold by the establishments. The recent improvements that have been made in the BLS Consumer Price Index program have enabled it to develop indexes of output and productivity for more components of retail trade.

Indexes of productivity based on deflated value of sales output measures reflect shifts among services with different levels of sales but the same trade labor requirements. Therefore, the overall industry productivity index can show movements without any change in component elements.

In retail industries a large portion of the value of sales is provided by the manufacturers and the wholesalers of the products sold. A measure of net output would be desirable since it would most closely correspond to the functions provided by the retailer. Unfortunately, measures of net output based on data with separately deflated final sales and cost of materials can result in large errors of measurement when the cost of materials is a large proportion of the final value. This is because all the errors in the current value of sales, the current value of material purchases, the Consumer Price Index, and the Producer Price Index affect this residual.

Gross or total sales will represent a good measure of net output or value added with less measurement error if the value added as a percent of sales (gross margin) does not change over time. Available data seem to indicate that for the industries published, average gross margins have not changed substantially over time. To introduce labor input weighting, the indexes for retail trade industries for the most part are developed in two stages. Deflated output measures are first developed for detailed merchandise lines. These are aggregated to higher levels, and the resultant indexes are then combined with labor-cost weights. For example, in retail food stores, sales for 13 key merchandise lines are deflated using specially prepared price indexes based on the BLS Consumer Price Index components. The indexes for the merchandise lines are aggregated to five department lines—meat, produce, frozen food, dry groceries and dairy, and all others. These in turn are aggregated with labor-cost weights to develop a measure of overall output for grocery stores.

Wholesale Trade

Until recently the BLS did not publish any measures for wholesale trade. Currently, only an index for scrap and waste materials dealers is published. The measure of output is derived by combining the quantities of various types of processed scrap into a broad product group and the various types of processed wastepaper into an overall wastepaper group. Measures for these two groups are then combined with employment weights to yield measures of overall output.

The BLS is currently examining three industries in considerable detail to derive reliable measures: metal service centers, petroleum bulk stations, and beer, wine, and distilled spirits distributors. These industries include about half a million workers, or 10 percent of the employment in the sector. Data on physical quantity are available to develop measures of output for these industries. The data on quantity for disaggregated commodities will be combined with fixed-period labor input weights reflecting the services provided by the wholesalers to retailers and other users.

Several measurement problems with respect to these industries need to be resolved. Some firms perform work on commodities that they distribute to retailers, but this practice varies substantially among wholesale distributors. Whether the labor input weights can adequately take this variation into account is questionable. In addition, in some instances a regional wholesaler distributes commodities to local wholesalers. This creates a problem of duplicate counting in the measure of overall industry output.

Finance

In the area of finance, the BLS publishes a measure of productivity for the commercial banking industry that reflects the three major services commercial banks render their customers—deposits, loans, and trust services. While banks also perform nonfund-using services, such as safe deposit services and customer payroll accounting, lack of adequate data precludes deriving a measure for them. However, because the proportion of employees engaged in such services is small, the overall validity of the measure is little affected by the omission.

There has been a great deal of discussion over the years as to the appropriate measure of the output of banking. Much of the discussion addresses whether the appropriate concept is one based on what has been called the liquidity approach or one based on a transactions approach.[1] In the liquidity approach the banks are viewed as providers of money to hold, and their output is measured in terms of the interest received on the volume of deposits held. Such interest received by banks is assumed to be equivalent to the income foregone by depositors due to their preference for holding deposits rather than for investing directly. The interest the depositors forego represents the value of the banks' services for such liquidity preference. This approach can be extended to all types of savings accounts, the assumption being that the foregone net interest is the value of the banks' services.

According to the transactions approach, the banks are providers of a series of services to their clients that are reflected in the transactions performed. The volume of the banks' output is proportional to the volume of the transactions handled. Thus the final output of commerical banking represents an array of services provided to bank customers relating to the depository, lending, and fiduciary functions of banks. In developing a measure of productivity for banking, the BLS adopted the transactions approach for the measure of output.

Estimates of the number of transactions in each of the service functions of banks are derived. In some instances, no direct count of transactions is available, and so the number of transactions is estimated from data on the total value of transactions and on the results of surveys of the average dollar-value of transactions. Although these estimates have some limitations, the derived count of the number of transactions is the measure used to reflect the quantities of services provided.

Deposit activity is measured in terms of the number of checks transacted and the number of time- and savings-account deposits and withdrawals. The data for demand deposit activities are derived ultimately from Federal Reserve Bank counts and official benchmark surveys. For time- and savings-deposit activity, the measure of output is derived from data published by the Federal Deposit Insurance Corporation and the Functional Cost Analysis conducted annually by the Federal Reserve Board. Lending services provided by banks are also measured in terms of units. As in the case of deposit activity and trust department activity, the BLS does not use banks' financial data to arrive at measures of component output.

Business and Personal Services

In the business and personal services sector, the BLS publishes measures for four industries—hotels, motels, and tourist courts; laundry and dry cleaning services; beauty and barber shops; and automotive repair shops. The output for each of these industries is measured by total revenues from the various activities of establishments within the industry adjusted by price changes. These measures are then combined with employment weights to derive an index of output for each industry. The BLS uses special price indexes derived from its Consumer Price Index program for deflating the receipts from the principal activities of each of the industries. For example, in hotels and motels, the receipts from room rentals, food sales, beverage sales, and so on are separately deflated by the appropriate price measures, and these measures are then combined with employment weights. It would be desirable to differentiate between all the separate activities of these establishments, but because of the limited number of price indexes that can be developed, some broader groupings have to be used.

Government

For the last 2 decades, the BLS has been conducting a program of developing indexes of labor productivity for all federal government agencies with 200 or more employees. Currently, the measures cover 390 organizations in 59 agencies that account for 60 percent of civilian government employment. The agency measures are grouped into functional groups representing relatively homogeneous activities, such as library services, loans and grants, and information services.

Where possible, the output of a government agency is defined as its final output—what it produced for use outside the government. Therefore, measures are also developed for agencies (and parts of agencies) providing services to other parts of the government, such as printing, personnel management, communications, and supply and inventory control. Because of the inclusion of intermediate activities and output, the index of overall productivity is not final for the entire government. The summary productivity measure reflects the average of changes in the productivity of the measured federal organizations.

The measures of output used in productivity calculations are diverse, including such indicators as inspections completed and reports prepared (for audit functions), statistical reports issued, maps produced, or weather forecasts made (for public information functions), food inspections conducted, drug arrests made, applications and licenses issued, drugs approved, and patents approved (for regulatory functions). Currently, output information is collected on about 3000 indicators.

Hospitals

For several years the BLS has been working to develop a measure of productivity for hospitals but has not yet determined whether the measure it has developed is adequate for publication.

Hospitals provide services designed to eliminate, retard, or prevent pathologies. Treatments, which can be regarded as producer technologies by which those services are rendered, are specified to produce desired outcomes. However, outcomes depend on factors other than, and in addition to, treatments, such as the pre-admission health of the patient. There is thus some question as to whether a measure of output related to hospital labor and other resources should be based on outcomes. The BLS does not adjust for outcomes in deriving its index of productivity for hospitals and instead uses a different approach.

Clinically named illnesses have been classified according to diagnosis, and diagnoses in turn are standardized into diagnosis-related groups—referred to as DRGs. A DRG implies a complex of treatments or procedures, which in turn are associated with the use of certain kinds and amounts of resources.

All diagnosis codes have been condensed into 23 major diagnostic categories (MDCs). The MDCs are generally based on diseases that tend to be diagnosed and similarly treated by specialists. Hospital discharges are first coded by diagnosis and then into DRGs.

The BLS measure of output for hospitals is derived from data on the number of inpatient discharges in each diagnostic category weighted by average hospital operating costs and the number of outpatient visits for each diagnostic category.

MEASURES OF LABOR INPUT

Productivity calculations require data on the hours worked of nonsupervisors, supervisors, unpaid family workers, and the self-employed. The principal source of data on employment and hours for all of the service industries for which BLS publishes indexes of productivity is the BLS survey of establishments' payrolls, the Current Employment Survey (CES). This survey provides good measures of the employment and hours of nonsupervisory workers by industry, but it does not provide data on the average hours of supervisory workers or on the employment and hours of unpaid family workers and the self-employed.

Information on the self-employed and unpaid family workers is derived from a survey of non-institutional households, the Current Population Survey (CPS). Based on 60,000 households in the United States, these data are adequate for aggregate measures such as those for the business economy as a whole or even major sectors, but they present limitations when used for such detailed measures as those for specific service industries.

Currently, the average weekly hours of supervisory workers are assumed to be equal to those of nonsupervisory workers in the service industries. This assumption presents fewer limitations for developing measures of change than for developing base labor input.

The most desirable measure of productivity is one that uses only the amount of labor actually involved in the generation of the services provided and excludes paid time off. The CES's data on hours are based on hours paid and include paid vacations, holidays, sick leave, and other time off in addition to actual hours worked. To the extent that leave practices change, the resultant measures of productivity overstate or understate the actual change in output per hour.

To develop a better series of hours at work, the BLS has been conducting an annual survey (now in its ninth year) of some 4000 establishments to collect data on hours at work and hours paid for nonsupervisory workers in the private nonagricultural business sector. From this survey, ratios are developed to adjust the present measures of hours paid (based on the CES data) to reflect hours at work. After careful study, "hours at work" was defined as time on the job or at the place of work and includes coffee breaks, short rest periods, paid cleanup time, and other paid time at the workplace besides actual time worked. Conceptually, this definition was considered to be the most acceptable one to use for extracting data from establishments' records. Although the appropriate information is available on hours at work at an aggregate level, a substantial expansion of this survey will be required to develop reliable data for specific service industries.

The BLS measures of productivity based on the hours at work for all persons assume that workers are homogeneous with respect to skill—that an hour of one worker's time is as productive as an hour of any other worker's time. However, a highly skilled worker can be viewed as providing more labor services per hour than a less highly skilled one. Shifts within the labor force from less skilled workers to more highly skilled ones because of increased education or experience are not reflected as increases in the measures of labor input. When skill differences are ignored, increases in skill levels are measured as increases in productivity.

To the extent that there are changes in the composition of the work force with respect to education and experience that result in skill differences, it may be desirable to reflect those changes in measures of labor input, since they will otherwise be reflected in measures of productivity.

To address this problem, previous studies have usually taken the position that relative wage- or income-level differentials associated with specific worker characteristics reflect marginal productivity of these attributes. Generally, the characteristics included are the number of years of schooling, age, sex, and possibly industry and occupation. Weighting the quantity of labor (hours of employment), classified by these characteristics of the work force, by relative wage or income differentials results in an aggregate measure of labor input intended to reflect the composition of the work force.

But this procedure is not without problems. For example, workers with similar characteristics have different earnings in different occupations and industries. However, the correlation between industry and occupation and earnings may also be due to influences other than productivity, such as regional differences in the cost of living, degree of unionization, and so on.

The BLS has developed some experimental measures of labor input based solely on changes in the amount of work experience and schooling workers have.[2] The methods used follow directly from the economic theory of human capital developed by Mincer[3] and Becker.[4] The method rests on the assumption that increased schooling and on-the-job training increase one's stock of skills and productivity. It also assumes that economic returns to higher education and additional work experience reflect the marginal productivity of these characteristics. The BLS has developed a multidimensional database that cross-classifies the annual hours of workers grouped by schooling and experience. The database has been developed from various models that make use of decennial census data, a matched sample from the CPS, and social security records.

As mentioned above, it is recognized that hourly wages differ not only because of differences in skills but also because of factors unrelated to productivity. Accordingly, simple averages of hourly wage rates for each education and experience group are not necessarily appropriate approximations of marginal productivity. Consequently, the BLS has developed an econometric model that provides measures of wages dependent on changes in education and experience but that simultaneously controls for other types of variation.

Skill-adjusted measures of labor input have been developed for the business sector as a whole, and this work is currently being extended to determine the feasibility of developing corresponding measures for specific industries, especially service industries.

NOTES

[1]Gorman, J. 1969. "Alternative Measures of the Real Output and Productivity of Commercial Banks," pp. 155-188 in *Production and Productivity in the Service Industries*, V.R. Fuchs (ed.), Columbia University Press, New York.

[2]Waldorf, W.H., et al. 1986. "New Measures of the Contribution of Education and Experience to U.S. Productivity Growth." Paper presented at the annual meetings of the American Economic Association, December 28-30, New Orleans, La.

[3]Mincer, J. 1974. *Schooling, Experience and Earnings*, Columbia University Press, New York.

[4]Becker, G. 1975. *Human Capital*, University of Chicago Press, Chicago and London.

Appendix D
How the Committee
Conducted Its Study

The Committee to Study the Impact of Information Technology on the Performance of Service Activities was composed of knowledgeable information technology (IT) executives from major service industries, nationally recognized macroeconomists concerned with productivity in services, executives from hardware- and software-producing groups, and representatives of government, labor, industry, and research. In addition, the committee sought input from chief executive officers, senior IT executives, and people with strong operating and financial evaluation experience in service industries, and it attempted to draw on the existing literature when appropriate.

The charge given to the committee was to examine the impact of IT on productivity in the service sector. However, after examining the macroeconomic data, existing surveys and publications on how IT has been used in services, the taxonomy of IT as it relates to performance, and the management practices of successful and less successful users of IT in services, the committee determined that the proper issue for investigation was not determining the impact of IT on standard measures of productivity in services, but rather understanding the impact of IT on the overall performance of service activities.

As discussed in the main text of this report, many dimensions of performance are difficult or impossible to quantify, let alone to collect reliable data on. Nonetheless, the committee chose to regard performance broadly, including such considerations as fulfilling mandated requirements, reducing costs, creating new products, increasing the quality or timeliness of output, avoiding loss of competitive position, developing new strategic capabilities, generating greater flexibility of infrastructure, improving capacity to handle complexity or customization, and so on. Furthermore, it included all aspects of IT investments and expenses (hardware, software, training, support, and operating) in its thinking, despite the fact that data on overall industry expenditures for software, training, support, and systems operations are generally difficult to obtain in any systematic manner.

The committee conducted analysis at the national, industry, enterprise, and activity levels. Thus it did not address international, individual, or group issues in any significant detail. Nor did it address small companies, although financial data on smaller companies were included in the data that supported the industry- and national-level analyses.

To conduct its national (or macroeconomic) analysis, the committee investigated the current data relevant to evaluating how IT has been exploited in the service sector. Much of this data is incomplete or inadequate in ways discussed in the text, and in any event such data cannot establish cause-and-effect relationships between investments in IT and the performance measured.

Once the committee went beyond the national level, the lack of systematically collected data became quite apparent. The committee therefore undertook to interview a large number of outside sources. The committee did not attempt to develop new databases, a task that would have been far beyond its expertise or resources to undertake. Instead, it relied on experts, both its own inside the committee (through committee deliberations) and others outside the committee (through interviews), as well as on other studies when available.

The industry-level analysis was primarily for context-setting. The committee drew on secondary literature and its own experts in the air transport, communications, commercial banking, insurance, retail-wholesale trade, and health care industries. These industries were selected because they had a wide range of measurable improvements in productivity, high levels of investment in IT, and different contexts in which to introduce IT; reflected important implications for employment and public policy; and exhibited extensive variety in the sophistication and scale of the IT installed. Good data were available for some of these industries as well.

At the enterprise and activity levels, the committee sought to shed light on the causal relationships underlying observed trends rather than merely to analyze correlations of data. The enterprise and activity levels are crucial for understanding these relationships, because decisions about investment in IT and use of IT are usually not made at the industry or national level; most are made by executives within the enterprises that employ them. Moreover, resources and appraisal procedures for investing in IT are generally developed at the enterprise and activity levels, and appraisals of investments, IT strategies, and system paybacks ultimately occur at these levels.

USE OF INTERVIEWS—APPROACH AND LIMITATIONS

To understand the causal relationships between IT investment and use and the performance of service activities, the committee drew extensively on a set of interviews it conducted with senior executives from firms in the service industries. The purpose of these interviews was to seek insights (both from the past and present) into patterns of behavior that could help explain why some companies or industries were—or were not—realizing more payoffs from IT. Thus the committee conducted these interviews and analyzed the questionnaires in an exploratory vein, rather than searching for high statistical reliability.

To select appropriate interviewees, the committee established a list of ten leading companies in each chosen service industry (financial services, transportation, retailing, wholesale distribution, communications, professional services, and health care). These companies were selected on the basis of size, rate of growth, profitability, recognition for innovation, and recognition as major users of IT. These firms seemed most likely to have given systematic thought to the problems of assessing and managing IT systems and to have encountered the full range of problems in both activities. Based on the committee's access to senior management, four companies in each group were then selected for contact. Such access was critical in order to obtain reliable responses concerning each company's practices, experiences, and results.

Executives from two of these four top-performing firms were interviewed in each industry, in all a total of 80 individuals at 46 companies. All together, these firms had nearly $500 billion in revenues in 1991 and employed nearly 3 million people.[1] Because the cooperation of key individuals was crucial, access to the firm was sought at the highest possible level. In each company, interviewers attempted to contact the chief executive officer or chief operating officer, the senior executives for IT, a major operating officer, and the chief financial officer. The individuals interviewed are listed in Appendix E. All quoted statements in this report were verified by those who made them as being correct at the time of the interviews.

These interviews were conducted in a semistructured manner, and they focused on the following concerns:

1. How companies decided to go ahead with a particular IT project;
2. How companies evaluated IT projects post-investment (if at all);
3. The results of such evaluations;
4. The impact of IT's use on organizational structures;
5. Performance measurement and changes in reward systems made to exploit IT effectively;
6. Causes of less-than-satisfactory returns from investments in IT;

7. How companies evaluated intangibles like quality, flexibility, response times, or complexity effects; and

8. What executives perceived to be the most important impacts of IT's use in their industries.

The introductory information sent to interviewees prior to the interview is given in Box D.1, and the interview guide for the interviewers is provided in Box D.2. To obtain more standardized data, a written questionnaire (Figure D.1) was submitted to each participating company after the oral interviews. Seventy-nine percent of the questionnaires were returned. Summaries of the responses to the questionnaire appear in Question Boxes 1 through 7.

In addition to the qualifications noted in Chapter 3, some further limitations of these interviews must be noted. Although each interview was conducted to gain understanding about both failures and successes in implementing IT in services, those interviewed understandably focused more readily on the successes of their firms, though most were willing to discuss some of their failures or problems. The selection of companies "near the top" of their industries and avowedly major users of IT resulted in a greater focus on the "winners" or "survivors." In addition, the focus on large firms—because of limits on committee resources—left a large gap in the committee's understanding of how small and medium-size firms use and manage IT. This is a gap that should be addressed in future research.

Although the data that emerged from the committee's interviews are primarily qualitative, such data help to interpret the quantitative macroeconomic data that do not adequately represent the wide range of impacts that using IT has had on the performance of firms in the service sector. Thus, semistructured interviews conducted by the committee were useful in defining (not measuring) parameters, in interpreting correlation data, and in providing support for causal hypotheses. Since the data from the interviews were not collected utilizing a statistical sample, common themes are reported in the text using qualifiers such as "virtually all" (90 percent or more), "a great majority" (70 percent or more), "most" (50 percent or more), "less than half" (30 to 40 percent), "a few" (10 to 30 percent), "a very few" (less than 10 percent), and so on. Conclusions are limited to the respondents' practices and views.

NOTE

[1] Revenues and employment figures for 1991 were gathered from a search of the Dunn and Bradstreet Market Identifiers database available through DIALOG Information Services. For a small number of companies, the 1991 data were not contained in this database, and 1990 figures were used. Thus the $500 billion in revenues and 3 million people employed should be regarded as rough estimates.

Question Box 1

Does your company have an overall IT strategy?

Yes	No	Only recently
70%	13%	17%

What is the time horizon of the strategy?

1 Year	2 Years	3 Years	4 Years	5 Years	10 Years
4%	12%	42%	4%	38%	0%

Does the decision process for IT differ from other investments?

Yes	No
37%	63%

Do the payback criteria differ from those for other investments?

Yes	No
31%	69%

Observations and Additional Comments

- Time horizons of IT strategy are around 3-5 years, generally with updates annually through capital budgets and specific operational plans keyed in at six-month to 1-year intervals.
- IT investment processes and payback criteria are essentially the same as those for other investments.
- In discussion with interviewees, a majority described long-range plans for IT investment and installation, rather than competitive positioning strategies.

Question Box 2

Do you routinely make PRE-project evaluations of IT investments?

Type of IT Investment	Yes	No	Occasionally
Cost Reducing	83%	7%	10%
New Product	64	11	25
Basic Infrastructure	67	17	17
Desktop IT	33	40	27
Mandated Systems	47	47	7

If evaluated, what do the returns tend to be?

Type of IT Investment	Indeterminate	Negative Return	Equal to Cost of Capital	Marginal Return	High Return	Comparable to Other Investments
Cost Reducing	0	0	0	13	48	39
New Product	5	0	5	16	42	32
Basic Infrastructure	11	16	16	11	16	32
Desktop IT	0	15	8	8	23	46
Mandated Systems	8	17	17	17	17	25

N.B. Percentages are based on number of responses to individual questions. Rows may not add to 100% due to rounding.

Question Box 3

Do you routinely make POST-project evaluations of IT investments?

Type of IT Investment	Yes	No	Occasionally
Cost Reducing	39%	32%	29%
New Product	36	36	28
Basic Infrastructure	22	52	26
Desktop IT	17	48	34
Mandated Systems	16	64	20

If evaluated, what do the returns tend to be?

Type of IT Investment	Indeterminate	Negative Return	Equal to Cost of Capital	Marginal Return	High Return	Comparable to Other Investments
Cost Reducing	0%	0%	0%	28%	22%	50%
New Product	8	0	8	8	25	50
Basic Infrastructure	14	14	14	7	14	36
Desktop IT	15	15	0	15	8	46
Mandated Systems	11	11	0	22	11	44

N.B. Percentages are based on number of responses to individual questions. Rows may not add to 100% because of rounding.

Observations and Additional Comments

- Post-project evaluations are less universally pursued than pre-project assessments.
- Most frequent post-investment evaluations are performed on cost reduction and new-product programs.
- Post-project audits tended to show higher audited returns than those projected, except in the case of desktop systems.

Question Box 4

How do you account for different costs in your IT evaluations?

	Capitalized	Expensed
Hardware	89%	11%
Software	34%	66%
Training Costs	11%	89%
Infrastructure Costs	17%	83%

Observations and Consequences

- A substantial portion of IT costs do not show up in "investment" figures.

Question Box 5

Overall, how, if at all, has use of IT influenced the organization structure of your company?

	Increased	Decreased	No change
Spans of control	68%	14%	18%
Levels of hierarchy	4%	63%	33%
Centralization	46%	24%	30%
Decentralization	44%	26%	30%

	Much	Some	Slight	None
Did IT facilitate organizational flattening, postproject?	27%	50%	12%	12%
Did IT facilitate significant use of self-directed teams?	8%	58%	19%	15%
Were performance measures changed?	11%	56%	4%	30%
Were compensation systems changed?	4%	33%	15%	48%

N.B. Rows may not add to 100% because of rounding.

Observations and Additional Comments

- The mix is about even between increased centralization (usually of data centers or databases) and increased decentralization (usually of operations).
- Most report increased spans of control, flatter organizations, more use of self-directed teams.

Question Box 6

Are users involved in the design of IT projects?

Rarely	Sometimes	Usually	Always
7%	7%	33%	53%

How were they involved?

Specifying Only	In System Design	Interactive in Design	Interactive Throughout
8%	6%	16%	69%

Are external customers involved in design of IT?

Specifying Only	In System Design	Interactive in Design	Interactive Throughout
46%	24%	18%	12%

N.B. Rows may not add to 100% because of rounding.

Observations and Additional Comments

- Users are involved in design of IT projects at design and implementation levels.
- External customers are often involved, but less frequently.

Question Box 7

What performance *metrics* are used?

	Measured Internally	Measured at Customer Level
Response times to customers	64%	50%
Quality of performance	57	50
Financial payback to company	82	14
Financial benefits to customers	43	43
Internal engineering metrics	54	4
Other important metrics	7	11

N.B. Percentages are based on number of responses to individual questions. Columns are not mutually exclusive.

Observations and Additional Comments

- About half of the respondents reported using formal techniques to monitor perceived quality from their customers' viewpoint.
- Formal metrics to measure the quality of service outputs are almost always engineering metrics (such as system response times, computer availability percentages, cycle times for operations, etc.) or customer survey data (expressing customers' view of the services of the company) that cannot be converted into financial measurements of output quality.

BOX D.1 Introductory Information Sent to Interviewee Prior to Interview

1. *Purpose of Interview and Follow-up Questionnaire:* Numerous publications have suggested a seeming paradox. They contend that the relatively high levels of investment in information technologies (IT) in services have led to little or no measurable productivity increases. This may be a problem caused by difficulties in measurement. This questionnaire is intended to understand better: (a) to what extent companies have, or have not, fared better and improved performance levels through use of IT, (b) how companies determine how much to spend on IT and set metrics for anticipated performance, (c) how companies build IT into strategic plans, (d) how companies evaluate benefits from their IT investments, (e) how these evaluations compare to anticipations, (f) what management techniques seem to work well or to cause problems in achieving productivity from IT, (g) what the most important impacts have been of IT on the organization's structure, management style, and industry competitive position.

2. *Definitions used in Interview and Questionnaire:* Information technologies (IT) include the hardware, software, and implementation processes for a cluster of technologies that provide transactions-oriented and interactive computer-based capabilities for: collection, input, processing, communication, storage, retrieval, and presentation of data and information. Respondents should consider the impacts of information technologies at several different levels: (a) *strategic uses* which change the nature and purposes of the entire enterprise, (b) *systems uses* which coordinate organizational units and databases to perform overall enterprise functions more effectively or efficiently, (c) *operational uses* which enable managing of single functions or units for greater efficiency or higher value-added, (d) *unit applications* which improve performance at a single workstation.

Services include all items sold in trade which are neither products nor constructions. The services industries include: financial services, retailing, wholesaling, transportation, communications, public utilities (such as sewer, garbage collection, electric companies, etc.), health care and delivery systems, entertainment, professional services (such as accounting, legal, consulting, design, research, etc. firms), computer software, entertainment, and so on. *Services activities* (which occur both within the "product industries" and the "services industries") may include logistics, applied research, process design, product design, plant engineering, warehousing, market research, marketing, advertising, sales, distribution, repair, post-sale services, legal, public relations, accounting, personnel, regulatory affairs, maintenance, basic research, or finance functions.

Continues

APPENDIX D

3. *Rules of the Interview:* All interviews will be taped for accuracy. All information will be held confidential unless specifically released by respondent. All quotes or paraphrases will be cleared *in context* with the respondent before publication. All publications will be sent to respondents free at the earliest date they are released for distribution. Interviews do not seek proprietary data, but useful patterns and insights having to do with measuring and improving the performance of IT in services activities. If copies of any relevant reports or company documents are available, they would help ensure accuracy.

4. *Outline of Interview:* We will be focusing on four central questions. For each of these there will be some detailed questions the interviewer will use to flesh out and make your responses compatible with those of other respondents. These questions include the following:

   A. Has your company made any major studies of the performance of its information technology (IT) investments? Please describe the breadth of the studies, levels of IT included, or if performed on individual projects, which projects were included. What were the results? What methodologies and metrics did you use?

   B. How was the technology developed? Internally? Externally? Joint ventures, other approaches? How was the IT function organized at the time? What were the most important problems encountered in introducing the technology? What have been, or are anticipated to be, the most important changes resulting from the new technology?

   C. How, if at all, have you used IT to affect the organizational structure of your company? Spans of control? Levels of hierarchy, centralization or decentralization of decisions? How has the technology affected your competitive edge in some aspect of your industry? How has it influenced the use of self-directed teams? Boundaries of units? Horizontal relationships and communications? Strategic alliances, and so on?

   D. In light of the above what would be your overall evaluation of the way IT investments enabled your company to improve services performance? What are the most useful insights or patterns that analysis of past projects offers for future IT investments?

BOX D.2 Interview Guide for Interviewers

1. *Has your company made any major studies of the performance of its information technology (IT) investments?* If so, when? Please describe the breadth of the study, levels of IT included, or if performed on individual projects, which projects were included? Were they successful? What performance measures were used? What was the general level of IT investment involved? In software? Hardware? Over what time periods were results measured? Why? What were the general conclusions concerning performance payoff? Could this be measured for discrete projects? Cumulative gains? What were the main sources of gain? What were the main causes of greater or less than anticipated benefits? What were the most important problems encountered in measurement? How did you deal with these? What were the major intangibles considered? How were they evaluated? Quality of outputs? Faster response times? Flexibility potentials? Greater knowledge about customers? Were software costs (development and licensing) included? Training and personnel development? If so, what were they? What would you say was the precision (+/-____%) of the measurements?

Please pick two or three major projects (in terms of cost, impact, or geographical scope) concerning which you are most familiar or for which such evaluations may have been undertaken. If possible, please choose some large-scale projects which "went well" and some which "did not go well." For each of these projects, what were the main goals of the project? What metrics were used in making the decision? What is the decision process for IT investments and how does that differ from other types of investment decisions? How is IT integrated into strategic planning? How was the actual evaluation carried out? By whom? How were various critical factors balanced or weighted? What was the approximate size of the investment? In software? In hardware? What was the cost vs. other information technology investments then installed? Was this a new activity for the company? The replacement of earlier automation? Replacement of people? Was there a specific investment return (hurdle rate) the project had to meet? How did this compare to other IT and non-IT hurdle rates? Were other criteria stated explicitly in advance? How well or badly did the project meet initial expectations, goals?

2. *How was the technology developed?* Through internal groups? Extensive outsourcing? Off-the-shelf purchases? Joint ventures? Who was involved at each stage? When were users involved? What was the nature of the development? How was the IT function organized? Where are standards set? Who had final decision authority? What important changes in organization or technical infrastructure were necessary to develop, accommodate, or exploit the new technologies? What were the

Continues

most important other problems encountered in introducing the technology? What have been, or are anticipated to be, the most important unforeseen changes resulting from the new technology? Did the technology change economies of scale? Economies of scope? From the operations level to the systems level, or vice versa? How were the effects measured? What time span did it take to introduce the project (from specification to outcomes)? Was the project organized as a separate division? Cross-functional team effort? Outsourced? What portions were expenses or capitalized? Why?

3. How, if at all, has the use of information technology affected the organizational structure of your company? Spans of control? Levels of hierarchy? Locus of control? Centralization, decentralization of decisions? Have there been shifts in staffing away from certain functions and toward others? Has the technology enabled your enterprise to shorten its response times? How much? What are the organizational, control, and motivational implications of these changes? How have they affected the use of self-directed teams? Boundaries of units? Horizontal relationships and communications? Strategic alliances? How has use of the technology affected your methods of performance measurement? Motivation systems? Control systems? What are the most important (or likely) impacts of the new technologies on job skills, training requirements, wage structures? How does your company approach the issue of "managing and developing people as intellectual assets"? Does the technology allow you to obtain a sustainable competitive edge in some component of your industry? How? What have been the major spinoffs or totally new directions new information technologies have enabled for the company? To what extent were these anticipated? Unanticipated?

4. In light of the above, what would be your overall evaluation of the way IT investments enabled you to improve services performance in your company? Why? What are the most useful insights or patterns that analysis of past projects offers for future IT investments?

SUMMARY QUESTIONNAIRE
INFORMATION TECHNOLOGY (IT) INVESTMENT PERFORMANCE

1. Has your company evaluated overall payoff of IT investments? Yes ☐ No ☐

	Indeterminate	Negative Return	Equal to cost of Capital	Marginal Return	High Return	Comparable to other investments
If so, what was the payoff?	☐	☐	☐	☐	☐	☐
What is your view of management's perception of overall IT payoff?	☐	☐	☐	☐	☐	☐

2. Does your company have an overall IT strategy? Yes ☐ No ☐ Only recently ☐

   What is the time horizon of the strategy? 1 Year ☐ 2 Years ☐ 3 Years ☐ 4 Years ☐ 5 Years ☐ 10 Years ☐

3. Does the decision process for IT differ substantially from other investments? Yes ☐ No ☐
   Do the payback criteria differ from those for other investments? Yes ☐ No ☐

4. Do you routinely make PRE-project or POST-project evaluations of IT investment?

Do you make routine evaluations?						If evaluated, what do the returns tend to be?											
Type of IT Investment	Yes		No		Occasional		Indeterminate		Negative Return		Equal to cost of Capital		Marginal Return		High Return		Comparable to other investments
	Pre	Post	Pre	Post	Pre	Post	Pre	Post	Pre	Post	Pre	Post	Pre	Post	Pre	Post	Pre	Post
Cost Reducing																		

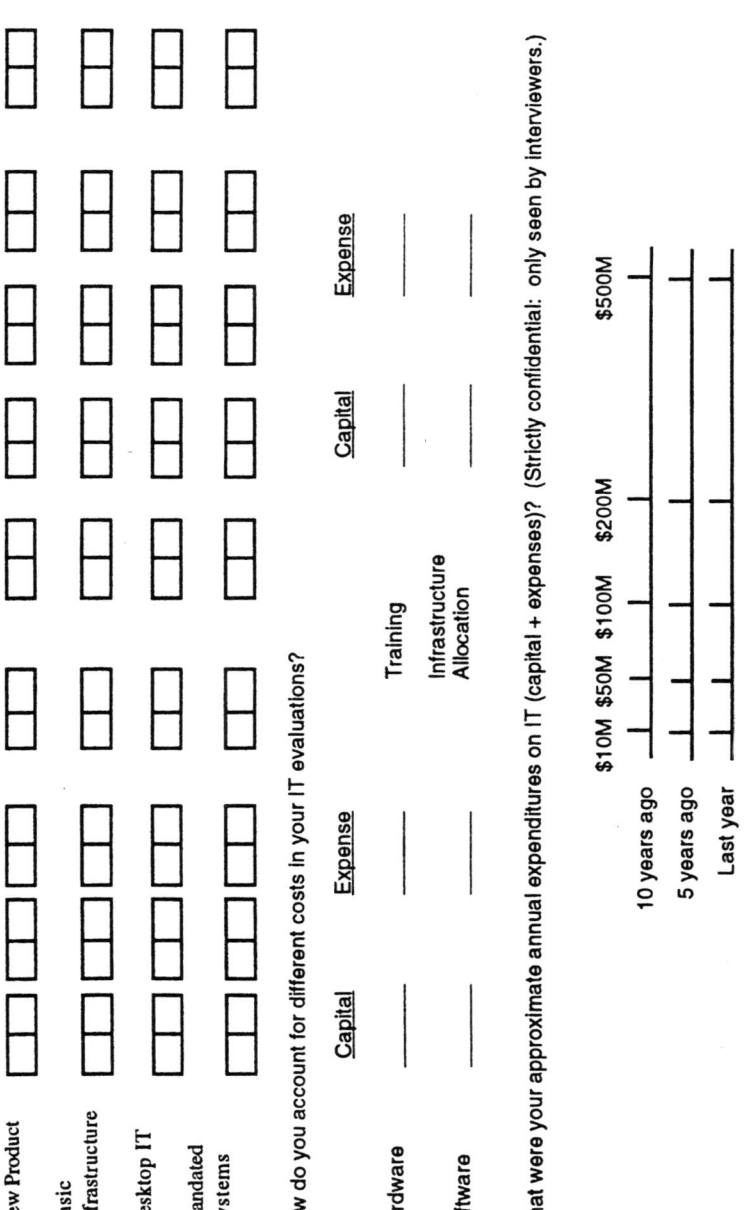

FIGURE D.1 Written questionnaire sent after oral interviews.

6. Overall, how, if at all, has use of IT influenced the organization structure of your company?

	Increased	Decreased	No change	Comment, if necessary
Spans of control	___	___	___	_____
Levels of hierarchy	___	___	___	_____
Centralization	___	___	___	_____
Decentralization	___	___	___	_____

Was flattening of the organization sometimes a stated specific goal, preproject? Yes___ No___

Did IT facilitate organizational flattening, post project?	Much___	Some___	Slight___	None___
Did IT facilitate significant use of self-directed teams?	Much___	Some___	Slight___	None___
Were performance measures changed?	Much___	Some___	Slight___	None___
Were compensation systems changed?	Much___	Some___	Slight___	None___

7. Are users involved in the design of IT projects?

☐ Rarely   ☐ Sometimes   ☐ Usually   ☐ Always

How are they involved?

☐ Specifying only   ☐ System Design   ☐ Interactive in Design Process   ☐ Interactive Throughout

Are external customers involved in design of IT?

☐ Specifying only   ☐ System Design   ☐ Interactive in Design Process   ☐ Interactive Throughout

8. What performance metrics are used?

	Measured Internally	Measured at Customer Level
Financial payback to company	——	——
Internal engineering metrics	——	——
Quality of performance	——	——
Financial benefits to customers	——	——
Response times to customers	——	——
Other important metrics (specify)	——	——

9. What were main causes when desired payback was not acheived?

	Most Frequent	Common	Infrequent
Management understanding of IT	——	——	——
Projects too large	——	——	——
Didn't reengineer process	——	——	——
Users not involved	——	——	——
Inadequate follow up	——	——	——
IT capabilities oversold	——	——	——
Poor implementation	——	——	——
Support systems not changed	——	——	——
Other _____	——	——	——

10. Were there other major benefits not captured by program measures?

	Most Frequent	Common	Infrequent
Benefits passed to customers	——	——	——
Added flexibility	——	——	——
Faster response times	——	——	——
Handle greater complexity	——	——	——
Empowerment of people	——	——	——
Other _____	——	——	——

FIGURE D.1 continued.

Appendix E
List of Executives Interviewed

Allen, Dennis
Assistant Vice President,
 Industrial Relations
BellSouth Corporation

Bacon, Lawrence
Senior Vice President, Information
 Systems Development
The Travelers Companies

Ballou, Roger H.
President, Travel Related Services
 Group (USA)
American Express Company

Barker, William G.
Chief Financial Officer (Retired)
CBS/Fox Company

Berardi, Greg
Director, Public Relations
BankAmerica Corporation

Bere, Richard
President
The Kroger Company

Bergonzi, Rino
President, Information Systems
United Parcel Service of America, Inc.

Blaser, Mitch
Manager, Management Information
 Systems
Marsh & McLennan Companies, Inc.

Brumbaugh, Mary
Manager, Management Information
 Systems
Sysco Food Services of Los Angeles,
 Subsidiary of Sysco Corporation

NOTE: Several executives interviewed preferred to remain anonymous and are not listed in this Appendix.

APPENDIX E

Campbell, Patrick E.
Senior Vice President, Technology Planning
NationsBank Services, Inc., NationsBank Corporation

Caron, J. Raymond
President, CIGNA Systems and Senior Vice President, CIGNA Corporation

Carter, Marshall N.
Chairman and Chief Executive Officer
State Street Bank and Trust Company

Chylinski, Ed
Vice President, Customer Accounting and Management Information Systems
NovaCare, Inc.

d'Alessio, Jon
Staff Vice President and Chief Information Officer (currently Treasurer)
McKesson Corporation

Dawson, Earl
The Chase Manhattan Bank, N.A.

Duchaine, Janet
Vice President, Direct Marketing Division
CIGNA Corporation

Elmore, Robert
Partner and Worldwide Director of Business Systems Consulting
Arthur Andersen & Company

Erbrick, Frank
Senior Vice President
United Parcel Service of America, Inc.

Evans, David V.
Vice President, Information Systems
J.C. Penney, Inc.

Ferkenhoff, Robert
Vice President, Information Services (Retired)
Sears Merchandise Group, Sears Roebuck & Company

Ford, James
Vice President, East Central Region
Kmart Corporation

Ford, Lafayette
Financial Manager
United Airlines, UAL Corporation

Fossett, David
Manager, Information Systems
Ford Motor Company

Foster, Tim
Vice President, Operations
NovaCare, Inc.

Garrett, Sharon
Vice President of Information Services and Chief Information Officer
Walt Disney Company

Gerbracht, Theodore
Vice President, Technology Planning, Global Information Services
Merrill Lynch & Company

Glaser, John
Vice President, Information Systems
Brigham and Women's Hospital

Goldman, Craig D.
Senior Vice President and Chief Information Officer
The Chase Manhattan Bank, N.A.

Hancock, John L.
Executive Vice President, Product and Technology Support
Pacific Bell

Hanway, Edward
President, CIGNA Worldwide and
Vice President, CIGNA Corporation

Hayes, Charles
Managing Director and Chief
  Financial Officer
Marsh & McLennan Companies

Heit, Steven
Manager, Information Systems Planning
United Parcel Service of America, Inc.

Heschel, Michael
Group Vice President, Management
  Information Systems
The Kroger Company

Heuber, Paul
Vice President, West Central Region
Kmart Corporation

Hoover, Richard
National Sales Manager
NALCO Chemical Company

Kinsolzing, Monique
The Chase Manhattan Bank, N.A.

Krau, Deborah
Vice President, Information Services and
  Chief Information Officer
Lahey Clinic

Lee, Dennis
Assistant Vice President, Operations
  Systems Planning
BellCore

Liebhaber, Richard
Executive Vice President and Chief Strategy
  and Technology Officer
MCI Communications Corporation

Loewenberg, John
Chief Executive Officer, Aetna
  Information Technology and
Senior Vice President, Aetna Life &
  Casualty Company

Looper, James
Director of Program Management and
  Systems Planning, Consumer Segment
MCI Telecommunications, MCI
  Communications Corporation

Macmanus, Christopher J.
Vice President, Information Services
  Organization
Johns Hopkins Hospital

Malmberg, David
Vice President, Inventory Management
  and Systems Services, McKesson
  Drug Group
McKesson Corporation

Maskovsky, Jerry
Managing Director, Information Services
Marsh & McLennan Companies

Massey, Calvin
Chief Information Officer
Scripps Clinic and Research Foundation

McLean, Douglas
Product Line Manager
Apple Computer, Inc.

McPherson, John
Director, Real Estate Planning
Safeway, Inc.

Michael, Joseph
Vice President, Customer Service and
  Logistics
Avery Dennison Corporation

APPENDIX E

Miller, Peter
Senior Vice President
J P Morgan & Company, Inc.

Miller, Randall W.
Management Consulting Partner
Deloitte & Touche

Morency, Bernard
Principal
Mercer Canada

Ollestad, Mel
Senior Vice President, Claims, Employee Benefits Division (Retired)
CIGNA Corporation

Pulliam, Larry
Vice President, Operations
Sysco Food Services of Los Angeles, Subsidiary of Sysco Corporation

Reed, William C.
Senior Vice President of Operations and Chief Information Officer
Geisinger System Services

Ripp, Joseph
Senior Vice President and Chief Financial Officer
Time, Inc.

Rodek, Jeffrey
Senior Vice President, The Americas and Caribbean
Federal Express Corporation

Sawyer, Thomas
Manager, Management Information Systems Planning
Dayton Hudson Corporation

Scholz, Garret
Vice President, Finance
McKesson Corporation

Schutzer, Daniel M.
Vice President, Emerging Technologies and R&D
Corporate Technology Office, Citibank

Sexton, David
Senior Vice President, Information Technology
State Street Bank and Trust Company

Sherwood, Blake
Vice Chairman
Marsh & McLennan Companies

Siegal, Richard
Chairman and Chief Executive Officer
Sysco Food Services of Los Angeles, Subsidiary of Sysco Corporation

Sinkula, W.J.
Executive Vice President
The Kroger Company

Smith, Dennis
Vice President, Management Information Systems
Bulova Division of Loews Corporation

Smith, III, H.S.
Vice President, Information Services
SuperValu Stores, Inc.

Sorgen, Howard
Senior Vice President, Global Information Services and Chief Technology Officer
Merrill Lynch & Company, Inc.

Stein, Martin A.
Vice Chairman, Automation and Support Services
BankAmerica Corporation

Stewart, James G.
Executive Vice President and Chief Financial Officer
CIGNA Corporation

Thompson, Douglas
Senior Vice President, Distribution
 Services, McKesson Distribution Group
McKesson Corporation

Valenti, John
Vice President, Southern Region
Kmart Corporation

Weston, Joshua S.
Chairman and Chief Executive Officer
Automatic Data Processing, Inc. (ADP)

Williams, Douglas
The Chase Manhattan Bank, N.A.

Woicke, Peter
Managing Director
J P Morgan and Company